They Fought in the Fields

THIS BOOK BELONGS TO

_____

_____

_____

NICOLA TYRER

They Fought in the Fields

The Women's Land Army:
The Story of a Forgotten Victory

SINCLAIR–STEVENSON

For Keith, Edmund and Alice

First published in Great Britain in 1996
by Sinclair-Stevenson
an imprint of Reed International Books Ltd
Michelin House, 81 Fulham Road, London SW3 6RB
and Auckland, Melbourne, Singapore and Toronto

A CIP catalogue record for this book
is available at the British Library
ISBN 1 85619 554 6

Typeset in $11\frac{1}{2}$ on $14\frac{1}{2}$ point Plantin
by Deltatype Ltd, Ellesmere Port, Cheshire
Printed and bound in Great Britain
by Clays Ltd, St Ives plc

*'The Land Army fights in the fields.
It is in the fields of Britain that the
most critical battle of the present war
may well be fought and won.'*

Lady Denman

Contents

List of Illustrations

Acknowledgements

[handwritten: Ann French FROM FIRST M. Millans,]

[handwritten notes in right margin: The column nod dor del y see thaun Ronald deusn]

To list all the people who have helped create this portrait of the land girl and her working environment would be a daunting task. But among those who entrusted me with their diaries, letters, newspaper cuttings, photographs, cartoons and treasured copies both of the stylish *Land Girl* and the workmanlike WLA county newsletters, there are some I would like to single out. The fact that I came to know so many one-time rat catchers, ditch diggers, tractor drivers and tree fellers is due in large measure to the efficiency of Jean Procter, founder and director of the British Women's Land Army Society. Until she set up the BWLAS in 1964, ex-land girls must indeed have felt members of a forgotten army, overlooked year after year at the nation's annual remembrance parades. I would also like to thank Mary Twyman, one of the Kent land girls who worked on fields and farms which, because they lay in the flight path to London of enemy aircraft became known as Bomb Alley. Mary Twyman, who received a bravery medal from the King, was to have written her own book on the Land Army but was sadly defeated by ill health. She passed on to me much of the material she had painstakingly compiled and encouraged me to incorporate it into this book. My thanks also to Penelope Greenwood, granddaughter of Lady Denman, Director of the Land Army, for memories which gave new insight into the private side of this remarkable woman; also to Charles Burrell, her nephew, for generously lending me both the entire bound collection of *The Land Girl* and Lady Denman's private photograph album which celebrates the land girl in all her varied callings.

Special thanks too to Dorothy Brant who, as Regional Officer for the North East, was one of Lady Denman's generals, to Marion Nicholson who took the campaign for post-war gratuities to the very top – a meeting with Prime Minister Winston Churchill at the House of Commons; to Margaret Drage, who arrived at Balcombe Place, the Land Army HQ, in 1939 as a seventeen-year-old typist, and to Joan Chapman, who was billeted at Sissinghurst Castle, home of WLA rep. and subsequent chronicler Vita Sackville-West; also to Peg Francis, Evelyn Elliott, Joan Pountney, Joan Collinson, Betty Green, Dinah Pengilly, Ivy Lemon and Johnnie Luxton.

CLARENCE HOUSE
S.W. 1

I was indeed proud to be Patron of the Women's Land Army for I remember so well their great contribution to victory in World War II.

No matter the weather, in snow, rain, wind or sun, women all over the country worked tirelessly to fulfil the programme of food production to sustain our Nation.   Their unsparing efforts earned our gratitude, and I would like here to pay my own tribute to all those who fought in the fields.

ELIZABETH R
Queen Mother

1996

Author's Note

I decided to write this book firstly because I realised that a generation has grown up who have never heard of the Women's Land Army and secondly because the story of all those inexperienced and idealistic young girls leaving their terraced homes in the cities to take on the task of feeding a nation has always struck me as rather moving. Their efforts may not have changed the lives of women coming after them the way those of the suffragettes did – in fact the daughters of land girls usually turn out to be a lot less practical than their mothers. Their sacrifices were not dramatic or life-threatening, as were those of some of the pioneers of women's suffrage. But the success of the WLA, which forced an initially deeply sceptical farming community to eat its words, showed what women can achieve when they are offered a level playing field. For this reason it is part of the women's story.

There is another reason for celebrating the WLA and that is the resolutely cheerful way they coped with what we have come to call the sex war. Most of the women in this book would describe themselves as any man's equal, yet few feel comfortable with the word feminist. To them it has a ring of hostility towards men which they do not recognise. Land girls were undeniably teased and tormented by men who felt threatened by their presence. Instead of crying unfair they got on with the job. Their moment of victory came when, at the announcement that the WLA was being disbanded, the biggest howl of dismay arose from the throat of the once-sceptical National Farmers Union. Girls growing up today are encouraged, quite rightly, to challenge discrimination and demand fairness. Their feminist role models, many of them crop-haired, steel-rimmed pugilists, urge confrontation with the enemy and are out for blood. The land girls made their enemy change sides – and kept their sense of humour. I'm sure we can learn from their example.

1 : Pioneers

'Dr Johnson, when asked his opinion of women preachers, replied that a woman preaching was like a dog walking on its hind legs: 'It is not well done, but you are surprized to find it done at all.'

Graphic, witty and scornful, the image is Johnson at his misogynistic best. Nearly two hundred years later, in 1939, it was with similar scorn that the British farming community greeted the prospect of a Women's Land Army. Their conviction that it couldn't be done is perhaps surprising since only twenty years earlier it had been done – and well done at that.

Most people associate the land girls and their famous uniform of green jerseys and fawn breeches with World War Two. But mould-breaking though these women were, they had an earlier even more pioneering precedent. The first Women's Land Army had been set up with tremendous haste in 1917 when, after three years of a harrowing war, starvation loomed. That year Britain was described by its Agriculture Minister as a 'beleaguered city'. Wholesale destruction of food-carrying

I

ships by the ruthlessly efficient German Navy, the run-down state of British farming and the unquenchable demand for men by the Services had reduced the country's reserve of food to just three weeks. Despite the prevailing view that the land was no place for any decent girl, forty-three thousand women patriotically applied to join the new force, though half were rejected as unsuited to the toughness of the work. A survey of 12,637 Land Army members in 1918 showed women at work in all fields of agricultural life; there were 5,734 milkers, 293 tractor drivers, 3,971 field workers, 635 carters, 260 plough-men, 84 thatchers and 21 shepherds. What is more, their efforts had proved highly satisfactory and won praise from both farmers and politicians. Memories are short, however, and by the time Britain's farmers learnt about plans for a new Land Army on the eve of the Second World War they had conveniently forgotten the unsuspected skills displayed by its older sister.

In most other European countries women have traditionally worked alongside their menfolk, herding animals, digging and planting in the fields, harvesting and haymaking. In Britain, however, farming had always been very much a male preserve in which the woman's role was limited to specific light farmyard tasks like feeding the pigs and calves, collecting eggs and tending the kitchen garden. Things are best done the way they always have been done has ever been the farmer's creed. Not that, as the war clouds gathered over Europe in 1938, British farmers had anything to be complacent about. British agriculture at the end of the Thirties was in a sorry state. The country was importing seventy per cent of its food, in stark contrast to the German Reich which by then was producing four fifths of the food it consumed. It seems incredible that successive British governments did nothing to remedy this dependency, which made it acutely vulnerable, especially in the face of Hitler's drive to reduce imports in Germany and the precedent of the First World War.

The situation in Britain was largely the result of a decision taken at the end of the nineteenth century that the route to prosperity lay through exporting sophisticated manufactured goods in return for raw materials and food imported cheaply from North America and the colonies. Things had reached crisis point in 1916 when a poor harvest and the announcement by Germany of a sustained submarine war forced the Government to intervene in farming policy. In December 1916 a new coalition under Lloyd George took office. County Agricultural Executive committees were set up with the mandate of bringing grassland back into cultivation and taking over badly run farms. Between 1917 and 1918 one and three quarter million acres of grassland were ploughed up to grow wheat. For the first time the Government introduced minimum prices for cereals and potatoes. During the years of peace which followed, however, the hungry lessons of the First World War were quickly forgotten. The policy of guaranteeing farmers a minimum price for crops was abandoned, as world supplies of grain grew and prices fell. Farming, like everything else, fell victim to the Great Depression of 1929. Over the next three years the price of agricultural land fell by over a third. More than a third of agricultural labourers left the land as farmers turned to less labour-intensive forms of agriculture, such as dairy farming, in an attempt to trim wage bills. Arable land returned to grass and thousands of acres of land were simply left untended, soon to be choked with weeds, scrub and bracken. Many farmers gave up altogether. The small number who prospered were those who switched to dairy farming.

By the early Thirties the Government was forced to reintroduce subsidies and marketing boards were set up to improve distribution. Import quotas were negotiated with foreign suppliers but the concept of Imperial Preference meant that between 1932 and 1939 supplies from the colonies rose by almost fifty per cent. The introduction of refrigeration meant that not only cereal but meat could be imported. It was only by the spring of 1939 that the British Government, realising that there would soon be a huge population of soldiers and factory

3

workers to be fed, decided that something had to be done. The dilatoriness seems particularly hard to comprehend, since Neville Chamberlain, the Prime Minister, had been a Cabinet Minister during the First World War, had seen the dire consequences of a blockade at first hand, and knew only too well how vulnerable Britain's supply lines were.

Under the new Minister of Agriculture, Sir Reginald Dorman-Smith, farmers were offered £2 per acre of grassland they ploughed up between 3 May and 30 September 1939. Incentives were offered to persuade farmers to grow grain. Tractor drivers and other agricultural mechanics were exempted from conscription from the age of twenty-one. Four days before the outbreak of war – the end of August 1939 – the Government's food policies were finally put into effect. The War Agricultural Committees, universally known as the War Ags., which had been formed in 1936 along county lines, each having a chairman, executive officer and secretary, were told to start work as a matter of urgency. The initial target of what was known as the 'battle for wheat' was to get two million acres of grassland ploughed by the time of the 1940 harvest. Commendably, in view of the hand-to-mouth nature of government policy, this target was reached by April 1940 with only eight counties failing to fulfil their quota. But labour shortage was an acute problem. By 1940, due to decades of farm workers leaving the countryside in the search for a better life, an intensive forces recruiting campaign in the spring of 1939 and then conscription, it was estimated that there was a shortfall of 50,000 agricultural workers.

It was to fill this gap that on 1 June 1939 – after a prolonged and often calamitous gestation – the Women's Land Army was reborn. Calamitous because war was imminent and because Government officials and civil servants displayed precisely the same indecision and lack of vigour in setting up the Land Army that they had shown in resuscitating British farming.

The idea of using women to fill the gap in the ranks of farm workers was first discussed at an official level a good eighteen months before the outbreak of war – on 9 April 1938. The Permanent Secretary at the Ministry of Agriculture called a meeting with four senior officials to discuss farming labour in the event of war. Exactly as had been done twenty years earlier it was decided, if war was declared, to set up a Women's Branch of the Ministry under the Directorship of a woman. Lady Denman, who had been a pioneer of the Women's Institute movement in Britain, seemed the obvious choice. Lady Denman had assisted Dame Meriel Talbot in setting up the first Land Army, serving a stint at the original Women's Branch at the Ministry of Agriculture and touring the country, promoting recruitment to the Land Army in 1918. A passionate and articulate champion of everything to do with rural life and, due to her Women's Institute contacts spread throughout the counties, a ready-made 'networker', it is easy to see why Lady Denman appealed to the men at the Ministry. At this stage her brief was twofold: to put forward a list of people qualified to act as her assistants in administering a national organisation and to explore the idea of setting up Land Army committees in every county, with a list of women qualified to act as chairmen. Lady Denman hesitated before accepting the Ministry's invitation. Her one fear was that any new role could limit her contribution to the work of the Women's Institutes. When she consulted the National Federation's Executive Committee, however, they urged her to assume her new role. She lost little time, for by the end of April 1939 she was hard at work at the Institutes' headquarters in Eccleston Street in London's Belgravia, sketching in the outlines of a Women's Land Army to go into action in the event of war.

On 14 May, assisted by Miss Farrer, the General Secretary of the WI federation, and using the Institutes' lists, Lady Denman wrote to the women she had personally chosen to be chairmen of each county committee.

2 : Lady Denman

Gertrude Denman was one of the last members of a breed that today has almost totally disappeared – the philanthropist. As her granddaughter Penelope, now Mrs John Greenwood, puts it: 'she had been brought up to believe that of those to whom much is given much is also expected.'

To us, with our black-and-white views on class, she appears an intriguingly paradoxical figure. Born Gertrude Pearson in 1884, she was the only daughter of the immensely wealthy first Viscount and Viscountess Cowdray. Sir Weetman Pearson had been elevated to the peerage in 1910, having made a fortune from construction. Among the monuments of the family firm, S. Pearson and Son, which originated in York-shire, were the Blackwall Tunnel under the Thames, the East River Tunnel in New York, and countless docks, harbours, canals and railways all over the world.

Gertrude, known to her friends as 'Trudie', had grown up in a world of chauffeured Rolls-Royces, luxurious country houses and African safari holidays. For her twenty-first birthday her millionaire father bought her her own 3,000-acre country estate. Yet throughout his life Pearson remained a dedicated Liberal, supporting a range of radical causes embracing Home Rule for Ireland, Women's Suffrage, old age pensions and sickness insurance. Her deep love of her father and respect for his values explains why Lady Denman's privileged background did not prevent her, unlike many other titled ladies, from feeling genuine compassion for those who were less fortunate than herself, and from displaying an almost ascetic approach to luxury which contrasts strongly with the hedonistic playboy life-style pursued by so many of the very rich, both then and now. Indeed she devoted much of her life to campaigning for better living conditions, better education and better medical facilities for the working classes.

After a sketchy education which included a spell at a girls' day school in Kensington, a governess, and a finishing school in Dresden, Trudie had, like other girls of her background, done the London season. In 1903 at the age of nineteen, much to the satisfaction of her ambitious mother, Lady Cowdray, she married into the aristrocracy in the shape of Thomas Denman, a twenty-eight-year-old Liberal peer whom she had met at a ball in London. Her first sight of him was at the top of a grand staircase, standing on crutches like the archetypally romantic wounded soldier – he had been invalided out of the Boer War. Thomas's immediate antecedents were unremarkable – his father was an unambitious and impecunious Sussex squire. The first Baron, however, had distinguished himself when in 1820 he appeared as one of the counsels for the defence of Queen Caroline at her trial at the House of Lords on a charge of adultery. The match between Trudie and Thomas Denman, an asthmatic who later developed a reputation for hypochondria, appears to have taken place more because it suited both sets of parents than out of any genuine passion on the part of the young people. In 1905 their first child Thomas, was born, followed two years later by a daughter, Judith. In 1910 Lord Denman was appointed Governor General of Australia, taking Trudie off to the southern hemisphere for four years. There she loved the Australian countryside but loathed the pomp and ceremony and the endless entertaining, that went with being the Governor's wife. 'The people I like best', she wrote to a friend, 'are the Labour people. They are very simple and nice.'

By the time she became head of the Women's Land Army, Lady Denman was known to the public chiefly through her association with the Women's Institutes. In the last three decades the WI has acquired an unfortunate, cosy, jam-making image, much derided by the ambitious career women of today. In 1917, however, when Lady Denman first became chairman, the movement was distinctly radical. Far from promoting home-making skills, the Institutes, which had originated in Canada at the end of the last century, had the express aim of widening countrywomen's horizons. The idea was to encourage them to come out of the damp, draughty cottages in which they spent a monotonous, careworn existence raising children they struggled to feed, and step into a new world of opportunity and education in which they could learn not only new practical skills, but self-confidence, self-expression, citizenship and self-improvement.

In 1939, aged fifty-five and not in the best of health, Gertrude Denman was at the height of her intellectual and organisational powers. A bungled operation years before which condemned her to wear a surgical corset did not inhibit her impressive energy, or prevent her playing tennis and golf regularly and riding to hounds whenever she could. Physically she was slim and rather masculine-looking. She took little interest in clothes and possessed a face that was characterful rather than pretty. What had once been flaming red hair and had now faded to pepper and salt surmounted a strikingly misshapen beaky nose (a younger brother had broken it during a game of croquet). Despite her limited education she was highly intelligent and naturally efficient – the kind of woman who in those days would have led a more fulfilling life had she been born a man. Domestic life didn't appeal to her and she was glad to leave the business of child-rearing to her domestic staff. By the time the Land Army was set up she and her husband, a somewhat lacklustre character, who, as far as his political career was concerned, had failed to fulfil his early promise, were leading more or less separate lives. Today Lady Denman might have been a businesswoman, a barrister or an MP. The naturally succinct and lucid way she expressed herself would have brought a breath of fresh air to the rambling nature of much contemporary political debate.

Lady Denman was regarded by some of her colleagues as having a rather cold manner. Those who knew her well say she was shy in the company of strangers, particularly those who were from a different social class – despite her earnest wish to be a good mixer. In 1926 the Denmans had suffered a personal tragedy which may have had some bearing on Lady Denman's reserve. On the eve of his twenty-first birthday their son, Thomas, who had made a promising start, having graduated from Eton to Trinity College, Cambridge, had undergone a severe mental breakdown from which he failed to recover. The celebrations were cancelled and Thomas was sent to a mental institution from which he never emerged.

The Women's Institutes were only one of a number of progressive social causes Gertrude Denman had espoused before the Land Army took over her life. In 1908, adopting her father's political convictions, she had joined the Women's Liberal Federation Executive to campaign for the introduction of votes for women. In 1917, after her return from Australia, she became involved in organising the first Land Army. The following year she spearheaded a national recruiting drive. In pre-radio days open-air rallies were deemed the best way to spread the word and Trudie and a friend drove round the Southern counties, dressed in Land Army uniform, which consisted not just of breeches, but, in those pre-rubber days, of leather gaiters, attracting the attention of passers-by with a policeman's rattle. Once this had been achieved she would address a rallying speech to the crowd, either from the steps of

9

her car, or occasionally from the stage of a local theatre. On one occasion in Portsmouth she followed a turn by performing dogs and won warm applause from a naval audience.

Another good cause which had attracted Lady Denman's support was the Land Settlement Association. This was the idealistic response of a small group of wealthy philanthropists to the general urban unemployment that characterised the inter-war years. Its aim was to provide smallholdings and allotments in the country for the jobless – Welsh miners were one group – in the hope that by becoming self-employed they might recover dignity and self-reliance. Lady Denman had herself helped one family move, housing and employing them on her own country estate, but plans to put this bold social experiment into action on a larger scale were put paid to by the war.

The campaign which best expressed Lady Denman's particular brand of courage and far-sightedness, however, was her championing from the beginning of the Thirties, of family planning. She became the first chairman of the Family Planning Association. Her readiness to promote this cause at a time when to favour birth control was tantamount to condoning promiscuity, was the direct result of her first-hand experience of the lives led by the wives of agricultural workers. 'Breeding and feeding children' was how she summarised their grim existence. Her support for birth control lay not so much in the fact that it prevented unwanted pregnancies, as that it helped mothers to space their children. This way, she argued, each had maximum chance of health and happiness. The movement was attacked by many branches of the Establishment and the Church in particular. Mrs Bramwell Booth of the Salvation Army denounced it as 'utterly wrong and not in God's plan', claiming in an article in the *Daily Mirror* that 'young girls were being destroyed in great numbers every year because of it'. The president of the Catholic Women's League forecast 'race suicide and moral degeneracy'.

In her fight to establish family planning centres in country towns so that all married women, and not only those who lived in city centres, had access to contraception, Lady Denman came face to face with the conservatism and prejudice of the British Establishment. This, combined with her own brand of moral courage was to stand her in good stead in her fight to establish the Women's Land Army.

Evelyn Elliot

(née *Webster*). Joined Land Army at 17.
Land Army 1946–50. Home town: Sunderland.
Civilian occupation: butcher's assistant.

I went from dead meat to live when I joined the Land Army. I left school at fourteen and went to work first in a greengrocer's and then in the butcher's. The reason I joined the Land Army was that the men hadn't got back from the war and there was a recruiting drive in Sunderland. I got sent down to a hostel in Reading for my training. I'd never been so far from home before. When you were being trained you lived in the hostel and went out to different farms in the day. Specific farms run by the local War Ag. took on trainee land girls. On these farms there would be an experienced land girl and it was her job to teach you what to do. My pay went down. I was getting 25 shillings a week in the butcher's shop.

When I joined the Land Army I only got 17 shillings. For the month of training we got our board and lodging paid by the Government. When I started work, which was in Henley-on-Thames, I got 2 shillings and 10 pence for a 48–50 hour week. In the summer it was longer. Sometimes you'd start at 5 a.m. and still be in the fields at 8 o'clock at night. If I worked on a Sunday or a Bank Holiday the overtime rate went up to 1 shilling and 11 pence an hour. But I had to pay for my keep out of that.

I chose dairy farming because I wanted to work with animals. But you were so green; I'd no idea that bulls behaved differently from cows. One day I was told to take feed and water in to the bull. He was in a pen and tied up. He was a Friesian, which is a big breed. He seemed about ten foot high to me. I walked gaily in with my buckets of water. First he knocked me off my feet with a toss of his head. Then, as I got up he gave a great kick and practically kicked me out of the byre.

3 : Prejudice

The contrast between the urgent, businesslike way Lady Denman set about her new task – she too remembered the beleaguered city of 1917 – and the procrastinating patronising attitude of the politicians and civil servants she had to deal with was striking. She grasped, in a way they seemed unable to, the central role the WLA would need to play in winning the war. As she herself wrote in the *Land Army Manual*: 'Germany is attempting to starve the British people into submission. To win the war our country must defeat the blockade. This is the joint task of the British Navy and of Britain's great field force of agricultural workers.'

No sooner had Lady Denman been invited to set up women's committees in every county, using her national network of Women's Institute contacts as a starting point, than she handed over the running of the Women's Institutes to her deputy, Miss Grace Hadow, and set to work. Installing herself at the headquarters of the Women's Institutes in Eccleston Street in London's Belgravia, with a handful of trusted assistants, Lady Denman drew up detailed plans for the administration of a wartime Land Army. She worked in circumstances of the utmost secrecy. It was vital not to hand propaganda material to the enemy, or to reveal the acutely vulnerable state of the country's food supplies. Within six weeks of the initial Ministry meeting – on 14 May – letters were on their way to the chosen candidate for each county committee. The Munich crisis of the autumn of 1938 brought the threat of war nearer than ever. Lady Denman followed up her initial approach to the County Chairmen designate by asking them to form their committees in readiness for war. The response of the Ministry of Agriculture to such efficiency was to do nothing. That autumn Lady Denman appealed to the Minister of Agriculture, Mr Dorman-Smith, to meet the chairmen to convince them that they would be needed and to maintain morale. Not only was this request ignored but Lady Denman herself was not granted an interview with him until March 1939 – just five months before war was declared. When she finally saw him she handed him a campaign plan urging the Ministry to instruct the chairmen to canvass farmers willing to take on land girls, to find who was prepared to offer billets and to establish a minimum wage. But behind the scenes in Whitehall her sense of urgency was the subject of sneering. The Treasury's extraordinarily complacent reaction to Lady Denman's proposals, expressed in a letter to the Minister of Agriculture, was that they were 'a sledgehammer to crack a nut'.

Towards the end of April 1939, pushed to the limits of her patience by the bumbling incompetence and sheer discourtesy of the officials with whom she was supposed to be in partnership, Lady Denman issued an ultimatum, threatening to resign if she were not authorised to appoint her own headquarters staff. Unlike the only other ultimatum she issued during her time as Director of the Women's Land Army, this had the desired effect. The Permanent Secretary at the Ministry wrote that her 'request was completely reasonable'. The suggestions outlined in the campaign plan she had presented to Dorman-Smith were authorised. Immediately she received the go-ahead Lady Denman appointed Inez Jenkins, who had been General Secretary of the National Federation of Women's Institutes, as her Personal Assistant. From now on things moved fast. Local education authorities and farmers were asked to be ready to train women for tractor driving and other skilled farm work. The county committees were officially recognised and allocated paid secretaries and other clerical staff and a national recruiting campaign was launched. Over a year after she had originally suggested it to the Minister of Agriculture, in June 1939, Lady Denman finally achieved her conference of County Chairmen. The Permanent Secretary of the Minister, who attended it, was impressed by Lady Denman's economical style of leadership, observing that he had 'never seen business dispatched so quickly and speeches so relevant and so short'.

There remained the question of a suitable headquarters for the Land Army. Again the administration dragged its feet. In February 1939 Lady Denman had offered the luxurious home her father had given her as a twenty-first birthday present, Balcombe Place, near Haywards Heath in West Sussex, but had received no response. Six months later – in July – her offer was finally accepted. The move, however, did not take place until the eleventh hour – 29 August – just five days before war began.

The clerical staff – fourteen officers, thirty-five clerks and typists – whose job it would be to create and maintain dossiers on each and every member of a force that would come to number 80,000 and would in its eleven-year life encompass a quarter of a million women, were supplied mainly from the Ministry of Agriculture's offices in Smith Square, off Millbank. They formed the shop floor. Lady Denman, Mrs Jenkins, by now appointed Assistant Director, and Margaret Pyke, the pioneer and champion of family planning and a great friend of Lady Denman's who had been released from her position as

General Secretary of the Family Planning Association, constituted the management triumvirate.

The immediate task facing the country in September 1939 was to bring in the peacetime harvest and get two million extra acres of land ploughed up and under crops by the following year. Thanks in no small measure to a rash of highly idealised recruitment posters featuring healthy looking girls in tight sweaters cuddling lambs, nuzzling sheaves of corn or leading dependable-looking cart horses there was no shortage of recruits. By the outbreak of war 17,000 women had enrolled and 1,000 volunteers could be sent immediately into employment, many of them trained. There was no doubting the keenness of the girls. One, asked how soon she could be ready, is said to have replied: 'Can you give me twenty minutes?'

This keenness, however, was in no way matched either by the farmers who were expected to take on the girls, or the farm workers who were to show them the ropes and work alongside them. To the intense frustration of Lady Denman and her staff at head office it proved extremely hard in those early months to find jobs for the girls who had volunteered and to keep those on the waiting list from giving up and looking for other kinds of war work. The agricultural workers, or at least the politicised trade-unionised element, were particularly scathing about the Land Army. To their instinctive misogynistic prejudice was added a fear that the girls would prove a source of cheap labour, which would hamper them in their campaign for better wages. The first land girls were indeed paid twenty-eight shillings a week, ten shillings below the average farm wage at that time. This is roughly equivalent to £32 in today's money. In July 1939 an editorial in the *Land Worker*, the magazine of the National Union of Agricultural Workers, reacted to the launching of a new Land Army with undisguised spleen: 'The Hon. Mrs This, Lady That and the Countess of Something Else are all on the warpath again. The Women's Land Army is here, and they have all got their old jobs back –

of bossing people, and of seeing that the farmers find a way out of their labour shortage without having to pay better wages.'

The agricultural workers continued to insist that the mere idea of women attempting men's work was ridiculous. An editorial in their magazine a year later sought to share the joke with an audience it knew was like-minded:

> In the House of Commons . . . Mr Lloyd George referred to the 'bad days of Eden, when Adam was turned out because he was a bad farmer'. There is no evidence of bad calculation in the garden of Eden, the story of which contains an agricultural moral always overlooked. It was a successful holding utterly wrecked by the employment of women in the fruit-picking season.

The conviction that women wouldn't be able to perform a whole range of farm work was not confined to farm workers. It was as if the valiant tractor drivers and ploughmen of the first Land Army had never existed. One farming commentator held his lapels and sonorously pronounced:

> Women can look after the chickens, but they cannot ditch. They can feed the pigs, but they cannot look after the boar. They can milk the cows, and if they have enough experience, which is not very often, they can attend to their calving, but they cannot look after the bull. They can drive a tractor with a hay-sweep or hay-mower, but they cannot pitch hay. They can drive a reaper and binder, but they cannot drive a big track-laying tractor. They cannot lay drains, they cannot cart or spread chalk, or spread dung or load it. They cannot pull swedes or mangolds or load them. In fact they cannot do any heavy work on the farm, and there is not a great deal of light work; the idea of substituting women for men on the farm is absurd.

The flood of negative publicity throughout the farming press proclaiming women's unsuitability for land work – and the Government's failure to counter it by a positive campaign of its own – caused considerable bitterness and disillusionment, not only at headquarters but among county staff during this first winter. The frustration was felt all the more keenly as the initial recruitment drive, with its stylish posters, had been such a success. The reaction of Miss Calmedy-Hamlyn of Brides-towe in Devon, a breeder of pedigree stock and a prominent member of her county committee was typical of the anger felt by WLA organisers at the Government's continued failure to accord the Land Army a high profile. Announcing her resignation from her county's WLA organising committee, she wrote: 'I feel that I have been deluded into recruiting girls and getting them to throw up their work, believing that they would get fed, clothed and trained and placed in suitable work on farms. Now they have found that there are no jobs, no uniforms and no places for them. They are being turned adrift while we who are the organisers of the Land Army are having our right of free speech stifled by being prevented from criticising these things we know are taking place.'

The pioneering work of the 4,500 land girls for whom jobs had been found by the end of December 1939 started the thaw in the farmers' attitude. The excessively wet October and November were succeeded by the hardest winter in living memory, with frost and heavy snow in January and a bitterly cold February. 'It was so cold you could cut your hand and not find you'd done it till hours later when your hands thawed,' one girl recalled. But the girls refused to be beaten by mud, snow and ice, keeping their feet warm by stuffing hay down their gumboots. Gradually the word got round that the land girls were not only tougher than expected, but frequently more biddable than male farmhands.

The spring weather brought a renewed demand for labour – the target of two million new acres to be broken to the plough had been successfully met – and by the end of May 1940, 6,000 land girls had been taken on, though still largely in the south where anti-female prejudice was less entrenched. This, however, was nowhere near enough to bring in the 1940 harvest. To cope with this shortfall Lady Denman decided to recruit an auxiliary force whose members worked for four-week seasons. But this time, due to an astonishing lack of support from the authorities, recruitment was not conspicuously successful.

An example of the extraordinary indifference of officialdom to the Land Army can be seen in two consecutive radio broadcasts in June 1940 aimed at farmers in need of extra labour. One was by an official from the Ministry of Agriculture, the other by Ernest Bevin, Minister of Labour. Both urged farmers to apply to the Labour Exchange or their local War Ag. The name of the Land Army wasn't mentioned. This seemed to Lady Denman to be the last straw. In tones of the deepest exasperation she wrote to the Rt Hon. Robert Hudson, who had taken over from Dorman-Smith as the new Minister of Agriculture:

> I was most distressed to hear Mr Hurd in his broadcast last
> night advise farmers wanting seasonal labour to apply either
> to the War Ag Cttee or Lab Exchange. This will give
> farmers the impression that the Ministry does not consider
> the Land Army seriously as a source of labour and it must
> add to the already loudly expressed dissatisfaction of the
> many volunteers whom the Land Army enrolled for seasonal
> work and who are now being told that they are not likely to
> be needed. Mr Hurd's omission is particularly unfortunate
> as, although I did not myself hear Mr Bevin's . . . I am
> receiving protests that when discussing agricultural labour he
> did not mention the Land Army. These broadcasts will add
> to our troubles here. For the regular force we have recruited
> about 3,000 of the additional 5,000 we were told to enrol.
> Many of these are already in training but as yet we have not
> got enough jobs for them. For the Auxiliary Force we have
> enrolled a very large number of volunteers on the estimate
> that these will be needed and that the need was urgent.
> Now even the small demands which we have received for
> Auxiliary Force workers are being cancelled partly because
> soldiers are being made available for farm labour at a very
> low rate. I shall be exceedingly grateful if you will help us by
> making very special reference to the WLA when you
> broadcast tomorrow.

Hudson evidently complied because when Lady Denman wrote she thanked him saying '. . . it was a pleasure to hear the Land Army mentioned individually and not as one item of a mixed bag of conchies, prisoners of war, unemployed etc!'

The appointment of Robert Hudson, affectionately known as 'Rob', as Minister of Agriculture proved a turning point in the success of the Land Army. Intelligent and responsive, he appreciated as well as Lady Denman the vital role which this huge force of willing female labour would be called upon to play in maintaining food production once overseas supply lines inevitably began to suffer. He also, like Lady Denman, enjoyed country life and got on well with farmers. Relaxed and amusing he regularly told stories against himself. A favourite was one which described a lunch to which he had been invited by a Yorkshire farmer and his wife. The spread had been generous, pushing to the limit the wartime austerity measure limiting meals to three courses. He thanked his hostess, adding a mischievous hint that the Ministry of Food would be less impressed with the copiousness of the fare. His hostess, who like many farmers thought that to deny those who were producing the food the opportunity of consuming it was unjust, was unrepentant. Fixing him with a stern look she observed, 'It is written in the Good Book – "muzzle not the ox that treadeth out the corn".'

4 : Land Girls

Who were they, these hopeless, feeble, ham-fisted, finicky, snooty, immoral townies whose coming invasion of the countryside caused such a flurry of disapproval and pessimism in the agricultural dovecote? Alice Fright and her friend Doris Taverner were parlour maids in rural Kent. 'Johnnie' Luxton was a Littlewoods pools clerk in Bootle. Phyllis Nichols was a cook in Devon, Jean Procter was a nanny in Edinburgh. Lily West packed tins of Andrews Liver Salts in a factory in Durham. Margaret Rayner was a shorthand typist. Evelyn Elliott worked in a butcher's shop, Josephine Sewell sold drapery at the Co-op. . . .

Unlike the other women's services, whose hierarchical structure, modelled on the men's, included an officer class drawn from the ranks of the socially privileged, the Women's Land Army was a one-rank force where hard physical labour was the order of the day. Where girls from upper-class families tended to be steered towards officers' rank in the Women's Auxiliary Service, the Red Cross, or even Intelligence as a socially acceptable form of war work, the girls who joined the

Land Army had often left school early and came in the main from modest backgrounds where daughters were expected to work for their living, just like sons. However, the ranks did include farmers' daughters – Dinah Pengilly was almost cut off by her father for lowering herself to the rank of humble farm worker. There were even a few girls from the gentry – Hilary Deedes, now the wife of Lord Deedes, had always wanted to farm and had her father's reluctant blessing, while Jean Barker, now Baroness Trumpington, worked for Lloyd George and had lunch with him every day. In the main, however, the girls were hard-working barmaids, factory workers, hairdressers, mill workers, waitresses, bakeresses.

A third of the girls came either from London or the industrial cities of the north. The ranks of the Land Army would have been considerably thinner without the cotton mills of Lancashire and the stocking factories of Nottinghamshire. Between 1939 and 1948 Lancashire supplied the Land Army with 25,000 girls, with Middlesex coming next in the recruitment stakes.

For most the new life was to prove a rude awakening. Dozens had chosen the Land Army for the most unrealistic of reasons – they fancied themselves in the uniform, they liked the posters featuring smiling glamorous girls carrying sheaves of corn . . . the freedom of life in the open air attracted them. For most of them animals meant dogs and cats and implements a knife and fork. Yet within a matter of days of leaving home, and often with minimal training, those who chose general farming would be expected to walk down pitch-dark lanes to fetch and milk recalcitrant cows; harness towering Shire horses, drive a pony and trap delivering milk, learn the facts of life in a hurry (and often in front of a sniggering crowd of onlookers) by taking the cow to the bull; drive tractors and wield unfamiliar weighty implements like scythes and pitchforks designed for male muscles.

Insulated by their city background from the unselfconscious couplings of the birds and the bees, their innocence was total.

Within days of arriving at her Devon farm Johnnie Luxton, then twenty-one, was asked if she would help the man castrate the pigs. 'I had no idea what that meant so I willingly agreed. The man in the pig hut told me to fetch a can of Jeyes fluid and a sharp knife. He told me to hold the can so that he could dip the knife in it each time it was used. The first few piglets he picked up were sows so all he did was clip their ears. Then he picked up a boar. Slash, slash went the knife. The piglet squealed, there was blood everywhere, he dipped the knife in the Jeyes fluid and carried on with the next one. Everything that fell to the floor was gobbled up by the dogs. The farmer said my face was a picture. "You didn't have the faintest idea what we were going to do, did you?" '

Naturally these girls who didn't know hay from straw, made mistakes. One, handed a bucket of soapy water and a cloth by the cowman on her first day and told to get washing (he meant the cows' udders) while he did something else, turned out on the exasperated cowman's return painstakingly to have washed one cow from head to toe. One girl was told to harness up the carthorse, a huge Clydesdale. 'I had to stand on a box to put his collar on. He put his head down so I could put the collar on. Then he tossed his head up. I was still holding the collar. Up in the air went I with him.'

The staff in county offices did their best to prepare volunteers for the toughness, exhaustion and, often, loneliness that were more than likely to be the real harvest reaped by their patriotic gesture. Many Land Army organisers believed the unashamedly glamorous image of pastoral life evoked by recruitment posters was deceitful. An instructress at a Farm Institute in Hampshire tartly rebuked the commercial artists of the day for showing a 'pretty girl nursing a lamb or an equally ravishing blonde in a picture hat, tossing a minute wisp of hay'.

You could join the Land Army at seventeen, though some, like Barbara Pawlowski, who was only sixteen, lied about their age and forged her father's signature to get in. Others, like Peg Francis in Grimsby, counted off the days to their seventeenth birthday in order to sign up. Most people in the Forties seem to have been a good deal more innocent than we are today. Many of the tens of thousands of teenagers who volunteered had led sheltered lives and were emotionally little more than children. Some, required to travel from their home in Lancashire down to a remote farming community in Devon, revealed they had never been on a train; others, used to sleeping in double beds with several siblings, cried themselves to sleep with homesickness in their unfamiliar bedrooms. This was one of the main reasons why it was decided to use bunk beds – regarded as more companionable than single beds – when equipping Land Army hostels.

It certainly wasn't hard to get into the Land Army. In fact many old land girls who suffered with back problems as a result of lifting, think the medical examinations should have been as probing as they were for the Armed Services. One girl remembers her medical as being over in a minute: 'All I had to do was open my mouth and say "ah". For that I was pronounced fit.'

Peg Francis's examination in February 1946 was almost as abbreviated. 'Dr: "I see you wear spectacles my dear. Read the letters please." I got nearly to the bottom line. Dr: "Never mind, I suspect you'd see a charging bull." '

Today we are used to the steady advance of women across territory once thought of as an exclusively male preserve. Increasingly, we see little odd in women driving buses, lorries and taxis, just as we accept women judges, bankers and surgeons. But in the conservative climate that characterised country life at the end of the Thirties the appearance of the land girl caused shock waves of seismic proportions. She was, of course, an interloper twice over, on sex grounds and because she often came from the more sophisticated world of the city, with its fondness for the latest fashions – make-up,

film-star hairstyles, impractical shoes. Imagine the men gawp-
ing and the women, threatened by this influx of self-conscious,
youthful, colourful frivolity, scowling.

Many of the older farmers never got over the incongruity of
seeing young girls carrying out tasks that since the dawn of
time had been done by men. Arthur Street, a successful
farmer–author, describes a female threshing gang: 'Recently
on a drizzly, cold afternoon, I visited several gangs. I saw
typists minding the chaff, mannequins on the strawrick, bank
clerks on the cornrick, and domestic servants cutting
bonds . . .'

And if Street's view of the land girl was that of an impostor,
albeit it a comely one, the general public's mental picture of a
land girl was even wilder. An editorial in the *Land Girl*
magazine in May 1941 enumerated with amusement the
variety of stereotypes adopted by the public when discussing
the land girls:

> A study of press cuttings leaves one baffled by the variety of
> vision of people who write to the papers. Some see the Land
> Army as a solid mass of amazons tossing the bull with one hand,
> and throwing a hundredweight sack with the other. Some have
> a vision of a pale anaemic female trying to do impossibly heavy
> work in appalling conditions; others fear land girls as dangerous
> and brightly painted houris, luring innocent farmers from their
> happy homes.

From the start the Land Army suffered from an image
problem, perhaps because it became associated with the low
status from which, quite unfairly, the agricultural worker has
always suffered in this country, compounded by the fact that it
was made up only of women. This certainly hampered
recruitment in the early days, a fact which policy makers in the
civil service were predictably slow to address. It was the thing
in certain quarters to look down on land girls. Women in the
Auxiliary Services seem to have been particularly snobbish.
One girl went into a pub with some other land girls and found

soldiers with ATS girls. 'They called out, "Here come the sod busters". The men were friendly and told us we were doing a good job. I remember how horrified my sister was when I told her I had enrolled. She was a WRNS officer and told me I was wasting my education and would soon be bored working with yokels who were "wood from the neck up". I said I had joined because I preferred to grow things than help destroy them.'

In those old-fashioned days when daughters lived at home until they married and a frequently highly authoritarian father's word was law, many girls joined the Land Army for the undreamed-of delight of getting away from home. This was the case with Jean Procter, who joined in January 1939.

> I had an old-fashioned father who thought women shouldn't work. He'd sent me up to Edinburgh to look after an elderly aunt. I was bored stiff. I wanted to join the WRNS but at four feet eleven they said I was too short. I didn't fancy the WACs and the ATS – a friend who was an officer said the girls were a coarse lot – so I got round my aunt and joined the Land Army. It was very different from the image in the posters of girls with fluffy lambs under their arms or carrying a sheaf of corn. I spent the first two weeks carting pig manure – loading it into carts, taking the cart to the field, coming back and starting all over again. At the end of a fortnight the farmer said to me: 'If you'll stick at that you'll stick at anything.'

Other girls had genuinely idealistic reasons. Few, however, had any idea how tough and how different from the picture on the romantic recruitment posters the life would prove to be. Valerie Hodge, a young artist living in an attic studio in Bristol, was the very first land girl to enrol. In July, after being presented to King George VI at a National Service Rally in Hyde Park, she explained why she had chosen the Land Army. 'Here was the thing for me – the service to serve England – the service to keep this land alive – and also a service in which one could help in the everlasting process of creation, instead of helping in destruction.'

A journalist writing for the magazine *Illustrated* in December

1941 gives an idea of what new land girls looked like as they arrived from the cities. Turning these delicate butterflies into strong uncomplaining workhorses must have seemed an uphill task to the farmers. 'They arrive unsuitably shod, unsuitably clad; with four-inch heels and eye-veils. Make-up masks their faces. They are finicky about their food . . .'

Aware that the war was forcing them to attempt a social experiment that might well prove as doomed as mixing oil and water, the Land Army organisers urged land girls not to regard their new neighbours as Neanderthal backwoodsmen and try to adapt to their new life.

Shewell Cooper, a veteran horticultural columnist, was the author of the *Land Army Manual*. The booklet, written in hearty, bufferish prose totally at odds with Lady Denman's economical style, was designed to imbue all volunteers with the correct patriotic spirit – 'farming work . . . mean[s] hard physical strain, but any girl who can endure it finds compensation in the knowledge that she is playing a very important part in National Service'. It aimed, in Cooper's rather ponderous way, to prepare them for country life. He warned in particular against a superior attitude.

> The town girl does not often find it easy to live in the country. She naturally misses all the amenities she is used to. She cannot pop into the local cinema when she feels inclined. She cannot even go round to the local fish and chip shop or to a snack bar if she wants a quick meal in the evening. She is not able to stroll down the High Street and have a look at the shops and see the latest fashions, and there are not, of course, the number of men about to go to dances with at the local Palais de Dance.
>
> Some townspeople are apt to look upon all country folk as country bumpkins. They have an idea that it is only the town folk who know anything, and because people in the country are not so slick, or are not so well dressed, or perhaps are not up to the latest fashion, they are apt to be labelled as old-fashioned . . .
>
> Actually country folk usually know far more than those who are bred and born in towns and cities. They may not know all the names of the film stars . . . but they do know the names of

the birds and their habits. They are able to tell whether it is going to be wet or fine the next day. They know which herbs are useful and all about the ways of wild animals . . .

Betraying his age with words like 'rouging', Cooper urged these exotic Birds of Paradise from the cities to lay aside their gaudy plumage and adopt in future the more discreet tones of the hedgerow sparrow:

> Town girls on the whole use far more make-up than country girls [he warns]. The WLA volunteer should therefore be prepared to 'tone down' her lips, complexion and nails considerably. A certain amount of make-up may be used at parties and local village dances, but long nails are quite unsuited to work on a farm, especially when covered with bright crimson nail varnish. The volunteer will soon find that, as the other girls from the village do not use make-up, she will prefer not to use it herself so as not to look conspicuous. She will find, too, that she will get such a healthy colour to her cheeks that rouging will not be necessary!

The land girl who goes into her new surroundings determined to 'show them a thing or two', Cooper is at pains to stress, will never thrive. Ignoring both clothes rationing and the fact that most land girls could not aspire to *haute couture* wardrobes he warns: 'She will only be stared at if she wears the very latest Bond Street creation at the local social or "hop".'

One of the aspects of the Land Army which distinguished it from the other Services was that, since land girls were employed by the individual farmer and not by the State, there was no real disciplinary system. It was thus vital to impress upon recruits the need to stay at their posts. Shewell Cooper: 'Every volunteer should remember that money has been spent on her equipment and training to make her a *specialist* for a vital job. She should not, therefore, *ever drop out*. She must feel that *she* is feeding the nation. If she drops out, someone may starve. The Land Army must have a motto – "Stick to it".'

To make sure the potential recruit would be able to cope

with heavy work, Cooper suggested strengthening exercises: 'It is quite a good plan to try carrying buckets full of water for half an hour or more at a time, and then attempting to pitch earth onto a barrow and then onto a shelf about breast high for another hour or so, to see whether she can bear the aches and pains entailed.'

If these outsiders were to fit in, they had to learn what today we would call the country code – one of the complaints of farmers who had employed land girls at the end of the First World War was that they couldn't stop them smoking, even in the ultra vulnerable stackyards, where an entire winter's hay crop could be wiped out in one blaze. 'The volunteer should aways be punctual in her hours; she should not smoke about the place, especially in farm buildings. She should shut gates behind her; she should put her tools back properly, so that the next person who wants them can find them; she should never leave a job undone just because she finds it difficult.'

Lastly Cooper urged humility: 'A farmer is not made in a month, and . . . some girls are inclined to try to teach the farmer his business, often with unfortunate results . . . Farmers have no time to bother with fussy volunteers. They expect girls who have offered to do the work to carry it out without complaint.'

There was also plenty of advice on the need to work at fitting in with village life: 'Be prepared to do some useful work in the village in your spare time. It may be that you can get into touch with the local representative of the WVS and do some knitting. Perhaps you will be able to help by forming one of the personnel of the village First-Aid Point. You can be very useful, too, by putting your name down as one of the fire-watchers. Join the local Women's Institute . . . Go to any socials there may be in the village and try to fit in naturally. Don't push yourself and so spoil things. Take part in all such activities in a humble manner and help to break down any prejudice there may be against women on the land.'

The land girl was left in no doubt that she was an employee

and was warned against acquiring ideas above her station: 'When living at a farm where a maid is kept the volunteer should remember that she also is employed by the farmer, and not by herself. She should not therefore expect the maid to wait on her, nor should she give the maid extra work and extra bother.'

Heavy-handed though much of this advice sounds to our ears it was well meant. There is an air of the fussy mother hen in the clothes list recommended by the *Manual* and by the inclusion of old-fashioned remedies against wear and tear for tender hands unaccustomed to rough physical work, even if it was often received with hilarity by its irreverent young readers.

In addition to your uniform, be sure to take with you:
    two complete sets of underwear (at least)
    two complete sets of night clothes (at least)
    a pair of house slippers
    another pair of walking out shoes.
    one or two frocks for changing into in the evening
    a woolly scarf to put round the head early in the morning
    woolly gloves
    a bicycle if you possess one
    ordinary toilet requisites

Remedy for roughened hands
    Put one ounce of olive oil and 1 ounce chopped beeswax into a jar in the oven till melted. Cool and when easy to handle roll into a ball. Rub lightly into the hands after washing. A little oat flour will remove greasiness.

Chapped hands
    After washing the hands work in soap till all is absorbed and the hands are dry. Apply glycerine night and morning before quite drying the hands.

Chilblains
    Exercise the toes and fingers whenever possible. Do not wear wool socks or stockings next the skin. Apply ointment consisting of 10 grains of menthol to one ounce of olive oil. Dress broken chilblains with gauze. Keep this on with plaster.

Cracked thumbs

Apply Zambuk, castor oil or oil of wintergreen and cover with Elastoplast or a thumb stall to keep clean.

Jean Procter

(*née* Young). Joined Land Army at 19.
Land Army Jan. 1939–Dec. 1945.
Home town: Heaton Moor near Stockport, Lancs.
Civilian occupation: Trainee nanny.

I can still remember those wonderful country smells I would never have discovered but for the Land Army; the almost indescribable smell of the bell-clear morning air just before daybreak when the whole world feels renewed. It is part earth, part leaves and part something beyond words – but it has this scent that is so special you feel you can grow on it. I shall never forget those pre-dawns, walking along lanes to fetch the cows with my eyes still closed, hoping I was going in the right direction . . . Gradually the beauty of it all, the sense that you were part of a huge majestic system that would go on for ever, overcame your sense of tiredness. You'd hear the birds making soft friendly noises to each other in the hedge, see a rabbit popping down its burrow flashing its white scut, notice the dew sitting in great gemlike drops on the spiders' webs in the hedge . . . There was the lovely smell in the cowshed, the smell of warm cows and hay, the comfortable feeling of burrowing in against the flanks of a warm cow on a cold morning . . . and later in the day the smell of burning wood as you lit bonfires of hedge trimmings on a frosty autumn morning.

There was this immense knowledge the old farmhands had that you never quite acquired, though you acquired quite a lot. When I joined the Land Army I could not recognise one cow from the other. The farmer would rip his hair out because I put them all in the wrong stall. But after a while your powers of observation increased. You could look at a sheep and see if it had foot rot or maggots. But you still couldn't look at the sky and smell wind or rain coming the way the old country folk could. 'Better get that bit of hay in, rain's coming,' they'd say, when to you the sky looked clear as a bell. They were always right. They may have been illiterate but what they didn't know about the country wasn't worth knowing. They knew what to put on a sting or a swelling. Once I twisted my foot quite badly. One of the old farmhands fetched some comfrey and put it on as a cool poultice. It took the pain away and reduced the swelling like magic.

It wasn't all poetry. There were dirty, sweaty, routine jobs, like cleaning out stalls and byres. There were jobs that were positively horrible. I spent four days carting and spreading lime. When the wind blew you got it all over you. Because it was caustic it made my eyes sting and my nose bleed. But there were jobs you did once in twelve months where the sense of satisfaction of having done well was immense – looking at a field that had been stones and scrub a year before all beautifully planted up with crops, taking the last cartload of corn in and looking back at the shaved field of stubble.

What the Land Army did was make me independent. I'm seventy-seven and I've just repointed a stone wall and lowered a ten-foot hedge from ten feet to six feet. I spent six weeks with the national hedge-laying champion while I was in the Land Army – my farmer wanted me to be properly trained. The local tree surgeon said I'd done a good job with my hedge.

5 : Balcombe

As long as the phoney war lasted procrastinating Whitehall officials saw no need to promote the Land Army, an outfit which they clearly found hard to take seriously. From 1940, however, Germany began her two-pronged assault on Britain in earnest. London and the south of England experienced first the deadly dogfights of the Battle of Britain and then the agony of the Blitz, as wave after wave of bombers appeared on their nightly mission to cripple the country's industrial power and batter the capital into submission. Meanwhile shipping in the Atlantic was targeted with deadly accuracy by German U-boats whose brief was the destruction of British supply lines. This forced the Government finally to give serious thought to raising the profile of the Land Army.

By the summer of 1940 the Government's plans to boost food production appeared to be paying off. The hot dry summer, increased use of machinery and a male labour force that was still reasonably plentiful – at this time farm workers were not called up till they were twenty-one – combined to produce a harvest up a tenth on the average in the years before the war.

But in Cabinet circles it was obvious that on the food front things could only deteriorate, with the intensifying of enemy action making the call-up of more and more able-bodied men from the land inevitable. In October 1940 Robert Hudson, the eloquent Minister of Agriculture, at last gave evidence of the Government backing Lady Denman and her assistants had been looking for in a rousing Churchillian speech to Land Army volunteers.

> The events of the past six months have made increased food production at home even more urgent. Total war is a war of endurance and to ensure winning it we must make the most use of all our resources, especially the land. Milking the cows, feeding the pigs and the poultry or driving a tractor day after day is unspectacular and at times may seem to you very dull. But without the food you help to produce the bravery of the fighting services would be of no avail and the machinery in our munitions factories would be silent and still. Famine could achieve what no bomb or blitzkrieg or invading force will ever bring about. It is your vital task to see that such a thing could in no conceivable circumstance arise, and is driven even further from the realms of possibilities.

Once the Land Army was up and running it was at Balcombe Place that Lady Denman set up her central office and spent most of her time. In this she was assisted by fourteen officers and thirty-five clerks and typists, mostly from the Ministry of Agriculture in London. Balcombe Place was a rambling, somewhat ungainly stone mansion set in 3,000 acres of Sussex countryside, had been built in the mid nineteenth century in Elizabethan style and had been Lady Denman's home since 1905. It was here that in 1907 she gave birth to her second child, Judith. It was from Balcombe that throughout the war Lady Denman drafted Land Army policy and campaigned in the teeth of resistance to secure its acceptance by members of Churchill's wartime government. It was from

Balcombe that she ran her enlightened campaign for a national minimum wage, and the right of agricultural workers to paid holidays, and from here that she pressed a recalcitrant Cabinet to accord the Land Army the same generous post-war gratuities as women in the armed forces.

The house had seen its heyday between the wars and, like so many grand houses, was destined never to recover its former verve after the Second World War. Today, its polished wooden floors blanketed in red fitted carpet, it is a very elegant, flower-filled old people's home. In the twenties and thirties, however, it hosted house parties almost every week-end. Politicians like Campbell Bannerman, the Liberal Prime Minister, Bob Boothby, rising star of the Tory Party and artist Neville Lytton were among the visitors who joined Lady Denman at billiards or enjoyed a set on Balcombe's tennis courts (two grass, one hard). Golfers could saunter round the nine-hole chip-and-putt course, or brave a bracing dip in the open-air swimming pool, which had started life as a lily pond. In those days the impressive stable yard housed, in addition to the hunters on which Lady Denman rode to hounds, half a dozen steeplechasers which Lord Denman not only bred, but rode, completing his final race at the age of fifty.

At the outbreak of war a number of Balcombe's younger servants joined the Services but the nucleus of senior staff, many of whom had served Lady Denman most of their working lives, remained there throughout the war. These were headed by Miss Missenden, the cook, known as 'Mrs *Miss*', Andrews the butler, Miss Young, who was Lady Denman's maid, her chauffeur Mr Burnett, and William Bott, the Odd Man. Penelope Greenwood remembers that Mrs *Miss*'s status was such that she was entrusted with government-supplied food supplies, stored in some of the ten rooms that made up Balcombe's vast cellars, and laid down against an invasion. The tins of meat and sacks of sugar and flour were never touched.

With an enthusiasm in keeping with her democratic ideals Lady Denman turned her family home over whole-heartedly to the young staff of the new organisation and the war effort. The rosebeds were dug up and planted with vegetables, the tennis courts sacrificed to livestock – rabbits, chickens, geese and even pigs were imported to foster the drive for self-sufficiency.

Lord Denman stuck out the invasion of his home by a noisy high-spirited army of young female working-class clerks and typists for ten days and then retired to a hotel in Brighton, whose sea air he claimed would be good for his asthma. From there he went to Scotland. The only reminder of his presence thereafter was the occasional carcase of venison sent down to swell the meagre meat ration, and received by girls from the inner city with muted appreciation.

When the Ministry of Agriculture staff arrived at the station from London they found all the Balcombe Place cars, including Lady Denman's Rolls-Royce, waiting to take them to their new home. On arrival at Balcombe they were given a cocktail while waiting to be shown to their rooms. The house had been completely redesigned to cope with the huge influx of people and equipment. Lady Denman installed her office in what was always known as the Business Room off the vast 'medieval' panelled hall. This became the typing pool for the junior staff. Inez Jenkins occupied the library, which in the evening became the social room where the senior staff met to chat or play cards. Six shorthand typists occupied the drawing-room. Six months after arriving at Balcombe Margaret Pyke launched the *Land Girl*, a monthly magazine which circulated Land Army news, published contributions – articles, drawings and even poetry – by individual girls and attempted to rally the scattered troops. The first issue, produced at a desk next to Lady Denman's in the Business Room, appeared in April 1940, reaching an eventual circulation of 21,000. What had been Balcombe's Music Room became the recreation room for the junior staff. Here they danced, either to gramophone records or to the piano, played darts, or slotted the odd piece into the giant jigsaw puzzles which were a favourite 'improving' pastime of Lady Denman's.

The city-bred youngsters ate the same food as Lady Denman and her assistants – including scones for elevenses, freshly baked by Balcombe's cook – and were free to go everywhere except into Lady Denman's bedroom. They were encouraged to start their day, that sunny autumn, with a dip in the swimming pool.

Margaret Barnett and her friend Barbara Bennett, both seventeen, had been typists in the bull licensing department of the Ministry of Agriculture in Smith Square. They arrived in company with their middle-aged supervisor, Miss Biggs, and recall the atmosphere as a cross between a five-star hotel and a benevolent boarding-school.

Balcombe was conspicuously lacking in male company, with the exception of the official the Ministry of Agriculture had rather patronisingly insisted on sending to run the Land Army budget and correspond with government departments and local authorities. He was a Mr Sutherland Harris. His title was Chief Administrative Officer and, though he ate lunch at Lady Denman's table each day, seems to have spent a lot of time trying not to look conspicuous.

Margaret Barnett says the luxurious atmosphere of Balcombe took them all by surprise: 'It was a real culture shock for us – this transition from working-class London homes to the realm of the aristocracy. The bedrooms were huge – I was in one with four other girls. Barbara was in what had been the night nursery for Lady Denman's children, with bathroom adjoining. We had monogrammed bedlinen and heated towels. There were at least half a dozen bathrooms. Lady Denman was very kind. If we went out at night when we came back milk and biscuits would have been left out for us in the enormous kitchens. During the Blitz we didn't go home much, but when we did we would be loaded up with flowers and vegetables from the garden.' For this munificence each girl paid a guinea (twenty-one shillings) a week which was deducted from her salary.

The thing Margaret Barnett found most difficult, coming from a modest background, was learning to address the domestic staff, who were often years older than herself, by their surnames. 'There was Burnett, the chauffeur, who always met us at the station in the limousine if we had been to London, and Andrews, the head butler. It did feel awkward but they were all very kind to us. We even started leaving our shoes out at night to be cleaned, which was rather naughty. Sometimes we'd play shove ha'penny with the footman in the butler's pantry.'

The girls' only complaint was that the stately meals, served in the dining-room in the old style by a full complement of staff, left them permanently hungry. This was partly due to rationing. Mrs Missenden brought in each girl's individual two-ounce ration of butter, cheese and sugar with the owner's name neatly written on a sandwich flag. There was, however, something of a tradition of people being hungry at Balcombe, even before the war. Penelope Greenwood says her grand-mother, who was by nature abstemious, decided that her house guests ate too much. Andrews the butler was accord-ingly instructed to serve four courses at dinner, instead of five. 'The experiment was abandoned soon afterwards. There was always a jug of milk and a plate of biscuits left out in the hall for guests who felt peckish on their way to bed. After the dinners were reduced Andrews told my grandmother that he felt the guests must be hungry as the plate was always empty in the morning.'

People who worked for the Land Army put the lack of filling food down to the inability, both on the part of Lady Denman and her staff, to abandon the old patrician standards. Though in many ways she went out of her way to be democratic, class distinctions did survive. One example of this was that when

Lady Denman was entertaining the Regional Officers of the Land Army she and her deputy, Mrs Jenkins, would drink wine while they were served water.

As part of the drive to cut the national consumption of food in the war years the Government decreed that households should not serve meals of more than three courses. Many county families embraced these democratic strictures enthusiastically, though sometimes their attempts to adapt to a simpler life-style produced results that were unintentionally comic. Dorothy Brant, who was one of the seven Regional Officers of the WLA, remembers a dinner at Balcombe.

We had been travelling all day and were really looking forward to our dinner. The food, brought in by the butler and footman, was beautifully appointed. The first course was a salmon, decorated as you would see it in Mrs Beeton. We were each given a minute quantity. The dessert was strawberries. They came in on a great dessert dish with a stand. The china was beautiful – white with a black rim and a decoration in gold. Solemnly the butler placed four strawberries on each plate. The Denmans had done their best to be egalitarian, but instead of serving cheap filling food like mashed potatoes, they were still doing things as they had when there were six, seven or eight courses at dinner. We talked to the senior residential staff at Balcombe and they admitted that they were permanently hungry because of the exquisite but totally inadequate food.

Margaret Barnett and her friends solved the problem by setting off every day after breakfast to buy a cottage loaf in the village shop and devouring it on the way back.

Lady Denman is remembered by the girls as an odd blend of indulgence and old-fashioned matronly strictness. She herself was a heavy smoker and there were always boxes of cigarettes for them to help themselves to in the drawing-room. The girls, however, were expected to observe certain standards of behaviour, many of which were unfamiliar. When the gong sounded for lunch, for example, they were not allowed to walk in, but were expected to form an orderly queue outside the dining-room. Margaret Barnett recalls Lady Denman's keen-ness on gardening, exercise and civic duty, all of which were regarded as character building:

> We all had to have our own little twelve- by eight-foot plot to grow greens and potatoes. We were shown how to double dig. Most of us came from London and were very young. We didn't find gardening that fascinating. Lady Denman also believed in regular exercise. Every lunch-time she would organise a hockey game. Most of us had never played hockey and we weren't too keen on that. We were made to do old-fashioned country dancing – the Sir Roger de Coverley and The Dashing White Sergeant . . . But the thing we dreaded was sitting at her table for lunch. We all ate in the dining-room and Lady Denman always sat at a table in the window, overlooking the swimming pool. Each day one of us was expected to sit with her. She did it because she was genuinely kind and wanted to get to know us, but she was a woman from a very different background and also from an older generation. I found the experience agonising.

Sundays, when Lady Denman expected the girls to be good citizens by visiting the hospital in Haywards Heath and helping look after wounded soldiers, became known among the disrespectful youngsters as 'hairs and scum day'.

Lady Denman made commendable efforts to cross the class divide and welcome the young women who had invaded her home. But there were times when she found the challenge of fraternising with the cockney typists a strain.

Penelope Greenwood, who was only seven at the outbreak of war, spent many school holidays at Balcombe since her mother, Lady Denman's daughter Judith, was very busy as chairman of the Land Army in Sussex. She enjoyed a closeness with her grandmother which Lady Denman had not experi-enced with her own daughter and recalls how Lady Denman solved the problem of taking a break from her office without having to bump into junior staff: 'Now and again she would be desperate to get away from her desk. But if she walked out of the door she'd be in the hall, which was full of typists. Rather than face them she had the Odd Man build a set of wooden steps leading from her office window down to the garden. From time to time she'd nip down unnoticed and have a quiet cigarette. Sometimes I'd meet her there and we'd build a bonfire together. That was one of her favourite occupations.'

With soldiers billeted at neighbouring Stonehall, a house dating from Stuart times and forming part of the Balcombe estate, only one activity was forbidden – there was to be no dallying with young men in the summer house at Balcombe. 'During the war we had double summer time so it was light till ten or eleven at night,' Margaret Barnett recalls. 'A couple of times girls were caught in there canoodling with soldiers. After that Mrs Jenkins used to patrol the grounds with her torch before locking up.'

Vita Sackville-West, who by this time was well known as a writer and gardening enthusiast, was a regular visitor to Balcombe where she helped Margaret Pyke select poetry for inclusion in the *Land Girl*. She was struck by the incongruity of Balcombe's baronial swagger coexisting with a prosaic office environment.

The red velvet curtains still hang heavily in their place, the oak panelling still makes a rich and sombre background, but the splendid rooms are now filled with office desks and trestle tables piled with card indexes and stationery, typewriters and telephones, pots of paste and Stickphast. Green and white posters of land girls leading horses, land girls carrying corn sheaves are tacked up with drawing pins against the wall . . .

One of the queerest sights . . . is the occupation by Land Army uniform of the outbuildings – the garages, the stables, and the squash racquets court. These evidences of luxury have become purely utilitarian; they have been turned into warehouses. There, from floor to ceiling, are stacked the familiar green jerseys, the brown breeches, the black gumboots, the fawn overcoats, the pale Aertex shirts. All so neat, so beautifully piled. It gives one some idea of the work involved in supplying the needs of eighty thousand girls.

Over all this the slim, vigorous figure of Lady Denman

presided, puffing constantly on her favourite Turkish La Piqua cigarettes in their characteristic orange and green box and clad unfailingly in a tweed suit. None of the Land Army administrative staff wore uniform. Though her town clothes were made for her by the fashionable couturier Worth, at Balcombe tweed was the order of the day. Lady Denman was intensely irritated by women who failed to dress in a manner appropriate to their environment. According to Penelope Greenwood, who now lives at Stonehall, less than a mile from her grandmother's old home, Lady Denman found Vita Sackville-West tiresome – not just for what she regarded as her 'arty crafty' attitudes and elaborately theatrical way of speaking, but for her insistence on wearing 'London clothes in the country' – London clothes consisting of 'rather smart dresses and inappropriate shoes.'

Dorothy Brant nearly fell foul of the Balcombe dress code before being appointed one of the Regional Officers. 'They asked me at headquarters what I would wear for the interview so that Lady Denman would recognise me in the restaurant where we were to meet. I said I would be wearing a pink and grey suit. When I arrived Lady Denman rushed forward with a welcoming smile, looked approvingly at my suit and announced, "You never said it was *tweed*." I discovered later that the reaction at Balcombe to the idea that anyone in the Land Army would wear pink had been intense dismay.'

A certain amount of Lady Denman's time was spent away from Balcombe touring the country visiting land girls in their various counties, meeting the women who ran the county offices, attending conferences and recruitment rallies and generally keeping up morale. Conscious of the need to conserve fuel she had the Rolls put up on blocks, travelling instead in her secretary's small Austin driven by Burnett, her chauffeur. According to her granddaughter these trips were anything but luxurious. 'They got lost . . . they became snowbound . . . she had to stay in horrid hotels and beastly digs, places where there was no fire and no hot water.' It cannot have been easy for a woman used to comfort and no longer young, but as Lady Denman would doubtless have observed: 'there's a war to be won.'

6 : Uniform

One of the main tasks for which the Land Army headquarters at Balcombe Place was responsible was approving and ordering a uniform that was comfortable and practical for physical work in all weathers. Looking at the grainy black-and-white photographs of bonny, smiling girls, taken, for the most part, over fifty years ago, the undeniably romantic appeal of the land girls seems to derive in large measure from what they wore.

To many people the Land Army and the famous uniform are synonymous. Nothing like the breeches and the slouch hat had ever been seen before or would be seen again either marching in parades or toiling in cornfields. The uniform of the WRNS or the ATS was merely a feminised version of the men's uniform. The Land Army had no male role model. Agricultural workers wore no uniform, leaving the designers of the land girls' uniform free rein. What they came up with was unique – a blend of countryside colours, the fashion of the day and a sporty look hitherto the prerogative of men's wardrobes.

Its straight lines and baggy contours were never intended to flatter the curves of the female figure, but these were girls in the prime of life. They were slim and fit and looked anything but masculine. Indeed the stiff garments seem to have accentuated their slightness, while the androgynous appeal of a woman in uniform was heightened when that uniform included trousers – a novel sight on women in the Forties. The Land Army uniform comprised fawn cord knee breeches, matching shirts, a green tie striped with red and bearing the letters WLA in yellow, and a figure-hugging green sweater, cropped at the waist. The legs were clad in thick wool socks which were worn turned down over the hem of the breeches and the shoes were stiff leather boots or brogues. On dress occasions the outfit was set off by a brown trilby-style felt hat (in 1949 this was replaced, to most girls' relief, by a fashionable green beret). A green felt armband with the letters WLA embroidered in red, surmounted by a crown, completed the outfit. Length of service was indicated by red diamonds which were sent out at six-monthly intervals by the county office. In the spring of 1942 the fawn officer-style greatcoat made its appearance. It was instantly admired – 'it's all that can be desired, and looks it' according to one fan. Worn with the Land Army green armband, the greatcoat was not only smart but extremely comfortable. This was thanks to Lady Denman herself. Aware that in cold weather the girls would wear their coats to work in and that they would therefore need consider-able 'give' across the shoulders, Lady Denman had asked Worth to design a shape that was attractive and practical. Unlike those of the other women's Services the Land Army greatcoat had two discreet tucks on the back. There was also a black oilskin mac and sou'wester while in summer the breeches were replaced by camel-coloured dungarees. Like almost everything else, the uniform was 'on coupons'. The system seems to have been extraordinarily cumbersome. As each new coupon book was sent out at the start of the rationing year every land girl received a letter from her County Secretary instructing her to surrender ten coupons straight away for uniform replacements. They were to be sent back to

47

the county office by registered post ('keep the receipt for the registered letter until the safe arrival of the coupons has been acknowledged from this Office'). Because of the harsh nature of agricultural work and the toll it took on clothing, anyone who worked on the land was entitled to an additional ten coupons to cover replacing work clothing. The idea was that later in the year each land girl would get her ten coupons back from the Employment Exchange. The County Secretary was at pains to stress that, despite being asked to surrender ten coupons immediately, Land Army members were better off than civilians. '. . . In the new rationing year you will have the same number of coupons as any other civilian in the country for private spending and, in addition, you will have the use of your Land Army uniform.'

To us, the uniform looks quaintly attractive – particularly when the dungarees were rolled up and turned into shorts to display tanned legs – but to those who had to wear it, distribute it, or supervise its wearing, it was often felt to be anything but.

Finding storage space for so many thousands of garments was, understandably, a nightmare. Penelope Greenwood remembers piles of stockings so tall they towered over people's heads in what is now her sitting room at Stonehall. One day a cat scaled the mountain to have kittens. Unfortunately the plateau at the top was so riven with crevices that some of the kittens fell down and starved. 'Being a child I was considered the only one small enough to burrow down between the piles of stockings to retrieve the malodorous dead bodies.'

Those who had the task of matching uniform to land girl found it at times almost overwhelming.

Dorothy Brant who, as one of the Regional Officers was responsible for the whole of the north east, now a distinguished-looking woman of eighty-nine, remembers the chaos, accentuated because the Women's Auxiliary Services took priority.

I joined in 1942 and we had a hideous time with the uniform. No one had anticipated that the Land Army would grow as fast as it did once women started being called up, which was that year. I remember the pressure on the Harrogate office as hundreds of girls needed to be kitted out. As soon as a girl had enrolled she had to come to the county office to get her uniform, to be told where she was to work and to get her travel warrant. There would be periods when there were suddenly no raincoats, or a shortage of shirts . . . or wellingtons . . . Head Office was always blamed and it certainly was not bespoke tailoring, but Britain was under great stress – the material to make the stuff had to be obtained for a start as there was enormous demand for uniform – from the Services, from the ARP . . .

Lack of overcoats were a major problem to girls who joined in winter. Ivy Lemon, who also joined in 1942, remembers the gaps in her kit. 'The uniform, which was delivered to my home, a week after I received my call-up papers, consisted of one pair of breeches, one pair of shoes, two pairs of socks, one pair of very stiff boots, a green pullover, two pairs of dungarees and one dust coat. No hat, no shirt, no coat, no mac . . . Fortunately I had a brother who had a few short-sleeved Aertex shirts. I managed to wheedle two out of him. I never did see any . . . shirts and the rest of the uniform trickled through when supplies were available.'

Once issued, the uniform was intended to last. Articles in the *Land Girl* regularly warned against profligacy: 'Uniform replacements are made free of charge only when the County Office is satisfied that the old garment has been worn out by fair wear and tear. Hats, breeches, boots and mackintoshes are normally not replaced until the end of the year. Stockings are replaced at the end of six months, as also are gum boots, overall coats, pullovers and slipper socks.'

In the early years problems with obtaining uniform frequently dominated the county news column in the *Land Girl*. Wellingtons were particularly scarce due to the drying up of the rubber supply after Malaya fell to the Japanese. Eventually they were restricted to dairy workers, the others being offered canvas gaiters as a substitute.

The problems caused by the shortage of uniform and its frequently poor quality became so pressing that they led to letters to the newspapers and Parliamentary debates. In a debate in the House of Lords Lord Bingley drew attention to the 'deficient equipment' of the Women's Land Army which, he pointed out, had to bear greater hardships and discomforts than other women's Services: 'Many of them are exchanging pavements for mud. Yet many have been working without greatcoats and with leaking boots and raincoats.'

A Buckinghamshire farmer was so concerned about the effect on productivity of defective outdoor clothing that in November 1942 he wrote to the *Daily Telegraph* about it. His letter provides graphic insight into what it must have been like to be a land girl.

The Women's Land Army has done yeoman's service already, and will continue to do so, but many of the younger members (in length of service) have often worked at a serious disadvantage. Two Land Girls who recently came here to work got soaked through the other morning. Their almost new oilskins leaked like sieves and their one and only pair of boots were pulp. As it was Monday their one spare change of clothing was not dry from the wash. They had, therefore, through no fault of their own, to stay in their billet for the rest of the day, thereby losing four working hours each.

This is only one example of what must be happening all over the country and during the winter the total hours lost will be most serious. Many of the WLA girls have not got their full outfit, and what are they going to do when they have to look after store cattle in the yards or be out on the market gardens? With their present equipment they will not be able during the wet days ahead to put in half a week's work. Rubber boots are now issued only to dairy workers and milkers, but there are many jobs on the land which need rubbers quite as much, if not more, than they do. The WLA have the hardest work of any of the women's services and yet they have been sent out with insufficient clothing which must result in hundreds of working hours lost . . .

Such a state of affairs would not be tolerated by the ATS, WAAF or WRNS.

But in wartime the British were nothing if not resourceful. By the middle of the war the Make Do and Mend campaign was at its height and the pages of the *Land Girl* teemed with tips on how to make the uniform last longer – from turning shirt collars to ingenious ways of repairing holed stockings – a recurrent nightmare as the leather of the boots was so hard – avoiding darning . . . The earnest, well-intentioned advice from head office provoked amusement among those who were actually doing the job, most of whom, after a long day of intense physical labour, felt they had better things to do than cut up their old shirts to make briefs to wear under their dungarees. They took the view that, whatever the instructions from head office, life was too short to place a bag of sawdust in their hat to help keep its shape . . . Many of the hints published in the *Land Girl* would be read out in the hostels for general entertainment. There was one girl who knitted shirts out of unrationed dish cloth yarn, insisting that they washed well and 'in time became quite white'. Another sent in a pattern for moleskin slippers which began with catching and skinning the mole before moving on to curing the skin by soaking it in paraffin. Some tips were useful. The following recipe for making an oilskin waterproof was given out by a committee member from Essex, who got it from a Scottish sea captain: 'A mixture of one part paraffin to one and a half parts copal varnish. If the oilskin is black a little powdered black lead can be added. This mixture dries quickly and prevents oilskins from sticking. Apply with a stiffish brush, sometimes giving two coats.'

If you were lucky enough to possess a pair, even worn-out wellingtons, or gumboots as they called them then, could, it seems, be usefully recycled: 'If your gumboots have gone in the foot but are still sound in the leg, cut off the sole with a sharp knife and trim the instep like an old-fashioned spat. Pull the leg on in the usual way and wear inside L.A. boots, lacing firmly in place. This looks quite tidy and efficient and keeps your legs dry.'

The official *Land Army Manual* put in its mite, though whether girls living on isolated farms had access to the arcane ingredients required by these old-fashioned remedies, is not known. Girls who had difficulty getting their gumboots on and off were urged to sprinkle the insides with French chalk, while those whose lives were made unduly miserable by the curse of leaking shoes were advised to paint them with a mixture of melted beeswax and castor oil. As for land girls whose stockings wore out, the suggestion was that they were not using common sense in looking after them. 'The volunteers should wear the three pairs issued to them in rotation. They will thus last much longer than if one pair is kept for best and two are worn to rags. Wash in good soap powder. Do not rub. Squeeze stockings gently and rinse in warm water. Pull to their proper shape before hanging up to dry.'

Some county reps used their own initiative to combat uniform shortages. Some held social evenings where land girls were invited to choose one item from 'Bundles for Britain' clothing from America. Clothing was in such demand that the girls had to line up in order of length of service. One girl who was second chose 'a gorgeously warm ski suit for sheer warmth' and remembers envying the first girl whose prize was a full-length sheepskin coat liner.

Dorothy Brant eventually split Yorkshire up into three separate offices with the express purpose of acquiring more space to store uniforms necessitated because land girls got bigger through working on the land. 'Whether it was the extra rations they were entitled to because they were working on the land, or whether it was that they became more muscular because of the heavy work, we found that after as short a time as six weeks many girls needed larger breeches, shirts and sweaters.'

For every land girl who loved her uniform there seem to

Recruitment posters for the Land Army
were criticised for portraying
an idealised picture of life on the land.

To join or not to join . . . A land girl shows the Land Army tie
to a civilian in March 1941. The setting is an Oxford Street store
which has been temporarily transformed into an information bureau
featuring war work for women.

*'We'll have to leave that bit, Farmer,
It's full of little bunnies.'*

*'Have you been at the dandelion
wine again, Florrie?'*

'Is it a bull or a heifer?'

*'Anyhow, that's final! Enemy tanks can't
come barging over Mr. Giles's earlies.'*

Cartoons in popular magazines show that the public
initially regarded land girls as naïve and amateurish.

'And to think I
used to buy mud
packs!'

'I take my bearings
from this field. They've
got a new land-girl.'

'All we know is, she comes from
Coventry.'

Pride and Prejudice.

The companionship of hostel life:
residents of Craiglea WLA hostel in Darlington, Co. Durham.

Flo Goodkey, from Hampshire,
later married a Canadian serviceman.

Betty Lee, from Bristol, had worked in
a cigarette factory before joining the
Land Army.

Girls from the industrial north converge on Victoria Station
en route to their new lives on the land in Kent and Sussex.

New recruits arrive at their training centre.
Veteran farming commentators noted sourly:
'They arrive unsuitably shod, unsuitably clad;
with four-inch heels and eye veils'.

have been two who complain that theirs never fitted, and that they never possessed the full kit. The Lancashire girl who attributed her six years' service (four and a half in the same job) without a day's sickness to the 'excellent clothing provided by the WLA' was probably heavily outnumbered. Many complained that the macs were too stiff to work in and, being unventilated, made the wearer hot and sweaty. Instead they preferred to waterproof themselves with sacks. 'We wore them round our waists, draped over our shoulders and tied to our legs, desperately trying to keep dry,' says one girl. The girls billeted on private farms, where there was never time to wash the breeches before they were needed again, seem to have suffered most.

Jean Procter insists her uniform was never remotely glamorous. 'When I went in you got any old thing to wear. For ages I had wellingtons which were two sizes too big and which were two left feet anyway. I didn't get an overcoat for four years; instead I wore a horrible mac topped by a yellow sou'wester. Your clothes rarely fitted. All mine were made for a girl of five foot seven, while I was only five feet. The dungarees you got for summer were far too hot. The breeches were all right. They were made of what we called whistling cord because they made a whistling sound when you walked. But you only got one pair and if you were working with animals they got filthy. If you were going out you wetted the front, took a sharp knife and scraped the muck off them. If you sat down in the pictures people would move away.'

Women who worked with machinery and whose uniform became saturated with oil and the paraffin that fuelled the Fordson tractors had additional problems. Margaret Hurst who worked in Hertfordshire as a full-time tractor driver used to go to the cinema with a young man who was in the Navy. 'I learned later that he told his friends he was afraid to light up a cigarette because the smell of paraffin coming from my clothes made him nervous.'

But while land girls thought they had a raw deal where

uniform and clothing was concerned female farm workers maintained land girls received highly preferential treatment.

A local paper in January 1943 considered the clothing issue so pressing it devoted its letters page to it. One, from three girls aged fifteen to twenty-two, reads: 'Farmers' daughters work long hours wading in the mud all day with no gum boots and no prospect of any, but the Land Army, which they are not allowed to join, get the boots and the mac . . .'

Another, from two experienced female farm workers, makes the point even more forcefully: '. . . We are often unable to obtain the clothing necessary for our work. This is particularly the case in the matter of footwear, really heavy shoes being practically unobtainable by a civilian even though they may be actually on view in the shops. In theory a farmer can get a permit to buy Wellington boots for his land workers, in practice it is not possible if *one* pair of wearable boots remains on the farm; while the Land Army are issued with a pair each and constant replacements.'

Land girls had a reputation – much to their leaders' dismay – for jazzing up their uniform in a way that was not an option for women in the Auxiliary Services, subject as they were to strict military discipline. Vita Sackville-West deplored this and scathingly denounced the girls who brought the uniform into disrepute. 'Uniform worn properly is smart, whereas uniform adapted to the personal whimsy of the wearer looks like nothing but a confused and unsuccessful fancy dress, . . . they would think it comical in the extreme if they encountered a soldier wearing a battle dress tunic on the upper part of his body, grey flannel trousers on his legs, and a trilby hat perched on one side of his head. Yet they themselves will cheerfully go about in a flowery frock showing under their khaki overcoat, or a magenta jumper combined with dungarees . . .'

Vita reserved her deepest scorn for the way some of the girls wore their hats: 'You cannot look fashionable in uniform; you can usually look only trim, neat and correct; but the land girl's uniform does offer the other alternative of looking picturesque.

This alternative she too often neglects in favour of trying to imitate the millinery advertisements in the illustrated papers. With dire results. She builds her hair up in such a way that no hat could possibly be expected to stay in place, adds a bootlace to her hat, and uses it as a chin-strap, trying, presumably, to make an ornament out of it, not realising that to the casual observer she looks as though she were suffering either from toothache or from mumps.'

Margaret Pyke took the same view and deemed the abitrary embellishment of the uniform so serious a breach of regulations that in August 1942 she devoted a leader to the subject in the *Land Girl*. Again it was the abuse of the hat which drew her ire.

> Volunteers are proud of their uniform, both for its looks and for its significance; it is a pity some of them attempt to improve on it. Uniform must be *uniform* or it loses all its point. Come out as gay or as shabby or as Bohemian as you like in civilian clothes, but don't try to express your personality in your uniform. This does not, of course, refer to tweed coats or old jerseys worn for dirty work on the farm or in the garden; but a volunteer seen in the streets of a large town . . . wearing a hat cocked on one side and tied on with red ribbon in a large bow under the chin, red tie and fancy shoes with otherwise correct uniform makes passers-by gaze at her with wild surmise as to whether it is she or the Land Army which has gone crackers. Nor do green corduroy trousers and the Land Army go well together.

When the weather was nice, however, and the girls good-looking, the uniform evidently did look delightful, a fact which Vita was ready to concede. Her lyrical, indeed transparently erotic description of girls sorting apples on what was clearly a perfect late summer day captures probably as well as anyone ever has the elusive charm of the land girl.

> One of the prettiest sights I ever saw was four land girls sitting on upturned packing cases under an oast house in the warm September sun. They sat round a huge sea of Orange Pippins, I don't know which were the rosier – the apples or their cheeks. It

55

was just a harmony of complementary colours, in browns and reds and greens. The browns came pale in the woods of the boxes, the wicker of the bushel baskets, the corduroy breeches, darker in the sunburnt hands moving among the fruit, and in the immense Mexican straw hats which for some odd reason two of the girls were wearing, giving them a startlingly foreign appearance in that very English farmyard; the reds came in the apples and in the red brown tiles of the roofs; the green in the few leaves still clinging to the stalks, and in the familiar jerseys, so close-fitting to the young figures. The whole picture seemed powdered over with gold from the latening sun, late in the day as it was late in the year; and the laughter of the girls seemed golden too . . .

Doreen Jakeman

(*née* Godfrey). Joined Land Army at 17.
Land Army 1941–50.
Home town: Whitstable, Kent.
Civilian occupation: left school at 16 to work in family seed and nursery
business.

Throughout my nine years in the Land Army I worked in dairy
farming – except for the time I spent in hospital.

One extremely hot September morning in 1942 I was in a
field at a farm in Wilsborough, just outside Ashford in Kent. I
was taking maize out to the cows, doling it out from the two-
wheeled dung cart. In those days it was grown for the leaves,
rather than the cob, and was used as a grass substitute – it had
been a very hot summer and the grass supply was running out.
There was just me, the horse and cart, my boss and twenty-
odd cows, mostly Shorthorns. All of a sudden there was a
terrific noise of engines and something like a huge grey blanket
appeared right over my head. It was no higher than the ceiling
in an average room. My boss shouted 'Get under the cart' and
I flung myself on the ground. The plane was a Junkers 88,
which was a fighter bomber, capable of carrying four bombs.
Their typical route was to cross from France to Folkestone and
follow the railway line up to Ashford where they'd drop their
bombs on the railway works. Because of the roar of the engine
I didn't realise they were firing at us – I was wearing khaki
dungarees and probably looked like a soldier – but when the
boss said 'get up. You're all right', I heard myself saying 'No
I'm not. I've been hit.' I touched my ankle with my hand and
found my hand was soaked with blood even though I couldn't

feel anything. A man shouted over from the other field 'Are you all right?' and my boss replied, 'no. Get a doctor quick. The land girl's been hit.' Then a doctor appeared driving across the fields. They had two stretchers – I expect they thought the boss had been hit too – and took me to Wilsborough Cottage Hospital. There were six land girls in the ward. One had been injured at Ashford station – standing too close to the rail when someone opened the door – the other five all had had appendicitis. This was a hazard of the job for people who weren't used to all the lifting and heavy work.

During the time I was at Wilsborough, Canterbury was blitzed night after night by German planes. One of the casualties was the County Headquarters of the Land Army. They had to start all over again, writing to each land girl in Kent, asking us when we joined and all our past history. The raids got so bad that the hospital authorities decided it was too dangerous and transferred all the patients to Pembury.

I had four wounds – two where the bullets went in and two where they came out. It did a lot of damage – cutting through the sciatic nerve – and left me with a dropped foot – I'm lame to this day. I was in plaster for a year, which was a mistake as it wasted the muscles. After that I had to wear a caliper for two years. This was a terrible nuisance in dairy work as I had a problem getting my gumboots on and off. If I got water down inside them I just couldn't get them off.

I stayed on the land for four years after the Land Army was disbanded. The life could be quite hazardous I nearly got killed by a cow. She was a Red Poll and she was very temperamental. I was the only person who could milk her. All the men were afraid of her. What I didn't know was that when she calved she was dangerous. The head cowman knew and when she was ready to calve he put her in a loose box near his house. I went unsuspectingly to give her feed and water and as I opened the door she charged me, bashing me right up against the wall and darned well near killing me. Then she backed away ready for a second charge. Somehow I managed to get out and get the door shut behind me but I was absolutely terrified.

I was determined to stay on the land and when the Land Army head office offered land girls who wanted to make a career in agriculture the chance of full-time training at the expense of their local council, I leapt at the chance. I spent a year at the Agricultural Institute in Moulton, Northants, learning every aspect of farming. After the Land Army was disbanded I went to work for a man who wanted to build up a herd of pedigree Ayshires. I worked for him for two years with no one helping me. I once went six months without a day off. That was as much as I could take. I was amused to learn that my boss replaced me with a man and a boy, because the man said there was too much work for one person.

I gave up the land in 1954 to marry a farmer who worked on land adjacent to my farm. We'd known each other for four years. We used to meet in the same café and talk about farming matters – the weather, the harvest, the cows . . . everything except romance. When he told his mother he wanted to get married she was against it because of my lameness. She didn't want him to spend his life looking after a cripple.

7 : The Rate for the Job

The chance to campaign on a national scale for improvements in pay and living conditions for country people was meat and drink to a woman of Lady Denman's progressive social attitudes and she seized the opportunity offered by her position as head of the WLA with gusto. At the outbreak of war the average wage for a male agricultural worker was 38 shillings a week (approximately £45 would be the current equivalent) – less than half the national weekly average for unskilled labour in other occupations which in March 1940 was estimated as 80 shillings. Lady Denman had to fight every inch of the way to secure a minimum wage of 28 shillings a week for the Land Army. From the start there was no question of equal pay as the Land Army administration did not believe a girl could do as much as a man. Vita Sackville-West certainly didn't. In her view 'Agriculture is . . . one of those professions in which a man is fully justified in receiving the high wage. He gives better value for his time and money. I think most farmers would agree that the ratio would work out at three women equalling two men.'

Even by the standards of the day it was a low wage. Girls with good office jobs in the towns and cities were earning around £4 and usually lived at home until they got married. Huge numbers took a substantial pay cut when they joined the Land Army, particularly after 14 shillings was deducted for board and lodging. Joan Chapman, who left a good job with ICI to join the Land Army in Kent, says girls who had come from London envied the local girls who lived at home and didn't have to part with the 14 shillings for their billet. Yet while most girls took a pay cut, those who had been in domestic service in civilian life thought Land Army pay and conditions paradise compared with what they were used to. Alice Fright, who had gone into service after leaving school at fourteen, had been earning 7 shillings and 6 pence for a six-and-a-half-day week as a parlourmaid in Kent.

The hours worked by agricultural workers in the war years, be they men who were born to it or land girl volunteers, seem exceedingly long by our standards. The basic week was forty-eight hours in winter and fifty in summer. Any additional hours – and at haymaking and harvest time farmhands worked till the light failed, which with double summer time could be eleven at night – qualified as overtime. It was typical both of Lady Denman's vigour and sense of fair play to want to get the farming industry regulated. Wages crept up throughout the war and by the time the official WLA Manual came out it was able to tell the would-be volunteer:

> The Ministry of Agriculture and Fisheries has laid down, as a condition of employment of a member of the WLA, that she should be paid a weekly wage of not less than 32s if she is 18 or over for a working week of up to 48 hours, with a minimum overtime rate of 8d per hour. If she is billeted in the farmhouse she must receive a minimum of 16s per week in addition to free board and lodging. Of course if the county rates are higher, higher wages are paid to the volunteer. In some counties . . . these are as high as 38s. [Girls who had volunteered to work as timber measurers for the Forestry Commission, in the days before the Timber Corps became a separate force, were being

paid the wage of 45 shillings as this type of work was regarded as skilled.] Before a volunteer goes on to the farm she will be told what is the working week and what is the county rate of wages. She will also be told whether Sunday labour and labour on days of public holiday are counted as ordinary overtime or as overtime on a higher scale.

Holidays with pay were highly uncommon in all areas of employment in the pre-war years and farmers were deeply reluctant to grant this perk to their workers. It was a cause dear to Lady Denman's Liberal heart, but it was to take years of patient lobbying by both her and Inez Jenkins before this victory was achieved. In the early years the most they could do was offer free travel, paid for out of Land Army funds, in certain circumstances. Land girls travelling to a training centre had their journey paid for, as they did when travelling to their first job, or from one job to another (other Services enjoyed general travel warrant allocations). On the question of holidays the *Manual* stated: 'There are no special WLA regulations about holidays with or without pay, but where a member of the Army has worked for six months at least 20 miles from her home she becomes entitled to a free journey home at the expense of the WLA. . . . the railway entitlement does not necessarily mean that the land girl will be able to obtain a holiday during which to visit her home, nor be able to take holidays when she likes. Her right to a holiday depends on the terms of employment and on any order of the County Agricultural Wages Board which may provide for holidays with pay. . . .'

An insight into where the money went in wartime Britain and just how tight things were for land girls is provided by an account compiled by two thrifty girls working in Somerset of their week's budget in the summer of 1940.

Rent	5/3d
coal and oil	3/7d
papers	11d
meat	3/8d

bread	2/1d
marmalade	6d
jam	8d
flour	6d
Stork marge	6d
sandwich spread	7d
cocoa	6d
coffee (Camp)	10d
milk	7d
tin milk	7d
matches, soap and soap flakes	1/1d
cheese	6d
sugar	7d
fruit, dried fruit and veg	4/7d
sundries	2/5d
total	£1 13s 1d

Marion Nicholson who was earning £20 a month in her job with the Pearl Insurance Company before joining the Land Army, says: 'We were very hard up. I remember being left with about 6 shillings and 11 pence after I'd paid for my billet and bought necessities. There wasn't any point in grumbling – that was what the pay was for agricultural work. But we did resent some of the perks the girls in the Services got. They got cheaper tea in railway cafeterias, and they got soap and sanitary towels provided. We had to buy our own and that represented a hefty chunk out of our wages.'

Every effort was made by the various agencies involved – notably the Agricultural Wages Board – to see that land girls remained fairly paid by the standards of the day and got adequate time off from their labours. In 1942 the minimum rate went up to £1.18s less £1 for billet. Overtime rates were fixed at nine and a half pence an hour. In the summer of 1943 pay rates for women agricultural workers increased again. As from 10 June 1943 women over eighteen were to receive not less than 40 shillings and 6 pence, rising to 45 shillings after a month. This compared with an increased minimum wage for men at that time of 65 shillings. Girls under eighteen were to get 34 shillings and two-pence ha'penny rising to 38 shillings after a month. For this in winter they were expected to work an eight-and-a-half-hour day on five weekdays and a five-and-a-half-hour day on an agreed half-day, while in summer the working week went up to a nine-hour day five days a week with five hours on the agreed half-day. Conscious of the fact that some land girls were charged a lot more for their lodgings than others, the authorities tried to even out unfairness by stipulating the minimum net wage a girl should receive – exclusive of overtime – after she had paid for her billet. For the first month it was deemed that all girls over eighteen should be left with at least 22 shillings and 6 pence, rising thereafter to 23 shillings and 6 pence. Seventeen-to-eighteen-year-olds should be left with not less than 18 shillings the first month and 20 shillings thereafter. Overtime rates varied according to when they were worked. For weekdays the rate was 1 shilling and twopence for all girls over eighteen and 1 shilling for seventeen-year-olds; on Sundays the rate rose to 1 shilling and 5 pence for eighteen-year-olds and 1 shilling and twopence ha'penny for seventeen-year-olds. On half days pay was calculated at the weekday rate for the first two hours and paid at the Sunday rate after that.

In 1944 pay rates rose to 48 shillings. Nineteen fifty, the last year of the WLA, and five years into the 'land fit for heroes' campaign of the new Labour Government, saw a raft of improvements, including special rates of overtime for public holidays and a reduction in the working week. A notice issued by Northumberland, Cumberland, Durham and Westmorland WLA shows that by this time the minimum rate for female workers for a week of up to forty-seven hours was:

21 and over 76/-. Maximum bd and lodging 27/-. Minimum net cash wage after billeting charge has been met 49/-.
18 to 21 70/-. Maximum bd and lodging 25/-. Minimum net cash wage after billeting charge has been met 45/-.
17–18 Minimum gross wage 59/-. Maximum board and lodging deduction 20/-. Minimum net cash wage after billeting charge has been met 39/-. *Overtime*: additional payment for hours worked in excess of 47 must be made at the statutory overtime rates fixed under the Agricultural Wages Board. Minimum rate for overtime.
21 and over weekdays – 2/-. On the agreed weekly short day, Sunday, New Year's Day, Easter Monday, Whit Monday, August Bank Holiday and Christmas Day 2/5d.
18–21 weekdays 1/10d. Special overtime 2/3d.
17–18 weekdays 1/7d. Special overtime 1/11d.

The main obstacle to standardising pay was that unlike the situation pertaining in the WAS, where the state was the employer, in the Land Army the paymaster was the individual farmer. Inevitably in a force so large and scattered over so many areas and types of farms, there were substantial variations. To try to protect girls from exploitation the Land

Army stipulated in writing that farmers whose land girls were billeted elsewhere should pay them sufficient to leave them with 'the Land Army minimum cash wage appropriate to their age group on a 48–50 hour week after paying for the cost of their board and lodging'.

In the early years the introduction of a minimum wage combined with the conviction that women were not strong enough for the hard physical work that farming entailed actually worked against the Land Army, making many farmers reluctant to take on land girls. They tended to opt instead for adolescent boys whom they could pay less.

As in so many other aspects of life in the Land Army girls who lived in hostels probably had the best of it. Every hostel had its own forewoman whose responsibility was to deploy her gang according to the requirements of the neighbouring farms. It was she who collected the wages from the farmer and if any farmer proved recalcitrant with money or unreasonable over break times he risked losing his labour force.

Lady Denman and Inez Jenkins were tireless in their efforts to win decent, standardised conditions for land girls. At the outbreak of war they had to be content with a minimum wage and a guaranteed minimum employment week. In July 1943, however, conditions had improved beyond all expectation and Mrs Jenkins was able to reveal the terms of what she, with justifiable pride, called the Land Girl's Charter:

> Gradually as the LA has grown in size and importance it has been possible to add to and improve the conditions on which its labour is supplied. Now revised minimum conditions have been published which give all LA members real and reasonable security. This is the Land Girl's Charter:
>
> A minimum wage after you have worked up to 48 hours a week in winter or 50 in summer and after you have paid for board and lodging of 22/6 if you are 18 and over and 18/- if you are under 18.
>
> Sick pay at full wage rates . . . reasonable working hours with a half day off each week, Sunday work to be reduced as much as possible (though it was acknowledged that with dairy work this

was not always possible). A holiday of one week in the working year and an occasional long weekend when working time lost may have to be made up.

Free travel to any job to which your Land Army office sends you and two free rail warrants on leave in each working year to any station in England and Wales.

This is what the LA guarantees for you and if your employment is not on these terms you must tell your local representative or County Office so that either conditions may be put right or you may be removed elsewhere.

In return for this protection the land girl had her obligations: . . . 'you will keep your promise of mobility and be ready to go to work wherever you are needed; that you will accept the job which the Land Army offers you . . . that you will not leave your employment without the LA's knowledge and approval and that while you are in your job you will give the good and cheerful service for which the LA has now rightly become famed.'

Exactly a year later the months of dogged campaigning paid off and Mrs Jenkins confounded the Land Army's critics in the agricultural workers' camp by announcing the hard-fought right for holidays with pay for the whole industry. In an editorial in the *Land Girl* of July 1944 she was understandably jubilant: 'Once more the Land Army has given a lead in the Agricultural industry. For over a year it has been a Land Army regulation that its members shall have one week's holiday on pay during the working year. Now a new order of the Agricultural Wages Board has made a week's holiday on pay the legal right of every agricultural worker. Under the Board's new order an agricultural worker qualifies for one day's holiday with pay after each two consecutive months of regular employment completed on or after Nov. 1st 1943. He may insist on having at least three days of any holiday for which he has qualified to run consecutively and he may also insist on having the whole of the holiday for which he has qualified between April 1st and 31st October, unless he himself agrees to take it during the winter months.'

In winning this right for all land workers Inez Jenkins also saw to it that farmers whose land girls forfeited their holiday entitlement through job changes paid wages in lieu – and got the agreement backdated. As she wrote: 'In the past it has sometimes been difficult for the Land Army to enforce its holidays-with-pay regulation where a Land Army member has changed her job during the year. Now in such cases the land girl will have the legal right to claim from the employer she is leaving one day's holiday on pay for each two months during which she has worked regularly for him since last November. When she goes to her new job she will at once begin working towards her next holiday and after her first two months there will have qualified for a day's holiday with pay.'

Lady Denman and Mrs Jenkins were conspicuously successful in regulating the Land Army in terms of standardising rates of pay and working hours. Applying the same approach to training proved more difficult. The *Land Army Manual* gave potential recruits an idea of in what circumstances they might expect to be given training. In practice, however, training for the Land Army proved highly random. Thousands of girls turned up on farms with no training whatever, much to the exasperation of the farmer. Ivy Lemon, a machinist from North London, who was making uniforms when she was called up, recalls her first day on an Oxfordshire farm. 'We'd been brought out from the hostel to a farm to hoe thistles in a field of wheat. We thought we looked marvellous in our new dungarees and dust coats with these terribly heavy Land Army boots. The farmer took one look at us and said, "I don't know whether I should let you destroy my wheat or leave it to the thistles." ' Marion Nicholson, who found herself designated a forewoman, in charge of a gang of land girls on Romney Marsh, had no training at all. Doris Taverner, on the other hand, was sent for six weeks to a training farm where she was taught to milk on a model cow with rubber udders. According to the *Manual*, which being a propaganda tool was keen to present the best possible picture of what lay ahead, training of volunteers was provided 'if the County Secretaries feel they need it.

'Volunteers who are accepted for training are sent for four weeks for a free course, either at an approved farm or at an Agricultural College or Farm Institute. Board and lodging is paid for by the Government and an allowance at the rate of 10s per week, less National Insurance and Unemployment Insurance contributions is made by the Government to the volunteer for her personal expenses.'

The Land Army was at pains to stress that volunteers sent for training would genuinely benefit from the experience and not merely be used as cheap labour. 'The farmers who take trainees for instruction must, of course, be those who have time to spare to give such instruction. Volunteers on such farms can be assured that they will receive genuine training . . . The training may be carried out on farms where the volunteer can be given special instruction in milking, tractor-driving, or the care of stock and poultry, or on those market gardens and private gardens where all-round instruction can be given under supervision. The trainee will not simply be used for the purpose of providing unskilled labour, nor will she be expected to stick to only one or two processes.'

One of the types of work for which training was necessary was timber measuring, which commanded the impressive wage of 45 shillings a week. At the time the *Manual* was written the Timber Corps had not yet been set up and this work was carried out by the Forestry Commission.

A good education is needed for this type of work and a short Government training of two or three weeks is given at the Forestry Commission Training Centre in the Forest of Dean before employment. At the end of their course of training, volunteers are placed in employment in couples in a forest or saw-mill at a starting wage of 45s a week. The hours of work are from 7 am to 4.30 pm with a half day off on Saturdays. Overtime must be worked if and when required. The work includes dealing with the commoner home-grown trees and principal timbers, the measurement of sawn timber, the stacking of boards and planks for seasoning and the care of tools. Practical work includes the measuring and cross cutting of poles for props, the stripping of branches and bark and the supervision of wagon-loading.

This work was obviously regarded as more skilled than straightforward forestry work: 'For this . . . volunteers receive no preliminary training but go into immediate employment at a wage based on the existing agricultural wage rate for women in the county where they are working. This is never less than 32s per week. The work includes the lopping and chopping off of timber for pit props and the planting of young trees.'

From its inception the Land Army was inferior to the women's Services in terms of the perks to which its members were entitled. Despite the fact that land girls worked infinitely harder than women in the Armed Forces, they enjoyed fewer holidays, were paid less, got fewer clothing coupons and even received fewer travel warrants. One example of discrimination which rankled in particular was that women in the Services were provided with underwear and sanitary towels while land girls had to supply their own. When a member left the Land Army she had to hand in most of her uniform and was expressly debarred from claiming the National Service medal which even civilians involved extremely peripherally in war work could claim. Women in the Forces enjoyed the same conditions as their male counterparts. This meant they were entitled to a week's holiday every three months compared to the Land Army's grudgingly granted one week a year.

In some instances the discrimination was extraordinarily mean-minded. For the early years of the war land girls were actually banned from canteens run by the forces and YMCA. They were not admitted until August 1942, after a campaign which reached Westminster. At a time of stringent rationing these canteens had first claim on what supplies there were. As a result, their subsidised meals and snacks were eagerly sought after. The unfairness of this was often got round by sympathetic servicemen offering to buy teas and snacks for land girls and bringing them out to them.

One girl was very upset when after a long journey from the north to work in Kent she was refused service in the canteen at the railway. 'I was tired, dirty and hungry and was told I could not be served.' Even after the discrimination was brought to the attention of Parliament land girls were often not allowed to buy the sweets and cigarettes reserved for the Forces. Far from being apologetic about this state of affairs, some canteen staff seemed to relish turning land girls away. Two girls who travelled constantly selecting timber for telegraph poles and road blocks, arrived at Shrewsbury station. They walked into the YMCA, as the station refreshment room was closed, only to be informed 'before a crowd of ATS and WAAF that they did not serve the Land Army'. A particularly petty piece of discrimination was the decision in the summer of 1942 to stop using metal for Land Army badges, substituting bakelite instead, even though brass continued to be used in all other uniforms.

A crucial area in which land girls enjoyed inferior treatment to the Women's Auxiliary Services was health. The Land Army was not responsible for its members, whose employer was the farmer, rather than the state, whereas in the Services members were under constant medical supervision. The land girl was expected to register herself with her local doctor. If he was not available the decision for her to stay off work rested either with the farmer who employed her or, if she was in a hostel, with the warden. Where it came to injury the land girl was expected to insure herself using a civilian insurance scheme.

Lady Denman endlessly lobbied the Ministry of Agriculture to increase the Land Army's meagre budget. As it was, travel expenses were often not forthcoming even when a land girl was on official business. A land girl who was a member of a gang working in Kent was killed while home on leave. Her forewoman, Marion Nicholson, was instructed by her county office to represent the Land Army at her funeral but was not given any expenses. 'I asked the way at a bus stop and the lady I asked took pity on me and took me home to lunch with her first.'

Land girls were frequently desperately short of uniform, since the Armed Services took priority. The whole question of inequities in coupon entitlement between the Land Army and the other women's Services were such a source of disgruntlement that in August 1945 Mrs Jenkins took the unusual step of devoting an entire editorial in the *Land Girl* to trying to convince her readers that, compared to civilians at least, land girls were well off.

> The Land Army member who is worst off is the one who joined before 1942 for she has had to make three annual surrenders of coupons for use of uniform and has given up 72 coupons in all. But during these three years she has received 196 coupons – 26 from the Land Army as special issue, three civilian rations of 48, 44 and 48 respectively and three occupational supplements of ten apiece. Now 72 from 196 is 124. Divide that by three and you find the 'poor land girl' after making her surrender, had 41 and a third coupons a year for private spending plus her full working kit. The ordinary person has 48 coupons a year for all purpose and no working kit. A land girl who joined after 1942 is even better off. If a member is released she receives back a proportion of the coupons she surrendered according to the stage in the rationing year at which she resigns and the length of time she will have to wait for her new clothing book.
>
> Now it does not take 41 and a half coupons a year to keep oneself provided with underclothing and the odd pair of woolly gloves. One should either have been able to buy other things as well or have coupons in hand. Let us be honest and admit that if the clotheless, couponless, discharged land girl really exists her sad state is in part her own fault.

When girls left the Land Army they were expected to send back their uniform, keeping only a shirt, a pair of shoes and their overcoat. They were refunded coupons for the returned clothing but this was not sufficient to allay the disgruntlement many land girls felt. Marion Nicholson: 'The men came out with gratuities, a coat and a suit. Admittedly the suits didn't always fit, but it was a gesture. You couldn't wear your Land Army greatcoat in civvy street. It was too thick and it just wasn't fashionable. I gave mine to the milkman. He drove a horse and cart and he was always frozen.'

The fact that the Land Army never achieved the same status as the Women's Auxiliary Services was in no way Lady Denman's fault. It had many factors against it. It was a new organisation, run by women who, though undoubtedly talented organisers, were none the less amateurs. It was patronised by tens of thousands of individual employers, and under the ineffectual protection of the Ministry of Agriculture, it was never likely to acquire the clout of the Army or the Navy with their centuries-old traditions and powerful Establishment supporters. Far from taking a supine line with the authorities Lady Denman ploughed all her energy into raising the profile both of the Land Army and the individual land girl. Passionately committed as she was, not just to the Land Army, which she realised was finite, but to the improvement of the lives of people who would remain in the country, Lady Denman spent the later years of the war battling for social reforms which would make the lives of land workers more comfortable; decent pay, guaranteed days off, holidays with pay, sick pay and extra rations. In 1942, conscious of the financial hardship faced by many girls in a pre-Welfare State society where if you didn't work you didn't eat, she set up the Land Army Benevolent Fund. The fund attracted contributions from a variety of sources; the Land Army itself raised money for it and the *Land Girl* recorded each county's contribution month by month, the Queen sent regular donations, as did the National Farmers Union and, interestingly, the Press. All the proceeds from Vita Sackville-West's book *The Women's Land Army* went towards it. The fund's purpose was to help fund girls suffering illness or disability, to give grants to girls out of work, to help with education and training grants after the war and loan capital.

Lady Denman lost no opportunity of reminding the world how undeservedly run-down and neglected living conditions in the country were. In a broadcast delivered in 1943 when the Land Army was at its peak strength of 80,000 strong she made an emotional appeal to girls returning to city life to join her campaign of social reform: 'I want all those of you who return to towns to keep with you always your understanding of the life and problems of the country, of the need for the kind of houses and education in the country which will give its dwellers and its children as good an opportunity as the towndwellers and their children get. And I want those of you who stay in the country to take your part in the fight for the conditions which are essential to a good life.'

8 : Farmers – and Farmers' Wives

Many land girls remember the farmers they worked for with deep affection. Hundreds found their new life so much to their taste that they never went back to their old city existence. Instead they married the farmer or his son or one of his workers and became countrywomen in their turn. Some went back to the towns but have remained in touch with their wartime hosts. Other were not so lucky. Farmers in the Forties were a disillusioned and embittered bunch, suspicious of outsiders in general and politicians in particular. Many were living in conditions which had evolved little since Chaucer's day and saw no reason why girls should be treated with kid gloves. They despised towndwellers and greeted the land girls' willingness to lend a hand with contempt. Times were hard and with the Government demanding more and more from a depressed countryside, they begrudged every penny spent on effete workers who had to be taught their agricultural alphabet from the beginning. Their wives, their own roles strictly defined along time-hallowed lines, resented the new equality and the financial autonomy it conferred on the land girls and not infrequently banned the girls from their territory.

Neil Farrow ran a mixed farm in Sedlescombe, East Sussex, where until 1942 they used only horses. Though Farrow, now an erect white-haired man in his late seventies, treated his land girls well, he maintains they did not measure up to male workers. Farrow's farm was a household where the conditions prescribed by Balcombe Place and the Ministry of Agriculture for the treatment of land girls were respected to the letter . . . Neil's wife, Jo, who remembers them as 'such nice girls', cooked for them three times a day – 'land girls were entitled to the same rations as miners – extra butter, margarine, cheese and meat' – and did their washing. The girls had separate bedrooms and their own sitting-room, were paid overtime if they worked after 12 on Saturday and had every evening free. Not for them long evenings hay carting in the fields till 10 p.m. at night. Of the three land girls who worked for him two still keep in touch.

It was frustrating for farmers to see skilled men replaced with absolute beginners, in Farrow's opinion. But he maintains none the less that many farmers expected too much of their land girls. 'Land girls could be a headache to a busy farmer. We were supposed to train them but we didn't have time to run after them and check up on everything. It wasn't their fault but they did tend to take too long on a job. I would have liked a hand with milking – we had twenty-five cows who all had to be milked by hand – but they didn't seem to get on with milking . . .'

Farrow was one of those who felt there was little point in trying to prove that men and women can do the same work. When he wanted extra help for harvesting or haymaking he used to recruit casual labour, either relying on older men or prisoners of war. 'I never thought it was right for girls to do heavy work – you could do a great deal of damage that way. After all these were young women who hadn't yet had their families . . .' His land girls spent their day hand-feeding calves, which he says they were outstandingly good at, and driving the lorry that delivered milk twice a day to houses and cottages in the area.

The hand-wringing that the prospect of female labour triggered among farmers, particularly as the older ones would have remembered the efficacy of the land girls of the First World War – strikes us today as pathetic, particularly when contrasted with the feistiness of the girls. Arthur Street, the veteran farming writer, was convinced girls would never master the art of tractor maintenance.

> The modern outfit (the tractor-plough) is a one-man job, requiring an expert in both branches, an engineer and a ploughman. He works alone, perhaps miles from the nearest human being. Therefore he must not only be an expert, but also physically capable of the strength necessary to cope with the various jobs to which even the most modern tractor and plough are heirs. That there are some land girls physically capable of dealing with these I am well aware, but I insist that the average girl is not fitted for such work. While the plough is worked correctly, any girl can drive the tractor merrily up and down the field, but when things go wrong a considerable amount of sheer physical strength is often required, for, as I say, there is no other help for miles.
>
> To my mind even the starting of the average tractor is not a job which the average girl should be asked to do . . .

Most land girls maintain that there were very few tasks on the farm that they couldn't do provided they were shown the correct way to tackle it. As for heavy lifting they found that after a few weeks they developed muscles they never knew they had.

Joan Pountney, who worked in Leicestershire, recalls struggling to carry the seventeen-stone sacks of wheat produced by the threshing machine. 'I only weighed nine stone. I could carry the fifteen-stone sacks of oats and barley, but the wheat sacks weighed seventeen stones. Usually, though, there was another girl to help you.' Joan only remembers admitting defeat on one occasion – for which she was severely ticked off by her local bosses.

> Another girl and myself were told to go and work for a farmer one wet Saturday morning. He had a reputation for not paying his bills and for not filling in his land girls' time-sheets so we were wary. When we got there we discovered he wanted us to unload a trailer full of fifteen-stone sacks of beans and carry them up a ladder to a loft above one of his barns. If it had been up steps with sides you could have held on-to, if it hadn't been wet and slippery, with us wearing wellingtons . . . I'd have tackled it. We put it to the farmer: 'what happens if we slip off the ladder?' So we refused and went back to the hostel. He reported us to the local War Ag. and we were given a severe dressing down.

Vita Sackville-West, who until she became a Land Army rep had had little contact with working farmers, painted a heavily romanticised portrait of the land girl in the bosom of her adoptive family, evoking the '. . . genial kitchen at supper time when the white tablecloth is spread under the lamp and the table is set with yellow plates and there is a huge loaf and a bowl of tomatoes and jade green lettuce in the centre. The fire glows behind the bars of the grate, the kettle bubbles gently. The man of the house sits in his shirt sleeves, reading the newspaper while he waits for his tea, the children stare, the dog gets up, the housewife comes out from the scullery wiping her hands, and there is the land girl in the midst of them, young, pretty, healthy, almost like the daughter of the family.'

Some girls fell on their feet and found themselves billeted with the kind of picture book country household Vita described. Evelyn Elliott, who came originally from Sunderland, worked for a dairy farmer in Cumbria where she was treated like one of the family. Her two years there were so happy that there were tears all round when she left and she is still in touch with one of the farmhands.

> Mrs Johnson, the farmer's wife, was really kind. She did all my

washing, except my dungarees which I did myself as they were always covered in cow muck. She was a wonderful cook. We had different dishes every day and I used to eat all my meals with the family, except the evening meal. The family had a maid called Maureen. She and I lived in what today would be called a granny annexe. We each had a bedroom with our own bathroom *en suite*. I was so hard up that sometimes when my wellingtons or socks wore out Mrs Johnson would buy me a new pair. They did wear out and you were only allowed two pairs a year from the Land Army. If they wore out after you had had your quota you had to buy your own. The Johnsons used to take me everywhere with them. I used to get invited to all the family parties and the Hunt Ball and all the Agricultural Shows. It was a complete change from the farm where I was before. There they had no electricity. Downstairs it was oil lamps; upstairs candles. All they wanted me for was housework. Every time the rep came I was washing the family car. I pleaded with her for a transfer because I wanted to be back with the animals.

Many land girls, in fact, far from being treated like a daughter, were served inferior food to that eaten by the farmer and his family and were expected to do housework or babysitting for nothing after a full day's work. Scores had problems getting paid and many were forbidden to enter the farmhouse. Girls describe autocratic regimes with the farmer's wife acting out the role of kill-joy matron in an old-fashioned prep school, clearly relishing every petty restriction she imposed. Some were made to go to bed at a certain time and forbidden to talk after lights out. One girl lodged with the cowman, whose wife forbade her to go to Land Army dances until her father wrote giving his permission. As a final act of spite this landlady would decline to serve supper on the nights her girls went out.

Some country folk, clearly unsettled by the eruption of all this unwonted youth and sexual energy in their midst, took an unhealthily voyeuristic interest in what the land girls did with their free time. One girl who lived in a cottage with five others says: 'Our farmer knew what we were doing at all times. We were expected to be in by 10 p.m. every night. If we went to the village dance which ended at midnight, we had to crawl on our hands and knees behind a wall and go in by the back door of the cottage. Nevertheless he still found out!'

It is impossible, from a distance of half a century, to determine which group was the more typical. However, from the tales so many land girls tell, many farmers come over as a churlish, hard-to-please, skinflint lot, reluctant to teach, ever ready to criticise and anything but chivalrous. One girl who worked for a farmer with five sons regards the weekly bath night arrangements as summing up his philosophy: 'There was no piped water so it had to be filled with kettles. They all bathed in the same water; the farmer first, then his sons. I was expected to be the last. Luckily for me my parents left London for Hereford just as I was moved from my former farm in Worcester to Hereford so I was able to go home for a bath.'

An awful lot of country men – war or no war – seem to have regarded the presence of women on the land as an impudence, a challenge to their authority and competence; to be fought off through teasing, intimidation and petty humiliation, sometimes on a daily basis.

Mary Etherington was assigned to the task of clearing a moor in Northumberland of trees so that the land could be ploughed. 'I was driving a big caterpillar tractor. I had to put these huge iron chains round the trees then drive the tractor away and pull them down. The chains were so heavy I couldn't lift them. The men were standing watching me. I asked them to help me carry the chains to the tree. They refused. "If you can do the bloody job of a man you get going," they said.'

What the men clearly found particularly hard to stomach was that mere women could on occasion prove more skilled at a particular job than them. 'They couldn't bear the idea of a woman teaching them,' says Kath Hickmott, who became a first-class tractor driver in Kent. 'I was asked by my farmer to teach a man, a conscientious objector, to plough. Knowing it was a bit sensitive I asked him if he minded. He said "no", so I told him what to do. He was with me for a week. He would plough while I watched and commented later. After he had left, some Italian prisoners who were stationed nearby came up and asked: "Has your teacher gone?" The chap obviously felt so unmanned being taught by a woman that he had told the Italians I was *his* pupil.'

Land girls, transplanted into a domain where, initially at least, they had no skill, were doomed to inherit the low status that has so unreasonably been the lot of the British agricultural worker down the centuries. Irritation at having to train and feed workers whose build and inclination made them, in their reluctant employers' opinion, unfitted for the work played a part. So, undoubtedly, did misogyny.

Land girls certainly feel they lacked status – even in those very country communities whose wheels their efforts helped to keep turning. Jean Procter, who was in the Land Army for seven years, says: 'Land girls were nothing. Nobody had a good word to say for you. You were there to work. That's all. I can remember many, many occasions when land girls were out working in the fields in the burning sun as thirsty as can be. The gardens of the private houses nearby would be full of people relaxing, but not one of them would ever offer us a cup of tea or even a drink of water.'

Land girls tell of farmers who wouldn't allow their girls breaks for meals, who stood over them as they worked in the field with whips, who fiddled their money and who refused them even a drink in the course of their working day. One girl, sent to work in the north-east, remembers the active dislike she and six other raw recruits encountered from the farmer and his workers on her first day potato planting in a muddy field on a chilly spring morning.

> Each of us was given a rough hessian sack to tie round our necks and were sent to the end of the field where potatoes from a cart were tipped into our sacks bringing us nearly to our knees. Plodding up the drill, bent double with the weight, we sat down when we reached the end, only to spring up when a great shout came from the far end, 'Get off your backsides. This is no

holiday camp.' The dust and grit got into our eyes and hair and when the planting was finished, our next job was to muck out the byres where cattle had been all winter (and several winters before it seemed to us). At 6 p.m. we staggered off duty, green-faced and strongly-smelling.

Farmers' wives could prove petty and mean-spirited, particularly if they thought their husband was paying too much attention to the fresh-faced, lithe-limbed young land girl. They often used food and drink, traditionally the female domain, as the weapons with which to wage a war of attrition on what they saw as their young rival. A girl who worked on a farm in East Anglia recalls that she was not allowed in the farmhouse at all.

> When I had finished milking I had to wash my hands at the cold tap in the yard. The farmer would go in and have a cup of tea and then the wife would come out and pour the tea left in the teapot down the drain in front of me. I arrived at that farm at 5 a.m. and didn't have a drink until 12 when I had my pack lunch. Later I learned that when some land girls, including me, walked past, the farmer and a friend had watched us. The friend had said something perfectly innocent like 'If only we were twenty years younger we'd be all right there . . .' The farmer's wife had overheard them and decided there was something going on. It all came to a head when the farmer asked me to have a word with his wife. According to him, she thought we were having an affair. I was shocked and embarrassed. He was sixty and only had one tooth.

The more spirited land girls, particularly the ones from the tougher parts of the big cities, gave as good as they got. They insisted that their employers teach them what they were meant to do, instead of leaving them with no guidance and then deriding their efforts.

One girl was given orders by the farm's foreman to harness the horse to the cart and then cart kale when he knew she had never harnessed a horse before. 'I asked him, "How would you feel if you were asked to perm a lady's hair?" The men standing round roared with laughter. He was furious and replied, "Don't be ridiculous." So I told him, "I have come here to be taught how to harness and saddle a horse. You can't expect me to know it all by instinct." '

Many land girls, however, were crushed by the harshness and obtuseness of their employers. Some farmers acquired a reputation for being unable to keep their land girls. A few overworked and underfed their girls so severely that they incurred the gravest penalty – being deprived of their right to farm by the War Agricultural Committee.

One girl who worked on a farm in the north-west went down from ten and a half to eight stone in a year. 'It was a terrible place, like being in Belsen. I was there for a year – not living in, thankfully. In all that time my employers never offered me anything to eat. They'd had thirteen land girls before me. I milked the cows but when I wanted a drink with my pack lunch I had to buy the milk from them. The girl that followed me became so ill and exhausted she had to be taken away in a taxi.'

For many farmers and farmhands the presence of a land girl provided an excuse for a particularly unpleasant form of sexual teasing. In the inadequate it brought out a streak of childish cruelty – as if the men, threatened in the very blood and bone of their being, felt the need to assert their supremacy in the crudest way possible. Nothing was considered out of bounds. Menstruation was quite a problem for land girls – although sanitary towels were not on coupons, many girls were not only billeted miles from any shops, but were out on the land all day. This was often the focus of much schoolboy sniggering. The girls dreaded staining their uniform – Peggy Wicks from Durham recalls: 'When you were pitching hay or shooks of corn up on to the wagon you would suddenly feel that gush and hold your breath, praying it didn't come through.' Another girl remembers that however careful you were the men always knew if you had your period. 'They would back away from you saying "keep away from her! She's got her —" '

The farmhands at one of the farms Jean Procter worked on

once teased her so unpleasantly they incurred the wrath of the farmer. 'It was humiliating at times. I wouldn't like my daughter to have gone through it. I was very proud of my uniform. One day one of the farm workers snatched my hat off my head and peed in it in front of me. I must say the farmer took him to task. He told him it was an insult to the Crown.'

Land girls were regularly given jobs the men knew they were afraid of or that they didn't want to do themselves.

Joan Pountney, who joined the Land Army in 1943 at the age of eighteen, moved into a hostel after bad experiences on private farms in Leicestershire. 'You were a land girl so you got all the worst jobs, all the dirty jobs. Then, after a hard day, you'd be expected to babysit for your employer in the evening. Once I even had to work on Christmas Day as it was too far to go home for lunch and be back for milking the next morning.'

Jean Procter says the men on the farms she worked on would invariably allocate a land girl to cleaning drains. 'There was a blockage in the sewer on one of the farms I was at. I was sent down to deal with it. Suddenly this horrible great rat appeared baring its teeth. The men gave me a stick and told me to crack it over the head – "whack, *whack*". I was shaking like a leaf.'

Doris Taverner, who grew up on a farm in Kent where her father was a stockman, had such an unpleasant time with a cowman on one of the farms she worked on that she complained and was moved. 'It was my job to tell him when one of the cows needed serving. He used to insist that I take the cow to the bull and then he'd shut me in the pen with him, which was downright dangerous and very frightening. Then through the door he'd say vulgar things about what was going to happen. He knew my husband was overseas so he'd say things like "let the old bull have a treat". I was only there for four and a half months but they were the worst of the whole of my five years' service.'

Occasionally, however, a tease would pick the wrong girl

and get more than he bargained for. One girl was only seventeen when she became the focus of the local sex pest.

> He introduced himself to me one day when I was hoeing turnips on my own. 'We'll be seeing a lot of each other,' he said. 'I know a lot about you land girls and what you get up to.' From then on I never knew a moment's peace. He would jump out from behind the barn door or somewhere else ands grab me. His favourite saying was 'give me a feel till the baker's been'. . . . Then came haymaking . . . I was detailed to partner Bill for the job of unloading hay into the lofts. I was using my pikol [pitch fork] and had just forked a load of hay at full stretch into the loft, when out came his hands again. I turned fast and the momentum carried the pikol forward. Bill had stuck his into the hay, with the stave just in front of his face. My prongs stuck into his stave just a few inches from his face . . . I was shouting and swearing, giving vent at last to all the pent-up feelings of the past months. I told him to leave me alone or next time I would kill him. He told everyone he wasn't going to work with me again. 'She's dangerous, she nearly killed me.' We never spoke again.

Many land girls remember being sent out on the hated task of weeding or singling (thinning) turnips in the pouring rain while the men found other tasks under cover. One girl on a farm in Lincolnshire recalls: 'My farmer was bone idle. I'd be sent out with three sacks to try to keep the rain off – one over my head, one down my back to try to keep my lower end dry and the third across my shoulders. The farmer would sit in the saddle room smoking – pretending to clean tack.'

Girls at a milk training centre in Suffolk learn the theory
of dairy farming, watched by their future victims.

Mastering the mysteries of the internal combustion engine.
Although sceptics foretold disaster, many land girls became skilled mechanics for
whom the temperamental iron-wheeled Fordson tractor held no terrors.

The young clerical staff who managed the Land Army paperwork found Balcombe Place, with its baronial Gothic proportions, a cross between a five-star hotel and a benevolent boarding school.

The Balcombe triumvirate. Lady Denman (right) with Margaret Pyke and Inez Jenkins, as they take a break from paperwork in the gardens at Balcombe.

Smiling and confident, the urban amateur settled into her new life with surprising ease and won over the most sceptical with her hard work and cheerfulness.

Land girls found rearing baby animals especially satisfying.

Land girls had to master implements that had been in use since the
dawn of civilisation, such as this simple plough and the team that pulled it,
as well as the latest caterpillar tractor imported from the States
specifically to tackle heavy land that had lain fallow since World War One.

Land reclamation was a vital part of the war effort as thousands of neglected acres were brought into cultivation in a drive to end Britain's dependence on imported food. Here a girl working on a land drainage scheme in Berkshire tightens the nut on a giant scoop before climbing into the cabin of her excavator.

A truly heroic effort. Stretching as far as the eye can see,
land girls driving Self binders bring in a bumper harvest from what,
at 400 acres, was believed to be Britain's largest wheatfield.

Today the combine harvester and one man does the lot,
but in the Forties harvest time meant fields thick with people.
Sheaves of corn were placed together, six sheaves to a stook,
and turned regularly so that the wind dried them.

Gumboots with shorts may look odd but ripe corn is razor sharp.
There is no mistaking the exuberance of these two girls
arriving at a farm in Surrey in September 1946 to help with the harvest.

Sylvia Parry

(née *Cresswell*). Joined Land Army at 18.
Land Army 1943–7.
Home town: Wednesfield, Staffordshire.
Civilian occupation: shorthand typist.

When I got my call-up papers I saw the name Glynllifon. I hadn't a clue where it was and showed it to my dad. He said, 'Your mum's going to go mad.' I'd asked for Staffordshire and I'd never been that far from home before. We had a big party to celebrate my joining the WLA – I wore my new uniform which I thought was the cat's whiskers. When the time came to go to Wolverhampton station the whole family turned out – Mum and Dad, aunts, uncles, cousins, my sister. I didn't feel homesick as there were ten of us travelling from the Birmingham area. The journey was wonderful, all along the coast through Rhyl and Colwyn Bay. At Caernarvon there was an open lorry waiting to take us the eight miles to our billet. This was Glynllifon estate, a wonderful place by the sea, which belonged to Lord Newborough. He had been told he would be taken over either by the WLA or the Tank Corps and he had thought he'd rather have the Land Army.

The house had huge stables where some of the old coaches were still housed. Over them were living quarters where the grooms and coachmen used to sleep. This had been converted into a hostel with two big dormitories, a dining-room, lounge and warden's quarters. It was a lovely place but being old it was full of wildlife. Bats used to fly about in the corridors. One of the girls had told us that once they got in your hair you couldn't get them out. Whenever we walked about we solemnly covered our heads with towels. It was also infested with mice. I found one on my head one night. I climbed into the bunk of the girl above me and the thing climbed up the sheet after me. It was fun in the hostel but the warden was very strict. You weren't allowed to be out after 10 p.m. The youngsters today don't know they're born. If you were late you'd be locked out. They'd shut the estate gates. If you did get caught you'd have to climb over the gates, which were pretty high, and walk up a very long drive which was dark and frightening, then under an arch. When you rang, the warden would keep you waiting for quite a while and then read you the riot act.

After I'd been at Glynllifon for a while I was sent to Hull for four weeks to learn how to drive an excavator for land drainage. When I got there I was in billets, but I had to spend most nights in the shelter as Hull was being bombed very badly. Once I was trained I spent a year in the Conway Valley digging ditches. When I look at those diggers now they look enormous. I wonder how I ever got into them. I can't climb on to a chair now. I went back to the Conway Valley recently. It's very flat there by the river. They are still digging ditches there today with the big excavators. Of course it's men driving them now. I was in lodgings while I was in the Conway Valley, in a house on the hill. The landlady used to give us sandwiches for lunch which were always jam and cheese – in the same sandwich. Coming back from my first weekend I got on the wrong bus and got lost. It was pitch dark and pouring with rain. In the end I found my way to a farm. They gave me a drink and put me on the right road. When I got back I had been locked out and my landlady was anything but pleased.

The last farm I worked on was in Cornwall. It was run by a bachelor farmer and his maiden aunt. I worked from 6 a.m. often till 11 p.m. and after I had paid for my keep I was left with the equivalent of £1.50p. The food was marvellous, but it was very isolated and lonely. I was only twenty or twenty-one and they couldn't understand that I wanted to go out. There was no bathroom or lavatory, which was quite a shock as we'd always had one at home. If you wanted a bath you had to manage with a jug of water. I had to wash my own clothes. The housekeeper only washed my bedlinen and towels. My main job was looking after the pigs, cleaning their sties and feeding them. One day I was taking two buckets of swill across the yard to feed the pigs. They should have been in their stye but the farmer had left them out in the yard by mistake. They made a rush at me, knocking me back into a pile of pig manure. The dog who was with me tried to protect me but only pushed me further into the muck . . . If you have ever smelt pig manure you will know how I smelt. Cleaning myself without the help of a bathroom was a pretty stiff challenge.

9 : Formidable Women

The Land Army was run by a pyramid of formidable women from educated backgrounds. At the top was Lady Denman and her assistant Mrs Jenkins. After her came seven Regional Officers, each in charge of several counties, whose job was to liaise between the regions and head office. It was a source of amusement to Lady Denman, a lifelong Liberal, that of her seven Regional Officers five had worked as organisers for the Conservative party. Forming the base of the pyramid were fifty-two county committees, responsible for enrolling, equipping, training, where this was possible and allocating the individual land girls to farms and billets. Each committee had its own Chairman, Organising Secretary, members and office staff. The larger farming counties were divided into two or sometimes three. The County Secretaries and County Organisers, who were the field workers of the county office, were all salaried, as were the office staff. Last came the voluntary representatives, known universally as reps, whose job was to form a link between the farmers and the land girls and the county office. The Chairmen, committee members and representatives were voluntary. Iris Tillett was the youngest County Secretary when she accepted the post for the Norfolk Women's Land Army in August 1938 and set up her office in Norwich. She remembers the difficulty of finding one's way round a country bereft of signposts. Maps and special permits were supplied to anyone with permission to enter the forbidden five-mile stretch from the coast inland. 'One of my staff got completely lost driving home one foggy night and accidentally drove on to one of the new airfields in the county. Fortunately she drove off again before being spotted.'

One of the most important jobs of the county staff was to inspect farms where farmers had agreed to train land girls in dairy work and general farm work, poultry care and horticulture. Care was taken to find a farm where conditions were fairly primitive by town standards in order to prepare recruits for the conditions which were likely to greet them. This was underlined at interview but many land girls didn't believe physical conditions would be as stark as predicted. One volunteer returned to her county office in tears after three weeks saying: 'it was just as you said it would be and I can't stand it.'

The County Chairmen were also members of the local War Agricultural Committees. Having experience of dealing both with the Ministry of Agriculture and the headquarters of the Land Army, the Chairmen were impressed by the contrast in the two communication styles. If instruction on a particular matter of policy came from the Ministry it would run to three or four pages of opaque bureaucratic jargon. Coming from Balcombe, the same subject would be dispatched in one page and in plain no-nonsense language. The Chairmen and the reps invariably came from patrician county families – old copies of the *Land Girl* show County Chairmen referred to time after time as Lady this and the Hon. Mrs that – having been recruited by Lady Denman through the Women's Institute network. This provoked criticism from Labour

Members of Parliament that the administration of the Land Army was 'too county'. Lady Denman robustly defended her choices, pointing out, doubtless with some justification, that if her Chairmen were to be taken seriously they had to be figures whom the farmers respected.

Once they had been allocated to a farm or hostel most land girls had little further contact with their county office. The reps were their main link with Land Army administration since they were responsible for their day-to-day welfare. Reps were supposed to visit every land girl in their area once a month to check that she was happy with her billet, that she wasn't being overworked or underpaid and that she wasn't too lonely. The reps' job also included seeing that all land girls had access to bathing facilities, though land girls who struggled to maintain their former standards of hygiene in primitive farm billets don't remember much official help on this score.

A note in the *Land Army Manual*, stated unequivocally: 'Where there is no bathroom in the cottage she will try to arrange for friends nearby to offer the use of their bathroom at stated times each week.'

The reps' brief included much of the self-improvement that was dear to Lady Denman's heart and which had inspired the Women's Institute movement. In addition to introducing the land girl to neighbours, the local Women's Institute and the Young Farmers Club, or encouraging her to set up a local Land Army club – the rep was supposed to encourage land girls to improve their qualifications and knowledge of agriculture. This could be done either through correspondence courses or by taking the Land Army proficiency tests. Most counties worked hard at improving the knowledge and skills of their land girls. Classes and lectures on horticulture or agriculture were arranged, as were demonstrations of specific farming techniques. Some county committees arranged tests and competitions in milking, ploughing, hedging and ditching, which were then judged by local farmers. Combined rallies were held at weekends, visits were arranged to research stations, Farm Institutes, or production centres for local crops, such as the sugar-beet factories of Norfolk or Lincoln.

As Shewell Cooper put it in his inimitable way in the *Land Army Manual*: 'It must not be thought that the LG is constantly going about on trips but it does make for *esprit de corps* and it does give a girl a feeling of being a member of an important army, if she can from time to time meet others and learn more of the profession in which she is employed.'

Though some land girls remember their reps with affection – Jean Procter approvingly recalls hers, a formidable maiden lady with a double-barrelled name, 'ruling her farmers with a rod of iron' – there was a difference in class between the reps and the land girls for whom they were responsible and it could prove a barrier. Vita Sackville-West, who in no way shared Lady Denman's socially liberal views and was an unrepentant snob, was herself a rep in Kent. Happy to describe land girls as capable of being 'unbearably tiresome' . . . and 'at times downright ill-behaved', Vita wrote candidly about the social gulf.

> Let us recognise that she [the Rep] usually belongs to a different class of birth and upbringing, and also . . . to a different generation. It is terribly difficult to adjust or even to modify an outlook which has grown up with you for half a century; terribly difficult to be tolerant and understanding of a code which may consistently outrage your own. It is perhaps a little unfair to set every well-meaning rep down as 'Lady Blimp', but let us at least recognise that some divergence of point of view must inevitably arise between the staid squirearchy of middle age, and gay wild youth out for all the fun it can get.

Vita Sackville-West herself was fairly well liked, even though her land girls regarded her as breathing a different atmosphere from them. Joan Chapman who lived in a flat in Vita's home, Sissinghurst Castle, in Kent, recalls: 'She always said she thought our pay was not too bad – yet she spent more on cigarettes than we earned for a week's work.'

Some reps were happy to bend the rules by providing

neighbours of their own class with land girls to help run their estates. Vita herself was guilty of this. Joan Chapman who had come from London found herself working as a private gardener for an elderly general who was a friend of Vita's. 'Nothing we grew was ever sold or went to help the war effort. At the time it worried me terribly. I spent my days picking raspberries for dinner parties, pruning espalier fruit trees – instead of growing food for a country at war.'

The class difference, predictably, did not always make for relaxed communication. Dorothea Abbot, working on an isolated farm in Warwickshire, remembers with amusement the sole visit she received from her rep.

> I had just collected the post by the main road when I saw a small woman approaching on an enormous hunter. She was in full riding habit and drew rein when she saw me. 'Is that you Abbot?' she called . . . 'I'm your Land Army representative. Do you want to see me about anything?' I told her I still hadn't received any gumboots.
> 'What's your number, Abbot?'
> '104076.'
> 'I hope you're not getting too much housework.'
> I told her I had no time to fit in any housework. As she rode off I was left wondering how, if I had had any personal problems, I would have managed to confide them to her at a height of sixteen hands.

Many girls, however, felt that they had been treated with genuine kindness and concern by their county staff. One wrote to her county office to express her gratitude. Her letter was published in the *Land Girl* in April 1945: 'When I joined the Land Army I didn't know that there would be a guardian angel watching over me to see that I got just what I asked for when I asked for it. But it seems there is one and I suspect it to be you. In the whole of my two and a half years' service I feel that I've been waited on specially and if you treat all girls the same they've no need for complaint.'

The administration of the Land Army was hierarchical and

functioned pretty satisfactorily. That was perhaps less true of the troops themselves. One of the factors which contributed to the Land Army being regarded as inferior to the Services was the fact that it was a force without officers. The most it could run to by way of rank were extra pips on the armband denoting length of service. After six months' satisfactory service a red half diamond badge was awarded, after twelve months a full diamond. Special armbands were presented for greater lengths of service with the ten-year armband being the most coveted. Where girls worked singly on isolated farms it was clearly impossible to instigate a hierarchy, but towards the end of the war as more and more land girls lived in hostels, it became head office policy to offer girls who showed qualities of leadership the chance of promotion to forewoman or gang leader.

The reality, however, was that the selection of forewomen was often pretty random. In 1944 a local paper in Kent announced that ten Kent land girls were to be the first in the country to be chosen for training as forewomen by Kent War Agricultural Committee. They were to spend six weeks in a farmhouse on the North Downs, have the right to wear an armband with an 'F' embroidered on it, earn an extra 10 shillings a week and would have the authority 'to report on slackers but not dismiss them'. War Ag. Committees in other parts of the country intended to run similar courses, it said, 'as part of a new deal for the Land Army to lift it above the "Cinderella" status of which so many of its members have so long complained'. Trainees would be asked to take all sorts of agricultural machinery to pieces, learning how to maintain it as well as use it. The chief practical training instructor was a man who had been a foreman for thirty years. 'There's only one way to control a gang,' he tells the girls. 'Do the job better than anyone in it.'

One of the women to be selected for training as a forewoman was Marion Nicholson (née Jeal). The only problem was that she had already been a forewoman for three years by the time she was called for training. Many girls found themselves promoted to forewoman merely because they had learned to drive.

Mrs Nicholson, who worked for the Pearl Insurance Company before joining the Land Army, had been a land girl for just ten weeks – and was still learning various types of land work herself – when the call came. The first thing she knew about her 'leadership potential' was when she received a letter from her local Organising Secretary appointing her to her first stint as a forewoman.

> Dear Miss Jeal,
> I think you had a message from me by Kathleen as to the possibility of you becoming forewoman at our new hostel, St Mary's in the Marsh. We have talked this matter over and . . . we are now definitely putting you down as forewoman for St Mary at 45/s a week.
> I feel sure that you will settle down more happily with a friend and therefore we are asking Miss Hyde to go with you. Nearly all the 40 girls starting with you next Monday will be raw recruits, knowing nothing whatever of the land so it will be a great help to have you to put them in the way of things.

The Secretary then wrote again warning that the domestic arrangements at the new hostel were in a state of chaos and suggesting that the new forewoman's leadership qualities might be needed inside as well as out in the fields:

> You will not find it such a comfortable hostel as Otford as it has only been temporarily adapted for the WLA for the summer months. The staff is not yet fixed and therefore I cannot give you the name of the matron. If domestic help is short at the beginning I know I can rely on you working with the matron to provide a rota of girls who will help in the hostel meanwhile. A cook has definitely been engaged.
> Although this hostel is situated in East Kent, and is in an isolated part of Romney Marsh, West Kent is definitely taking charge of it for the time being. Miss A. Roper is the District Representative . . . and will welcome you all on

arrival at the hostel on Sunday. The hostel is half a mile from the village of St Mary's-in-the-Marsh and three miles from New Romney. You are fortunate in that owing to the destruction of a bridge on the main road the East Kent buses to Hythe and Folkestone now pass the hostel which is a great advantage as it is in such an isolated spot.

Instructions for Sunday. Please be at the County Hall, Maidstone at 3pm where you will meet the rest of the girls . . . to be taken straight down to the hostel on lorries. I enclose a voucher to be used on Sunday.

With the best of good wishes for this new venture and don't forget to let me know if there is any way in which I can help you,

yours sincerely,

VMM Cox, West Kent Organising Secretary.

Miss Jeal's experience at the new hostel, where she was every bit as much a 'raw recruit' as the forty Yorkshire girls she was supposed to be in charge of, proved to be a true baptism of fire as the next day was D-Day.

We knew something big was going on. We were surrounded by troops. But we woke up that morning and there wasn't a scrap left, no tents, no litter, nothing . . . We had a funny old matron who wore a long Victorian nightdress and did her hair up in paper curlers at night. She couldn't stand the action triggered by D-Day – we were right next to an airfield, surrounded by guns, and there was gunfire and searchlights . . . all night trying to shoot down German planes and doodlebugs. One plane was shot down and landed on a steam train on its way to Lydd. We just carried on, though. If anything came over we'd dive into a ditch or hide under the shooks of corn. But the matron couldn't take it. She resigned in a panic, leaving me and my assistant forewoman to run the domestic side of the hostel as well as the working gangs. The only other help we had in the hostel was a couple from Yorkshire. She did the cooking and he was the stoker. They were very good at that work but they couldn't read or write, which meant we had to take over when it came to ordering and accounting.

Girls who worked in hostels under a forewoman went out to

95

work each day in gangs. The way the system worked was that farmers wanting land girls for particular jobs applied to the local War Ag. who then arranged for small numbers of girls, each with a gang leader, to go out to specific farms on a daily basis. The job of the forewoman was to teach the girls how to do the job they were there for and at the end of each day check their time-sheet with the farmer, seeing to it that all the girls got paid correctly at the end of the week. It was also to her that the farmer complained if he was not satisfied with the quality of the labour he had been sent.

'What happened, in practice, as I was a novice too, was that the foreman showed me what to do and I showed the girls,' Marion Nicholson recalls. 'That winter we spent most of our time land clearing – sawing and chopping down orchards ready to plough up for the next year's crops of potatoes, sugar-beet and corn.'

Problems between land girls and farmers did occur. One of the gangs at the Romney Marsh hostel complained to Miss Jeal that they had worked for one farmer for three weeks solidly without a day off. 'They were worn out. It was the summer so they were working all hours in the day and having no time off at weekends to wash their hair, wash their clothes or even write letters. I told them to create a rota so that two of them took one day off and two another. I was ill in bed with a stinking cold when the farmer in question came striding up the dormitory. He was a big man, he was wearing shorts and he was furious. He bellowed at me: "what do you mean by telling my land girls to take time off?" He threatened to report me to the War Ag. But I got in first. My complaint was upheld and they took all his land girls away.'

Running work gangs outdoors and playing the role of ringmaster within the hostel proved quite taxing, particularly as there was an RAF camp next door. 'We had a couple of girls come back drunk at night so we had to slap on a ten-o'clock curfew. Working all day in the fields we couldn't deal with those problems as well – bikes getting punctured, girls not fit to work the next day . . . We used to let the RAF use our dining-room as a social gathering place as they had nowhere at their camp. One night a girl came to me and said there was a man in her bunk. I went to investigate and found an RAF chap dead drunk, wrapped in a flag. We had to send for his officer to get him home.'

After hands-on experience in practically every job on the land – from potato planting to harvesting, from milking to land clearance – Marion Jeal was finally selected for training as a forewoman and sent to Frimingham Lodge, a private house near Detling aerodrome in Kent. Here they rose at 5.30 a.m. The curriculum, which had been specially tailored to Land Army requirements, was wide-reaching. From 7 a.m. to 10 a.m. was devoted to practical work. From 10 to 12 there were lectures on agriculture, dairy work, the use and care of tools, First Aid, citizenship and leadership. There was even a session on income tax and on how to entertain girls in a hostel. At 12 they broke for lunch. In the afternoon they either did more practical work or toured a selection of training farms. In the evenings they were expected to write up notes on the day's events.

Nicholson: 'On the work front the training course didn't teach me much that I didn't already know – except how to sharpen tools, perhaps. But I did emerge with more formalised authority. I became more involved with land girls' welfare problems, though on an unofficial basis. Every morning the girls from the hostel used to meet up with a group of girls in billets in the town, and they were often unhappy. Landladies had an awful cheek – expecting girls to do the washing up, or babysit . . . Land girls weren't there for that. They'd enough to do in the fields. Sometimes I used to go to the landladies direct, but they'd often give me a dusty answer. If they wouldn't co-operate I'd contact the rep.'

As a result of her training Marion Nicholson was promoted head forewoman. Her letter of appointment, from the Labour Officer of the Kent War Ag., dated April 1945, shows how much progress had been made towards the creation of a structured national agricultural labour force by the end of the war.

> Dear Miss Jeal
> In order to secure uniform treatment throughout the country, of Supervisory Workers employed by War Agricultural Executive Committees, the Standing Advisory Committee of the Agricultural Wage Board has recommended, and the Ministry of Agriculture has agreed, that Supervisory workers shall be classified as follows. Head Forewoman; forewoman and gangers.
> It has also been agreed that Head Forewomen shall not receive payment in respect of overtime, but will, in future, receive an inclusive weekly wage.
> In close consultation with the Assistant Labour Officer under whom you have been working I have decided to grade you as a Head Forewoman and your wage will accordingly be increased to £3.17.6d per week inclusive as from week commencing Friday 13th April 1945 and I sincerely trust that you will prove worthy of this increase.

Lady Denman had always favoured improving the professional standing of land workers. One way the Land Army sought to help its members increase their own sense of value was through encouraging them to take correspondence courses and instigating a system of proficiency tests in the various branches of farming. In 1943, 1,275 land girls did correspondence courses in agriculture and 630 in horticulture. The proficiency courses, which were judged by staff from agricultural colleges, were taken in general farmwork, milking and dairy work, poultry, tractor driving, gardening, fruit work and pest destruction. Successful candidates were awarded a rather unappealing brown bakelite badge with an accompanying certificate, and qualified for a bonus payment of two shillings and sixpence. This system was launched in 1944 with the best of intentions and produced a mixed reaction. From the start the tests had the reputation of being over-intellectual and taxing, while many girls felt, understandably, there was little point in having a piece of paper confirming that you could do a job which you already had been doing for several years. The degree of pomp and circumstance with which the badge was presented varied according to the status of the land girl herself. Those working on the big estates of the artistocracy received theirs at special award ceremonies, while girls working for ordinary farmers had theirs pushed unceremoniously through the letter-box.

Enid Barraud, working in Cambridgeshire, thought it almost a patriotic duty to sit the test. In the *Land Girl* in March 1944 Miss Barraud explains: 'There is, perhaps, a tendency to think "oh well, I've got along very well without any badge so far. I know the job pretty well, there isn't much point in going through the hoops now." There are these two points, as I look at it: your county wants to come well up on the list when the totals are made up, and you yourself owe it to yourself to secure official recognition of your conscientious fulfilment of a tough job of work. Go on now! Send in your application and hitch that little star to your wagon.'

Miss Barraud had been more than happy with her test, which she was at pains to present as a fair assessment: 'We really did have an ordinary job of work under proper working conditions, with all the proper tools and so on, and when it came to the oral questions, you felt the examiners really only wanted to see that you knew the job . . .' Her description of her test – the practical part of which was muck carting – reveals just how detailed a working knowledge of agriculture land girls were expected to possess.

> First some of us had to go into the stables and harness up a horse apiece, lead them out and yoke them into the carts. My mate had this job . . . and then got down to the job of filling the carts. We were all mighty glad to be doing something to warm us up and I think those carts got filled in pretty near record time. Then we had to lead the full carts out of the yard, down a lane, along the main road, up another lane to a muck heap, and there we emptied them – forking the stuff out, not tipping.

Those who had harnessed and yoked in and led the horses on the outward trip now stood back and the rest of us reversed the process. I found myself leading a lovely Percheron, in his prime, and dappled like the authentic rocking horse of nursery days. He was as docile as he was beautiful and soon I had the cart backed into the cart lodge and was unyoking him . . . I led the horse back into the stable and unharnessed him, and then we piled back into the tiny cars that formed our cavalcade and went off to a hostel for the oral part of the test.

. . . For the oral, we were all put into one room, and then taken one by one to another room for questioning. Questions stuck very closely to the little syllabus, and – as promised on the syllabus – were related to our actual experience.

My own first question was: What do you know about the rotation of crops? What is the object and principle? . . . Then came: what processes of cultivation would you use to prepare a field which had grown clover, ready for wheat? First ploughing. Yes: How deep? What next? When would you sow the wheat? How much to the acre? How much oats to the acre? Then we got on to the stock. I said I had not had much to do with pigs, except in an emergency if the pigman was away ill. All right: if I came one morning and found he was ill what would I give the pigs? I told them that I knew the consistency for swill and should mix up accordingly, and give the animals a troughful, adding more if they cleared it too quickly, cutting down next time if they left some. I mention this answer because I think it gives a good idea of the atmosphere of the whole test, an atmosphere of intelligence and common sense as well as academic knowledge. My last question was as to the symptoms of ill-health in cattle, and this didn't worry me very much. Our small herd has been rather unlucky this winter and I have had plenty of opportunity of learning what to look out for.

In other parts of the country, however, examiners seem to have been a bit over-enthusiastic, subjecting land girls who had picked up practical knowledge on the job to the sort of detailed theoretical exam that agricultural students would have had three years of studying to prepare for.

Jean Procter was one of the first four girls in the north of England to take her proficiency test. Although she passed with 96 out of 100, the other girls were way out of their depth and she feels the test was ludicrously tough.

The test began at 6 a.m. and went on till 6 p.m. with a half an hour break for sandwiches in the middle. At the end of the day I was absolutely exhausted. They took me into a field – a completely dry field – and asked me to dig a ditch. Fortunately I'd done ditching, so I knew it had to be two spadefuls deep and that I had to slice off the top in a special way to stop the sides falling in. Then the examiner took a handful of hay out of the rick and asked me to identify each of the different grass types. I knew because I had always been curious and the farmers were delighted if you showed a bit of interest. The other three girls just said 'it's hay'. I had to sharpen a scythe and then demonstrate using it. The other girls had never even seen a scythe, let alone used one. I had to harness and groom a horse, which bit me on the arm. The harness they provided was so neglected and stiff it was almost impossible to undo the buckles and I told them it hadn't seen saddle soap in years. I was asked how to diagnose and treat colic in a horse, foot-rot in sheep, mastitis in cows . . . how to take a cow's temperature. I knew it was up the backside, but one of the other girls who, funnily enough was a farmer's daughter, said 'in its ear'.

The thing I lost marks for, apart from criticising their tack, was a question on swedes. They gave me an imaginary field and asked me how many tons of swedes I would expect to get from it. I tried to imagine how many cartloads I might get out of it and had a guess. 'Your farmer would not be very pleased with that tonnage,' they replied. I thought they were daft questions to ask a girl.

10 : Bunks and Billets

In the early days of the Land Army most land girls were billeted on private farms. The lucky ones were welcomed like daughters, given pretty, comfortable rooms in houses possessing all the comforts and mod cons they had left behind, allowed free access to bathrooms and expected only to work their eight-hour shift. Five thousand liked it so much they continued to work on the land after the Land Army was disbanded.

Others were less fortunate. Many found themselves transported back to another age, a time when a lot of the things they took for granted – electric light, hot water on tap, flushing lavatories – had still to be invented. Many city-bred former land girls remember breaking the ice on the jug of cold water that was expected to suffice for their daily ablutions, the candle that threw such menacing shadows on the sinister, centuries-old walls, the straw mattress infested with fleas . . .

To compare life in the British countryside in the Forties with life in the towns and cities would be like likening Chad to New York today. It wasn't only land girls who found themselves stepping back in time. Evacuees from London who took cottages in counties as 'civilised' as Sussex discovered that well water, oil lamps and horse travel were still the norm. The depressed state of farming meant that many farmers lacked the money or the will to modernise tied cottages while the absence of telephone, television and swift transport kept farm workers relatively unaware of the march of progress elsewhere.

Anticipating the dismay that would afflict town girls who took for granted facilities like electric light and mains drainage Land Army headquarters did its best to highlight the positive side of rural life. An editorial in the *Land Girl* urged new girls to be open-minded in their dealings with their rustic hosts:

> Do put it out of your head that town life is the only life that matters; town people the only people that know anything worth knowing and that your job is to convert the ignorant yokel to your civilised standards. The countryman is a lot more civilised, intelligent and better-mannered than you are inclined to think at the first glance. They have a depth of kindliness you will go far to find amid the rush and tear and every-man-for-himself ways of the town. Country folk hang together and will see to you in a tight corner, and although you will come across gossip and feud, they are only on the surface, and you will always find someone to lend a hand. They may at times seem slow, but it is the slowness of people who always look before they leap, so that they may be a real help and not just give flimsy lip-service and facile advice. As soon as you have realised this one essential point of the sterling worth of country people, you will begin to appreciate their way of life . . .

The advice was good public relations and, as Lady Denman was herself devoted to country life, was doubtless sincerely meant. None the less adjusting to conditions which hardly seemed to have changed since the Middle Ages, and which the Land Army officials would never have to experience at first hand, proved understandably hard for young girls used to better.

Girls billeted on isolated farms in cut-off parts of the

country – Wales, Scotland and the West Country seem to have suffered most. Life could be dull and very lonely. Harsh treatment, uncomfortable living conditions and underfeeding by unsympathetic, parsimonious or downright unscrupulous employers when you were as young as seventeen, away from home for the first time and at times working up to a sixteen-hour day, must have made an already exhausting and uncomfortable existence almost unbearable. It is astonishing that so few land girls gave up.

One girl in Cumberland was on such an isolated farm that the once-a-week bus that took people into town only came within three miles of her. In order to take part in a Land Army rally in Kendal she had to walk six miles to catch a bus and six miles back home again, the return journey in darkness.

Two land girls who worked as pole selectors for the Home Timber Production Department, tramping the countryside in search of timber straight enough for use in telegraph and ladder poles, lodged in 232 different billets. Describing some of the more unusual they managed to see the funny side of exposing townies to the primitive side of rural life.

> Once a foreman was instructed to get a billet for us but forgot all about it, and when we arrived in the pouring rain (as usual) no foreman, no billet. When we got hold of him he told us to wait in the village shop, and after three quarters of an hour came back and said he had found us a lodge for one night and would move us the next day. We were shown into a dirty room, which contained a rusty stove and a wheelbarrow . . . We were so hungry that we got some rations from the shop and some wood and borrowed two cups from the young man's landlady. She brought us an orange box with a piece of newspaper for a cloth, so we had our meal, but decided we could not stay the night there, but would go to the next village. We asked the landlady how much we were in her debt and she thought it was worth 5 shillings each.

It wasn't just uncomfortable conditions that took getting used to. Many landladies were martinets who ran their households with the rigour of a military operation and didn't take kindly to newcomers with their own ideas. Two girls looking for digs in Wales found themselves in a room with seven others, having guilelessly agreed that they wouldn't mind sharing. 'On the Saturday we both had a bath, and when we were having dinner in the café attached to the place the good lady comes in and inquires in a loud forbidding voice of the forty or so people dining there, "Who had a bath?" In a very small voice Miss Tuffield said, "I did." And me, "I did," and we are informed that it is not a hotel.'

Many girls discovered there was an arbitrarily imposed 9 p.m. curfew in their digs – and that failure to observe it provoked punishment of the most rigorous sort. A girl working on an isolated farm in Hampshire was persuaded to go to the annual fair in Petersfield by a couple of young farmhands. When she got home, hours later than 9 p.m., having walked for miles in the dark she found a note pinned on the door. It read simply: '9 p.m. Cushion, blanket and cocoa in shed.' The door was locked.

Over and over again it was the sanitary arrangements that proved the biggest shock. A girl who lived in on her farm can still see what was to be her lavatory fifty years later. 'The farmer was a very dour man of few words. After tea I was given a tour of the farm and finally taken to the bottom of the garden to a wooden shed. To my horror when I pushed open the door I saw a large box affair with two holes shaped in it. A vision flashed before me of the farmer and myself sitting side by side each morning while he gave me my orders for the day. The contraption was moved at intervals and another hole dug . . . As I carried my candle up to bed that night I wished I was back home and shed some tears until I finally fell asleep.'

Many land girls will recognise their rustic host in the following description, which is half Dickens, half Whitehall farce. This girl had grown up in the city and had left a far better paid job in a munitions factory to join the Land Army.

The farmer used to dress downstairs by the fire in the mornings and after knocking at my door (closed with a bent nail as the farm didn't run to door handles) he would say, 'Don't get lighting any candles yet till I've found my trousers.' He would throw sticks on the fire saying the kettle boiled quicker with sticks, put the tea in the cups, and then pour on the boiling water; it tasted horrible and the leaves floated on top. There was a fly sticker fixed on the low ceiling coming down over the centre of the table where it stayed all the winter till the following summer. As it dried the flies fell off. When we had blackberry jam I didn't have any.

For many land girls cold, dirt, discomfort and hunger are what they remember about their bucolic experience. The lack of hot water is a recurrent theme in land girls' recollections. One girl, inquiring of her landlady how she would bath as there was no piped water in the house, provoked the defiant confession: 'I haven't had a bath for fifty years . . . there's always the river.' Another searing memory is beetroot or paste sandwiches. Land girls were entitled to extra cheese, eggs and butter to help them with their taxing manual work, but thousands were sent out each day with a round of not very filling sandwiches. One girl, who lodged with an elderly carter and his wife, lunched regularly on bacon pudding which was made of bacon rinds, parsley and onions, rolled into a suet crust and boiled in a cloth. 'What happened to the bacon the rinds came from I never knew. I certainly never saw any of it.'

It was the norm in the country to provide hot water for personal ablutions only at weekends. One girl who was billeted with an elderly lady along with two other land girls recalls that, despite the dirty nature of their work they were only allowed to wash in hot water on Saturdays. 'On that day we were allowed a pint mug each of hot water for our all-over washes.'

A girl billeted in Scotland describes graphically the challenge to personal hygiene of sanitary arrangements which, half-way through the twentieth century, still relied on well water. 'Water is carried (after being pumped into pails) and put in the hens' pots (normally used for boiling scraps for poultry and the pig). Fill an old zinc bath with a couple of pails of cold water and light a fire under the large hens' pot. Wash top half of body – dry – put on warm jersey and try to sit in the bath for the bottom half of body.'

It seems incredible, when the whole country was facing the most serious threat to its survival in a thousand years, that the land girls, many of whom were only teenagers, should have encountered such mean and shabby treatment. But stories of extreme hardship are widespread. Many girls were freezing cold in their bedrooms because of inadequate bedding. A couple of girls in Cornwall were given just a blanket – no sheets – to sleep under at night and expected to eat off orange boxes covered with newspaper.

In some cases girls were left inexcusably short of food, never seeing the extra rations of eggs and cheese to which they were officially entitled. In stark contrast to the cosy picture Vita Sackville-West paints of the host as expansive stand-in father, many land girls had a diet inferior to that enjoyed by the family they lodged with. One girl who had never been away from home before describes a life that many land girls would recognise:

Our last meal was at 6.30 p.m. after milking and there wasn't even a drink before bedtime. Each day the farmer's wife gave us tea in a small bottle (a lemonade bottle) which of course was cold when we drank it mid-morning in the field, and two slices of bread and cheese wrapped in newspaper. In the afternoon we had the same out in the field but with jam instead of cheese. We all sat for meals in the kitchen (except Sundays when the farmer, his wife, son, Joe and daughter, Sue, disappeared into the front room for their dinner and tea – I expect they had nicer food than us).

On one occasion this girl fell asleep on a Sunday afternoon out in the field and was late for tea. 'The farm lads had eaten theirs and gone off, leaving me one crust of bread. I had nothing more till 8 a.m. next day after two hours' work.'

Many must have thought they had wandered into a

timewarp. Like this girl working in Wales. 'I often think of the bleak, comfortless kitchen of that first farm. Only a wooden settle and a few wooden chairs for seating. One large scrubbed wooden table and one small circular table. During the long dark evenings the oil lamp sat on this table and the farmer wrapped his copy of the *Farmer and Stockbreeder* round the lamp preventing anybody else from reading . . .' This girl's abiding memory was hunger:

> The farmer would thump on my bedroom door about 5.30 a.m. He would have made a pot of tea by the time I got downstairs but this was all we had until we had finished milking twenty-plus cows, by hand of course. When we came in several hours later it would be to a heap of sliced bread and margarine. Later, if I found time to make butter we would have butter as a change from margarine, – so our 'breakfast' consisted of just that and more tea. Later, at lunch, there would be a bowl of potatoes – often nothing else. Sometimes there would be vegetables if they were available in the garden – very rarely meat.
>
> Tea-time would be a repeat of breakfast – occasionally jam would appear . . . The only day I recall 'real food' being served was when the threshing machine arrived and neighbouring farmers came to help.

Some land girls, instead of living with the farmer, lived in billets near the farm, private houses with a bedroom to spare. Though there must have been some kind, motherly landladies who fed their girls properly and gave them warm comfortable beds to sleep in, here too stories of meanness and eccentricity abound. One land girl in Kent, left to fend for herself while her landlady went hop picking, was pestered by a drunken soldier who tried to force his way in. She found out subsequently that her billet was the local brothel. A girl in Wiltshire was not given a hot meal for three months because her landlady preferred the blandishments of the pub to cooking.

Complaints poured into county offices in their thousands via the reps. To try to improve conditions as the Land Army grew, the idea of hostels was introduced. Land Army hostels, with their double rows of bunk beds, their boarding-school style bathrooms, their institutional dining-rooms were created out of any available property – private houses, hotels, converted stables, hutments, sports pavilions or even hen houses requisitioned by the Ministry of Works for the war effort. By 1944 there were 696 hostels throughout the country accommodating 22,000 land girls, about a third of the total force. Girls who lived in hostels, usually in groups of thirty to forty, had a much better time than their counterparts on farms. The overwhelming advantage of living in a hostel to girls in their late teens and early twenties was that it provided a ready-made social life, with many playing host to servicemen camped locally for dances, concerts and amateur dramatic productions. Hostel land girls rarely complain of the loneliness and even depression suffered by girls working on isolated farms, some of whom never saw anyone their own age from one week to the next. The other plus was that physical conditions, by and large, were reasonable. The food may not have been of a very high quality, but at least it was plentiful. Wages were paid promptly and distributed by the hostel forewoman, who was also responsible for seeing that the girls got to and from work, either on bicycles or by lorry.

Land Army issue bicycles were something of a joke and took some mastering, particularly where girls had never learned to ride a bike before. Every part of them was painted black, including the bells. They had been designed for export to the colonies. This explained their huge heavy frames that may have been perfect for pedalling along unmade-up roads in the African Bush but were slow and cumbersome on English lanes. The challenge was further stiffened by trying to pedal in the rigid Land Army boots and any girl who had her own lightweight bicycle at home brought it with her at the earliest opportunity.

Considerable thought was given by the District Officers when selecting a building for use as a hostel, to the girls' comfort and well-being. Dorothy Brant, who was Regional

Officer for the north-east, says there were regular protests from the Ministry of Works representative who was obliged to accompany her on visits to potential hostels, as they were footing the bill, at the numbers of bathrooms and lavatories she deemed necessary. 'They would always compare what I wanted with the other women's Services, implying that we should be treated the same. I pointed out that land girls, unlike women in the Auxiliary Services, didn't spend their days filling in forms in offices, but worked extremely hard, got extremely dirty and needed adequate bathing facilities.'

Some girls complained that life in the hostels was like a return to boarding-school. And there were similarities. There was a weekday curfew of 10 p.m. – often a school playground bell was rung – strictly enforced by the wardens. These were frequently elderly spinsters with a penchant for military-style discipline and a deep distrust of men, who indeed sometimes styled themselves 'Matron'. One girl arriving in the bitter winter of 1942 at a hostel, remembers her dismay at finding how regimented hostel life was to be. 'When we were settled in the dining-room the newly appointed warden . . . spoke about the hostel rules. We were to be woken at 6 a.m. (groans), followed by breakfast at 6.15. After the day's work and our evening meal we were free to do as we pleased. If we went out we must return by 10 p.m. (more groans) and the doors would be locked at that time. We were free to go home for the weekend at 1 p.m. on Saturdays (cheers), but must return by 10 p.m. on Sundays.'

Conditions were often pretty basic, especially if a hostel had been recently requisitioned. One girl describes the intense cold. 'That winter [1942] it was bitterly cold outside and not one degree warmer inside. The only heating in the whole house was one small open fire in the sitting-room; quite impossible for the twenty-five of us to get round it all together. For those of us detailed to sleep on the top floor, going to bed at night was like retiring to an ice block. We slept in everything

we could lay our hands on – pyjamas, socks, dressing-gowns –
the lot.'

Girls who had to bed down in temporary accommodation
while a hostel was found for them must have questioned
seriously their wisdom in joining the Land Army. A letter from
a land girl to her fiancé overseas shows how young girls fresh
from the city must have felt about the service they had
volunteered for.

> This place is really horrible . . . We sleep on stone floors in old
> disused army huts. To start with I had an awful night's sleep,
> not being used to sleeping on the floor on a paliasse – how my
> shoulders ached! There are sixty-six new recruits in charge of a
> Lt.-Col. who calls us up by blowing his whistle at 6.15 each
> morning. . . . Breakfast is from 7 to 7.15 and lorries depart after
> that . . . We started picking spuds until it rained at 4.30 p.m.
> then packed it in and walked most of the way back. It really
> rained then and I got soaked to the skin. I've had a hot bath in a
> filthy tub and some half cold grub. I can't find anywhere to
> hang my wet clothes, so they are here in the hut at the moment,
> which is not exactly a healthy state to sleep in – what a life! So
> picture Beryl and me lying on our stomachs on our divan-like
> beds, with the smoke of the oil lamp, our only light, getting up
> our noses, and the rain falling heavens-hard on the tin roof. I've
> already killed two spiders – again, what a life!

In other hostels, however, a quasi-family atmosphere prevailed with Land Army officials and motherly hostel staff doing
their utmost to make the girls happy and comfortable. Where
possible the girls were provided with bunk beds, not to create
an institutional atmosphere, but to make them feel more at
home. Dorothy Brant says, 'We were discovering that some
girls had never slept by themselves in a bed before. Many of
them came from quite poor backgrounds where there were lots
of children. They were used to sharing beds with their sisters
and they felt isolated and miserable in single beds.'

In many situations the hostel warden found herself assum-
ing the role of surrogate mother as well as being responsible for
cooking, housekeeping and running repairs. Cath Miller, who

ran a Land Army hostel near Reading, dealt with problems as disparate as headlice and pregnancy. 'To my horror I was instructed to finecomb each girl's head. My splendid fore-woman volunteered to be my first patient. We found only one infested head; one of the girls kept her hair in curlers all the week and only took them out on Saturday to go to the local dance. She washed her hair on Sunday morning and then put them in again!'

The girl who became pregnant – by an American service-man – encountered considerable support and sympathy from the other girls. Miss Miller suspected the girl was pregnant when she arrived and tried to persuade her to tell her about her condition. 'She, however, insisted there was nothing wrong and that she had eaten too many plums when they were fruit picking.' Three weeks later a friend came to her and informed her that the baby was due. 'It seemed all the girls knew about her condition and had been helping out with her work. The doctor was called and was marvellous . . . Jenny had a strapping boy within an hour of arriving in hospital. The father . . . had no idea about her condition, but British and American Red Cross and other charitable organisations provided toys and clothes and her friends clubbed together to buy a pram. Eventually the father was informed, so we hope there was a happy ending.'

For the lucky few hostel life meant all the creature comforts of a country house hotel. One girl was sent to a lovely old house between Cardiff and Newport. 'We were joined by other girls, mostly Welsh, with some from Yorkshire, London and Lancashire. They were a grand lot and we mixed well together . . . We had a very good warden. There was always plenty of hot water for baths and plenty of food. Miss Hayden was a splendid pianist and often entertained us in the evenings. On certain evenings a beautician came to give us a few hints on beauty care and at other times a member of the Women's Voluntary Service came to show us how to make slippers and gave us other useful tips . . . Two of the Land

Army Secretaries were very kind to those of us who lived long distances from home. At weekends they often took us out in their cars.'

The most privileged land girls were those who were selected to work in the gardens of Land Army officials who invariably came from the landed gentry and who therefore had plenty of domestic help. Two girls were chosen by a Scottish Land Army official to work in the gardens of her home near Glasgow, swapping the rumbling stomachs and blistered hands of their farming sisters, for the good life. They were trained in growing vegetables by the head gardener and their employer often worked alongside them. 'In our leisure time she taught us to play the recorder and took us to musical evenings and to visit her friends for coffee. One of my loveliest memories was sitting under a large oak tree with Nancy having our elevenses prepared by the cook – a flask of tea and home-made buttered scones . . .'

Linda Shrigley

(née *Lawson*). Joined Land Army at 17.
Land Army . . . 1943 – 7.
Home town: Dipton, near Consett, Co. Durham.

When I joined the Land Army I'd never even been on a train. I had a sister and two brothers. We lived in a little village and we hadn't very much money. My father had been a miner, but he had been wounded in the foot in the First World War and he wasn't able to go back down the pit. He just did labouring. I worked for my grandmother, cleaning the house and helping with the cooking. I had four uncles who all drove machinery above ground at the pit. There always had to be a good meal ready for them. I'd bake bread twice a week and make pies and puddings. She paid me 4 shillings a week. Other girls found the Land Army pay meagre. After they had stopped your keep you were left with 16 shillings and 11 pence. But to me that was a lot of money.

When I decided to join the Land Army I had market gardening in mind. Several girls I knew had joined up and were working locally, so I assumed I would get something nearby. I didn't want to go far as we were a very close family. The first hostel I went to was not far away – just a bus ride. There wasn't any market gardening available so I was sent for tractor driving. But within two months they told me I was going to Hull to be trained to drive an excavator for land clearance. Hull! It seemed so far away.

I got on the train at Bishop Auckland feeling really scared. I had to change trains to get to Hull and there I met another land girl and a man from up north who were going to the same place. It seemed such a long way to travel. There were no seats left on the train so we sat on our cases. When we arrived in Hull the station had been bombed flat. We had to take a tram out to where we were living. The boarding-house had a great big crack in the wall from the bombing. I was terribly homesick and cried at first but it gradually wore off. I really took to driving the excavator once I got used to being away from home. The other girl didn't like it at all – she was sent back to Durham by the foreman. There were meant to be two of us on the same job, taking it in turns to drive the excavator. The foreman said, 'Can you manage on your own Linda?' And I did. We had German prisoners of war clearing out trees from the river banks. We pulled the trees down with our machines and they sorted them out. Then we had Italian prisoners. They were very nice boys. They would say, 'I have a sister. She wouldn't do that work.' Even the English officers in charge of them were amazed when I got out of the machine. I was only four feet nine and a half.

I grew up very fast. My father came to see me when I was cleaning out a river in Newcastle. I didn't know he was there. He told me afterwards how impressed he'd been. He'd no idea the machines were so big. I met my husband while I was doing that work. He drove another of the machines. We got married while I was in the Land Army. I carried on afterwards because the job was still there.

11 : Acceptance at Last (or 'Girls like this cannot help but win the war')

Lady Denman worked tirelessly to raise the profile of the Land Army. Knowing, from her experience in the First World War, that women *could* do the work and realising how vital their contribution would be as the inevitable blockade tightened and more and more men were drafted into the Services, she travelled the country attending recruitment rallies, presiding over morale-boosting 'county' conferences in London and toiling over her recruitment broadcasts. Though she never felt she had the bureaucrats on her side she had enthusiastic support from Buckingham Palace. Queen Mary and Queen Elizabeth, the latter every bit as dedicated a countrywoman as Lady Denman herself, were Women's Institute members. In March 1940 the Queen (now the Queen Mother) attended a tea party in Goldsmiths Hall for which the Goldsmiths Company invited 250 land girls from every county in England and Wales.

Throughout the early years of the war the shortage of labour on the land was acute. Conscription was the main culprit, but the Government's constantly increasing food production targets put farmers under immense pressure. At the outbreak of war most land workers were eligible for call-up at twenty-one. But labour to bring in the 1941 harvest was in such short supply that the Government was forced to backtrack. In March 1941 they raised the minimum call-up age for male farm workers to twenty-five. At this time the Land Army still numbered only 14,656, It was a situation which could not last.

As the demands of the war intensified the call-up age was progressively reduced. By the end of 1942 all farmhands over the age of eighteen were required for the Services, draining agriculture of 100,000 men. With urgent government targets to meet – the quota for 1941 was for one and three quarter million new acres to be put to the plough to grow vegetables such as tomatoes and carrots – farmers were increasingly desperate for labour. The solution lay in the young women of England.

In the spring of 1941 Lady Denman had succeeded in wresting control of the Land Army away from the Ministry of Agriculture. This made her responsible for all administrative decisions and appointments and for overseeing the Land Army budget. As soon as she had secured her position she pulled off a significant public relations coup which did a great deal to improve the Land Army's unglamorous image and boost recruitment. In December 1941 Queen Elizabeth agreed to become patron of the Land Army. It was a post she carried out conscientiously, right up to the end, sending special messages at Christmas, 'thank you' letters to girls leaving the Land Army and reviewing land girls when on tour. In July 1943 the Land Army celebrated its fourth birthday with a party held at Buckingham Palace to which 300 land girls from every county in Britain were invited. The Queen broke with tradition and held the party indoors so that the girls might enjoy inspecting the ceremonial state rooms of Buckingham Palace, in preference to spending just another day in the open air.

In January 1942 the Government announced that from now

on women would be drafted for war work. Faced with the choice of monotonous, if well-paid jobs in noisy, congested aircraft or munitions factories or the Armed Services, huge numbers of women chose the open-air life. In a year the numbers more than trebled so that by June 1942 the WLA stood at 40,000. The following year the force again doubled, with the Land Army reaching its peak strength of 87,000 in July 1943. By now enthusiastic volunteers were joining at the rate of 4,000 a month. Because of the Government's ambitious new food targets work existed in the countryside for 100,000 land girls. The food production target for 1943 was for 600,000 more acres to be dedicated to wheat growing while another million acres of grassland were to be ploughed up. In August 1943, however, in a bid to force women into other less popular types of war work, the Government banned further recruitment to the Land Army.

It is ironic that the Government dammed the tide of girls flowing into the countryside just as the farmers woke up to their worth. The spring of 1942 had brought a desperate shortage of food as the result of the disastrous losses to British shipping in the deadly Battle of the Atlantic. In March alone U-boat action sank 275 merchant ships *en route* for Britain, most of them carrying grain. Cinema 'food flashes' at the time showed sinking grain ships and urged people to use potatoes to save flour. Now, as soon as a girl volunteered she was put to work – often without the month's training she was meant to undergo. By 1943 land girls were employed in every task in the farmer's year-long diary. Confounding the prophets of doom, who had warned that women would not be able to pitch hay or feed the bull or start a tractor, they were doing all that and more. They were thatchers, rat catchers, ditchers . . . they cut and threshed corn, built ricks, drove giant excavators . . .

The gradual acceptance of the Land Army by the initially suspicious, sceptical farming community, its discovery that what the girls lacked in experience and strength they made up for in dedication, and open-mindedness, is a heartening story. What so many farmers were discovering, of course, was that women would conscientiously do what they were asked, whereas a seasoned farmhand as often as not would do what he wanted. As one farmer who employed land girls put it, 'The girls were slow, but they were thorough, whereas the men would be watching the clock and seeing how quickly they could get the job done. Even the *Land Worker*, which had done its fair share of sneering, was forced to change its tune. In August of that year it proclaimed in the hyperbolic tones typical of wartime public relations:

> No industry is more essential to the prosecution of the war than agriculture. Land workers are playing their part just as sure as soldiers, sailors and airmen. The gallantry of them would come to nothing if hunger invaded the home front, or if any proportion of ships bringing imports to this country could not be employed for transporting troops and ammunition to overseas theatres of war. Each land girl volunteer is aware of the urgency and importance of her job. The measure and success of the Land Army is the demand for volunteers. Earlier in the war it was difficult to place recruits, but now there are not enough to go round. These women have to their credit magnificent records of successful efforts. They are doing the most valuable work and their organisation is essential to our war effort.

An employer from Montgomeryshire wrote to the *Land Girl* saying: 'I have 215 acres, including 90 acres arable, a TT herd, as well as other stock, and these three girls, with only one man for heavy work, run the whole job. Long live the WLA.'

A Kent farmer wanted his appreciation of his land girls made known (*Land Girl*, August 1942): 'We started with one girl in May 1940, and now we have 20, with three more waiting for the sunshine. This gang is probably the best that we have had. We have "rabbits" of course, but there are jobs for "rabbits". We have grumblers, but not half as many as we used to have. These girls have no clubs to go to and when we are busy they are given little freedom or sympathy, but there seems to be something that makes the landladies like the girls and the girls like their work.'

More than one farmer informed his County Secretary that the replacement of his old male staff by land girls had actually increased the farm's productivity. A dairy farmer wrote from Devon, 'Last year, with three men and a boy, we produced the record yield of 867 gallons per cow. This year, with only one man, who is sixty-six years old, and two girls, we have maintained last year's production, and at the present time are producing ten gallons a day more milk than at the same period last year. I think these figures speak for themselves.'

A delighted colleague in the same county, who found his milk output had first doubled and then quadrupled wrote (*Land Girl*, August 1945) to say that in his experience land girls were more successful as dairymaids because they were more adaptable and more conscientious than their male counter-parts.

> Joan Balogh took over the cattle and cows on Oct. 1st 1944. The increase in output of milk is as follows: 1944 – Oct. 157 per cent, Nov. 157 per cent, Dec. 137 per cent. 1945 – Jan. 201 per cent, Feb. 210 per cent.
>
> These are actual increases on corresponding months of the preceding year. You will conjecture that the production figures for the previous year were very low. I quite agree, they were – but they were figures I got, after employing successively, a foreman, a practical farmer and finally an experienced cattle-man from an estate of very large acreage. The secret of the success of these milk production figures is, I think, that a land girl . . . is amenable to the adoption of methods which can be found in any handbook on milk production and of rationing systems and will conscientiously follow out instructions to the letter.

On occasions the dedication so many farmers observed went beyond the call of duty and entered the realms of the heroic. The scope for acts of outstanding bravery was fairly limited in the Land Army but a farmer in Leicestershire was, understandably, lost in admiration for the courage of his land girl, a Miss B. L. Potter. 'My neighbour's Black Poll bull broke through the fence and got in contact with my Shorthorn pedigree bull, and consequently a desperate fight took place. On hearing the disturbance Miss B. L. Potter detached the two bulls from the herd and brought them across a 21-acre field to the homestead entirely on her own and separated them. I consider this a very brave act and no doubt saved damage to valuable livestock at a very great risk to herself.'

Some countrymen were impressed simply by the dogged commitment displayed by girls whose city upbringing had not prepared them for physical endurance. An employer from Northants expressed his gratitude in a moving letter to his county office (*Land Girl*, March 1942):

> With reference to Mary Hall, the land girl you sent to us last September, I cannot speak too highly of her, as it has been no easy task for a girl to go through the wet and cold we have had this winter. She lives two miles away from the farm and cycles up and down, and she has never missed a day or been late at any time through all the severe weather we have had. I have been on a farm all my life and fully understand what this work means to a girl who has spent all her previous years in office work. Today the snow was too deep for her to cycle, so my son took the car to fetch her, but Mary was nearly here, walking through the snow. I am afraid I have thought land girls summertime workers, but Mary has proved to me I am wrong.

That the land girls proved to be good with animals is perhaps no surprise. But they could also excel at traditionally 'male' accomplishments like ploughing. Many land girls who had found themselves driving and maintaining the temperamental iron-wheeled Fordson tractors from their first day on the farm saw no reason why they shouldn't enter ploughing competitions and were often successful. A veteran Yorkshire farmer, observing the West Riding Ploughing Competition in 1944, was entirely won over. 'I would not have believed they could have done so well with so little experience. In the main they are a lot better than the lads. They take more care and they're not in too big a hurry to get finished.'

By the time the Land Army was at its peak strength it commanded a respect and affection among the general public unique among wartime occupations. It was not only the farming community who realised the extent of the Land Army's contribution to victory. An extract from a letter written in 1944 by a gunner to a land girl in Yorkshire movingly expresses the admiration and gratitude many felt for the volunteers.

When the call for duty rang out, I was one of those thousands who decided that our homes and farms were worth fighting for. We left behind those who were so often termed the weaker sex – our wives, sisters and sweethearts. They in turn decided that their menfolk were worth all the help and backing they could give. I have lived all my life in the heart of England's foremost agricultural county and have experienced the hard way of living which the WLA have chosen. To see them now, doing exactly the same jobs, experts at all they undertake, is a sight that fills us with admiration when we come home on leave. They are giving us something to take back with us – the knowledge that our land is being safely tended and preserved during our absence.

I have spoken with several of the girls of this vast organisation in different parts of the country. They are the happiest of all the war workers I have yet seen, happy in the knowledge that they are doing a grand job and that they are helping their menfolk to frustrate the efforts of the enemy to rob them of their heritage. I am sure I speak for all the boys when I say, 'Thank you, Women's Land Army.'

The main objection to the Land Army had been that women were only capable of doing some of the lighter jobs that needed doing on a farm. A farmer in Farndon, Notts, had put his girls to anything and everything and could find no fault.

During Sept 1939 I needed extra men on my farm, and being

unable to get them, employed two Land Girls. One was over 21 and had a science degree and the other was 17 years old . . . Both were keen and most anxious to do their best. They learnt to pitch and load a heavy second crop of seeds and kept the men on the stacks busy until all was stacked. They drove a tractor, harrowed up twitch [couch grass] which they carted and burned, had a whole week's threshing, one on the cornstacks, one on the strawstacks, taking a man's place in each case, and keeping pace with the men. They fed and cleaned out pigs and learnt to milk daily; they picked potatoes and took on four acres of beet, of which they made an excellent job, afterwards helping to load the beet into the lorry. I found them cheerful and willing, with never a grumble in rain or storm, always sensibly clad and happy. Girls like this cannot help but win the war.

12 : Strange Tasks

The story of the Land Army is inextricably entwined with the disappearance, in little more than a decade, of farming methods which had been in use for thousands of years. Land girls learned to use implements which Victorian, Georgian and perhaps even Tudor farmhands would have recognised – hay knives, billhooks, scythes, the jacks and combs of the thatcher, the woodsman's spokeshave, horse-drawn implements like ploughs, hayrakes and harrows, the binder and the threshing machine. Land girls were probably the last group of farmhands to use them. Fifty years later these tools and implements are museum pieces, their obscure function requiring clarification on printed cards. The extent to which mechanisation of farming advanced during the war years is illustrated by the fact that in 1939 there were 55,000 tractors in use, while in 1945, thanks in great measure to imports from the United States, that figure had amost tripled to 175,000. It was not, however, simply a question of hand-milking giving way to the Alfa Laval machine, the pensioning off of Shires in favour of Fordson tractors, or the snuffing out of the ancient art of hedge laying by the mechanical hedge cutter. The centuries-old look of the countryside and the farmyard has changed, while the need to work in co-operation with nature and the elements has largely been overcome by technology. Instead of the black-and-white Friesians we see everywhere today, there were many different breeds of cattle, each with their own characteristics – Short-horns, Ayrshires, Devon Reds, Red Polls . . . In the days before artificial insemination nearly every farm had a bull who could be extremely troublesome. Before intensive farming destroyed the rules of stockmanship by confining creatures to cages, sows and piglets ran free, and hens roamed the fields in search of spilt grain.

Today after the field has been ploughed, harrowed and planted it remains unvisited till harvest time, the army of workers that formerly had the task of thinning and hoeing the growing crops made redundant by chemicals and machines. We have grown used to seeing hay and cornfields shaved bare in a day by one man on a combine harvester, whereas fifty years ago fields teemed with workers at haymaking or harvest time. We are so accustomed to those giant rolls of straw that stay in the fields half the winter it is hard to remember the traditional way of harvesting. Then the stooks of corn, placed together in groups of six like a wigwam so that the wind blew through the middle and dried the ears, would stand, turned each day, until the farmer deemed it was safe to build the rick. Cornstacks no longer exist, thanks to the combine harvester. Modern haystacks are merely bales heaped up in a pile kept weatherproof by Dutch barns with their roofs of corrugated iron or by plastic sheets. Then they were built using loose hay and required the sort of skill and experience that went into building a dry-stone wall. Finally both they and cornstacks were roofed with thatch which would be put on by a master craftsman with as much care as if he were roofing a cottage.

It was into this arcane world of complex skills, honed down the centuries, handed on from father to son, that the land girls were pitchforked. A few public figures appreciated just how tough it must be trying to penetrate this world and urged the farmers to be kind. Sir Bruce Fraser, the Third Sea Lord, addressing a local celebration of Warship Week, was in a position to see just how vital the Land Army's role would be as the sea blockade inevitably tightened. He described the Land Army as one of two women's Services directly connected with the Navy: 'They are growing more and more food to help us. Employers should remember that they are doing hard work and strange tasks and a little consideration, a kind word or deed, not only makes for happiness, but also for efficiency.'

What were these strange tasks?

To describe in detail every job undertaken by the Land Army would be impossible, since everything that had to be done on the land they did. Girls who couldn't ride a bike found themselves driving eight-ton excavators or starting recalcitrant iron-wheel tractors whose crank handles had a way of spinning backwards that threatened to take your thumb off. Food was being produced from every possible source. One girl spent her nights driving a lorry round the West End right through the Blitz, collecting rubbish from the dustbins of luxury hotels to turn into pigswill for her local pig club in North London. Others turned out after a day's work to pick wild fruit like rosehips and blackberries urgently wanted by food preservation centres.

Two things, perhaps, are of particular interest to the modern reader. Firstly the way land girls mastered those skills which, due to mechanisation, have disappeared from the farmer's calendar – building and thatching ricks, hedging and ditching, threshing, droving; and secondly those occupations which even in our days of equal opportunity still have the words 'man's work' stamped on them – dirty jobs like ratcatching, husky jobs like land reclamation and timber-felling . . .

Rats in wartime Britain were regarded in the evil stakes as only slightly inferior to Hitler himself. In 1940 there were fifty million rats in Britain – five million more than the human population – and many of them spent the winter devouring the grain that had been so painstakingly harvested that autumn. With many male ratcatchers fighting the enemy overseas it fell largely to the Land Army to defeat 'Hitler's helper' on the home front. Articles in the *Land Girl* helped nerve the girls for their grisly task by deluging them with fascinating facts: that one rat eats a hundredweight of food a year, which means that fifty million rats are eating two and a half million tons of food a year. During the war rats had grown so bold that in one knacker's yard they would gnaw the carcases which were in the process of being flayed.

Buoyed up by patriotic fervour, land girls took to ratcatching with enthusiasm, even though, on occasion, the cruelty involved did upset them. Betty Mace, who made playing cards in a printing works in Wakefield before being sent to Devon as a ratcatcher, says looking back the work was horrible, though at the time they accepted it.

> I'll always remember once near a rick seeing a mother rat caught fast in a trap with her babies still suckling. Half the time the traps didn't kill them and you had to finish them off with a stick. We used to hate pick-up days, when you collected the dead rats. Their tails were usually covered in sores and their bodies literally heaving with fleas. We had no gloves and nowhere to wash our hands between doing that and eating our lunch. We used to pick dock leaves and use them to protect our hands. But the thing that upset us most was killing rabbits. We'd put gas down the holes. That wouldn't kill them, just make them dopey. Then we had to wring their necks. An old man who had worked on farms all his life showed us how to do it. You had to pull until the neck went 'click'. Some of us had had rabbits as pets as children and rabbits aren't as horrible as rats.

In all, the Land Army boasted one thousand ratcatchers, among their number girls who in civilian life had been waitresses, hairdressers and even tap dancers. By this time the traditional methods of ratcatching were dying out and gassing and poisoning were taking over. In Devon in one year 24,000 rats had been killed by trapping but nearly 100,000 by the more modern methods.

In some parts of the country land girls formed themselves into anti-vermin squads. Four girls in North Wales travelling around by bicycle, killed 35,545 rabbits, 7,689 rats, 1,668 foxes and 1,901 moles in fourteen months.

Ratcatching, like many of the other jobs land girls had to tackle, was often picked up on the job. Some girls, however, were given special training. Mrs Sylvia Knight remembers trying to put her newly acquired theoretical knowledge into practice.

We went to a nearby village and on to premises where circus animals and sideshow animals (such as five-legged calves) were being housed. Professor Ashton gave us each a number. Mine was 10, and when he shouted that I was to stand in a shallow, smelly dyke and then put my arm down a nearby rat hole it made my flesh creep but with true Yorkshire grit I obeyed. When I plunged my arm in quickly and yelled out which way the hole ran, withdrawing with even greater speed, the girls on top of the bank started pumping cymag gas into another hole . . . Seconds later a huge rat ran out of my hole, incidentally the first I had ever seen. The shock was great and I landed on my back in the smelly drain. The reason why the site was overrun with rats was because there were two lion carcases lying a few yards away.

A girl from Leicestershire who wrote to the *Land Girl*, had clearly taken the patriotic message on board:

On the estate where I work we have in use one or two ancient looking cars, which in summer help to move the hay cobs and many other jobs on the farm, and one of these, an old Morris, has been the means of helping the war effort. One of the estate men and I got the car in running order and took it about half a mile to a field where the barley stacks were, and leaving the engine running, fitted a length of rubber tubing . . . on to the exhaust pipe. Next we placed the far end of the tube right in one of the many rat holes. Arming ourselves with sticks we waited till the poisonous fumes from the exhaust pipe wound their way into the underground labyrinths of the rats' holes. Suddenly, out popped a brown head with two beady eyes. Bash! One more of Hitler's helpers was removed; only a little helper maybe but one who can cause a great deal of damage to our country's corn supply.

After allowing the gas to enter each hole we stopped it up with frosty clots of earth and went on to another. The rats as a rule will not show themselves but are gassed in their holes. They have to make up their minds quickly whether to come out or no, for if they hesitate they are soon suffocated by the fumes. A large number can quickly be destroyed . . . Such are the joys of ratcatching, but we *must* all go out in order to protect our country's grain stacks, the nation *must* 'have bread'.

One of the ancient rustic skills which land girls took particular satisfaction in acquiring – and in many cases acquiring in a matter of days – was thatching. In the Forties this was not merely a picturesque way of roofing a cottage. In the days before nylon sheeting and grain silos it was the way of waterproofing hay and cornricks until they were needed either for feed or for threshing.

Most farms had a field set aside to grow the thatching 'reed' which in reality was a type of wheat whose stalk made it particularly effective in waterproofing. When it was cut it was put through a reed comber, a cousin of the threshing machine, to separate the ears from the straw. The thatchers started work immediately after the rick was built. Techniques varied from county to county, but all the girls wore stout leather knee pads to protect their skin from the sharp corn. In some areas girls had to learn to make not only the spars – bent into hairpin shapes from pliable hazel wood – that anchored the thatch to the rick but the corn rope that held the thatch on.

Ivy Lemon, who learned to thatch after a week's training, says normally girls worked in pairs with one girl putting the pads, or 'tiles' of thatch in place while the other brought up fresh supplies of reed from below.

It was the job of the girl on the ground to damp the reed a bit, otherwise it would slide off the rick before you had fixed it. She would pull the reed out from the pile of straw and make it into 'tiles'. These were pads measuring ten inches across and about three inches thick. These she placed in what was called a jack, which was the thatcher's equivalent of the builder's hod. It was a wishbone-shaped piece of hazel, cut complete from the shrub and standing about three feet high. It had a hook on one side of the 'Y'. When the jack was full of tiles the hook was pulled across and fastened to the other side of the 'Y' clamping the straw in position. Then it could be carried up to the thatcher and clamped on to the ladder until all the tiles it contained were used up when you could unhook it and let it fall to the ground.

Thatchers started at the eaves of the rick leaving an overhang so that the rain dripped on to the ground and worked upwards towards the apex in overlapping layers. As they worked they combed the thatch smooth with a specially made wooden comb. Every so often a pointed stake was pushed in and string tied round it with a looped hitch knot which would then be looped round the next stake. Ivy Lemon says: 'The stakes had to be put in so that the end pointed up towards the apex of the rick to prevent the rain running into the rick.' Twine grew increasingly scarce as the war progressed, particularly after the Philippines, the main source of imported hemp, fell to the Japanese. In Oxfordshire, where Ivy thatched, not only corn and hayricks but on one occasion a cowshed, from September to Christmas four years running, they saved the twine that the binder put round the sheaves of corn at harvest time. 'When they took the rick apart for threshing they cut the twine and then knotted it all together. Next year it would be used for thatching.'

In Devon, whose inhabitants have traditionally enjoyed a reputation for thrift, they made their own thatching rope from corn. Johnnie Luxton, who says she received the briefest explanation of the technique before being put to work, demonstrated the technique of corn rope making on the back of a lorry in a recruitment parade in Exeter. 'You had a bale of wheat beside you and a frame, a bit like the old-fashioned television aeriel that you pulled against. You fed handfuls of corn stalks in with one hand so that it all got twisted into one long strand.'

Thatchers in Devon were expected to make the wooden 'spars' that held down the thatch. 'An old man showed us how to do it. It was usually hazel as it's so pliable. It would be pointed at both ends. You took it in your right hand and twisted it in a certain way till it bent into a U shape. We wore leather pads on our hands as well as our knees. We used our hands to push home the spars. Occasionally one would break. If you didn't have protection you could have had a nasty injury.'

The great thing about thatching, unlike so many other farm tasks, was that there was something permanent to show for it. Johnnie Luxton: 'When all the ricks were up after the harvest, to stand back at the end of the day and admire your work, that was something.'

With the Government demanding that hundreds of thousands of new acres be put to cultivation each year land reclamation formed a significant – and oustandingly successful – part of the Land Army's work. A girl from Hertfordshire was the first woman in the country to work a Cub excavator and demonstrated her newly acquired skill to an awe-struck Press corps. In August 1942 twelve land girls from Kent were sent to the training centre in Hull to learn to drive excavators, prior to embarking on drainage work in Romney Marsh. Staff at Hull observed that the girls had performed better than the men.

Land clearance was hard work with bracken to uproot, boulders to shift, stumps to drag out, trees to fell . . . before the plough could even be thought of. Seventeen-year-old girls who in peacetime would never have expected even to learn to drive a car were plonked on giant excavators and told to get digging to the consternation of fathers and amusement of brothers.

Land reclamation projects were going on all over the country from Durham to Devon, from Norfolk to Wales. In

Devon the fight was on to turn part of the moor, with its tenacious scrub, gorse and bracken, into potato fields. In some parts the Land Army took charge of the entire process. This involved clearance, the first ploughing, the harrowing, the second ploughing, the planting and the ridging up. In one part of the county 110 girls were solely responsible for producing 1,300 acres of potatoes from hitherto derelict land. They ploughed, prepared the soil, planted, ridged, hoed, picked, clamped and graded for market.

No land was deemed unsuitable for cultivation, provided the will was there. One London girl ploughed a bracken-infested field whose one-in-three slope made ploughing downwards the only way. The slope lifted the plough out of the earth and the only way it could be made to stay down was when the farmer, his wife and their young son hung on to the back of it.

Like thatching, land reclamation was a task which provided considerable job satisfaction. Linda Shrigley was seventeen and only four foot eleven inches when she joined the Land Army, having done no work apart from help her grandmother with housework. After working as a tractor driver in her native Durham she was approached by her foreman and told she was going to Hull for a week's training as an excavator driver. 'I had never been on a train before and the idea of such a long journey on my own terrified me.' Having got through her course with flying colours, Linda was sent to work on a huge project, dredging the River Skerne in Durham, which, through years of neglect, had created a thirty-mile-long flood plain on either bank. Linda worked alone with three men and a foreman, getting up at 4 a.m., cycling for an hour and working a 6 a.m.-to-6 p.m. day often six days a week. She was so passionate about her work – 'I got the hang of it straight away' – that she gave a radio talk about it at the time.

My grab works three or four times to the minute. A grab is a big shovel affair, with teeth, that digs into the bottom of the river and gouges out 8 cwt of soil and clay and stones at a time. Then back goes another of my levers, and up comes the grab. Another lever turns the whole excavator round; then I press a pedal with my foot and tip the whole lot out of the grab on to the top of the river bank, just where I want it.

Soon I shall have to cross and start on the other bank. That's a whole day's job. You've got to tip enough stuff into the river to make a bridge to carry the excavator across, then you've got it all to dig out again. But actually we are not simply scooping out of the river bed all the time. Making the bank straight and sure – what we call 'champfering' – is just as important. We've got to see that this river is wide enough, as well as deep enough, to take all the drainage water that it should have been taking all along. That is why there has been this terrible flooding – just because the river was too sluggish and jammed-up and twisted and shallow to get the water away. So part of the time we hack away at the banks with the grab, and throw all the soil and clay well back. All this stuff goes to make a thick low wall right along the river, in case it ever tries to flood again.

As well as deepening and widening the bed, we've got to be always on the look-out for old drains that have been stopped up perhaps for hundreds of years. It never takes the men long to get them open – and that means that fields maybe half a mile away are starting to be drained at last. Then we've got to watch for obstacles like big boulders and trees. The men get the boulders out; we drag the trees out.

I think it's a real man-size job, this. We start the paraffin engines ourselves every morning, then we just slog away all day. We do about 60 or 70 yards a day, and each of us shifts about 200 tons every day. This is supposed to be one of the biggest drainage jobs in the country – and one of the fastest too. If we carry on like this we should be through in another eight months. And when it's done we shall have reclaimed about 60,000 acres for real safe cultivation.

. . . I wouldn't swop this job for anything; I really wouldn't. It does get a little monotonous at times; you don't do much travelling in an excavator, and you could get sick of seeing the old grab swinging up and round, round and down, all day long. But if I ever feel like that, I've just got to look down the river. All the way to Darlington it is now running freely in a deep, wide bed with safe banks, draining land that's never been drained before. And then I compare it with up-river where we haven't reached, with its narrow, twisted banks sometimes only a foot above water level. Or I look round at the poor wretched fields around here – abandoned, covered with rushes, the soil so *cold* after the flooding that nothing else will grow. Next year I shall come along here and look at the crops of barley and wheat and I shall think '*I* had something to do with that. I helped to wake up *that* weary river.'

One of the most hated jobs in those pre-mechanised days was picking Brussels sprouts, a harvest the more bitter because it is reaped in the coldest part of the year. Vita Sackville-West, trying to convey the all-pervading damp and cold of winter fieldwork, compared it guilelessly to a partridge shoot, the irony of the fact that this was a gentleman's leisure pursuit willingly undertaken perhaps escaping her. '(Take root crops) . . . This is a heavy job and a wet one. Anyone who has walked through a field of roots after partridges will know how wet it can be. The top leaves seem to hold water as nothing else holds water, except, perhaps, a pond. You are drenched to the knees after five minutes . . .'

A girl who actually had to do this describes it more graphically. 'Sprout picking all day in a biting north-easter, with intermittent showers of sleety rain when we just have to stop. We look like monks from the Middle Ages, standing there with sacks round our middles, another over our heads like a cowl, and our numbed hands tucked up our sleeves for a moment's respite.'

Planting vegetables – potatoes, celery, cabbages . . . another task now totally mechanised – was back-breaking to those not used to it. Peg Francis, a former factory worker, who worked in the vast vegetable-growing fields of Lincolnshire, describes the labour-intensive way it used to be done.

First two tractors preparing the land, then 'wag' (wagoner) would open the ground for setting – then Reg on his 'dobber' making regular small holes for the taaties. There would be three wagoners and their teams of beautiful horses bringing out the boxes of chitted (sprouting) taaties from the greenhouses, several men to hand them down to us and collect the empties. So two of us to a box – one either side the rhythm went – pick up three taaties, move on carrying the box whilst placing the taaties nice and tidy please, chits uppermost. Glance back down the rows . . . it all looked quite nice really – and then we'd groan, pick up the box and one-two-three oooh! Bending down was very hard on our tender leg, back and shoulder muscles – blisters formed on our soft hands . . . Getting out of bed the next morning was agony! I could roll out of my top bunk, gritting my teeth at the pain and go round helping the girls out and down from their bunks. It was awful till we got toughened up, though sometimes the fields seemed endless. In fact the row ends disappeared in the mist.

We planted celery six inches apart down a shallow row. The plants were four to six inches long and I went down on my knees for this lot. We dressed celery with dry fertiliser; we hoed celery and in the winter we knocked frost and snow off celery, tied up bundles of twenty with string – no gloves – or filled wooden crates with celery and trimmed off celery tops level with the tops of the boxes . . . We set spring cabbages, we set cauliflowers too and glowed when neighbouring farmers complimented us on our work . . . Then we would go with wagoner George and his team of lovely horses to load up ready for the trip to market – very nice in the fine weather, but if it rained hard I'd change three times in a day and shoulder-push behind the carts to get them out of the mud. We hand-dibbed our cabbages in – back-breaking work. We dry dressed them out of buckets. We planted at the right length between plants – the foreman measured.

Where it came to working with horses, land girls were expected to acquire overnight at least the rudiments of skills the old male carters and stockmen had taken years to perfect. One girl wrote in a letter home. 'Took a ton of sprouts to the station. Kitty is a maddening horse: she looks down suspiciously and steps coyly sideways at every puddle on the road. . . . Had to put my sprouts in the very end truck and when I came to get away had to back Kitty through a space only half an inch wider than the cart, between a lorry and a pile of sleepers. The Army watched breathlessly, but if they expected to see me scrape the paint, they were disappointed! The corporal grinned as I extricated myself. "Old bus goes quite well in reverse," he said.'

Girls who worked exclusively with animals seem to have found their days particularly fulfilling. One who had come from a Lancashire cotton mill and became a shepherdess in Lindsey wrote a vivid account of her new life which shows that road rage is nothing new.

My job is to look after the male lambs born the previous year. We begin work at 7.30 by looking round the sheep to see if they are all right – maybe one is on its back and must be put on its legs again. We then fetch their cake out of the hut . . . The cake is put in troughs and when it is eaten we move the troughs to a fresh fold and fill them with cut swedes. There is one trough for every ten sheep – last year we had 400 lambs so there were forty troughs to move; they are difficult to carry on your shoulder when it is sludgy or windy. After the sheep have eaten we move them to a fresh fold, . . . Taking up the last day's nets and cutting a few swedes occupies us up to lunch-time and after lunch there is more swede cutting and trimming . . . In the summer there is a lot of droving to be done; the only thing that gets me flustered is when motorists who honk their horns will not wait until the sheep are put to one side and so make them run which is very bad for them. Another horror is when the sheep dash into an open gateway or through a gap in the hedge. Off you have to dash, round the field shouting, barking like a dog and nearly choking yourself in the attempt until you finally get them on the road again. I have taken sheep eleven miles at times and by the time I have walked from one side of the road to the other pushing the sheep along I have done perhaps double. On long journeys I rest the sheep when they start to tire. My longest day was when I first took sixty-eight ewes and sixty-seven lambs eleven miles and then later drove ninety sheep to my home village. I got there at 11 pm.'

From time to time the head man on a farm would fall ill and the land girl's recently acquired skills would be seriously tested. This was the case with Violet Turpin, who had been in service before becoming a shepherdess at a farm in Dorset. Her employer wrote: 'Miss Turpin works with a pedigree flock of 300 Hampshire Down ewes. She can pitch hurdles and work a sheep dog – in fact, during the summer when she takes the sheep on the downs she works the dog by herself. Like many of us she likes the spring best when the young lambs are growing and she has the necessary patience for dealing with their suckling problems. During the heavy snows and bitter frosts of last January the head shepherd fell ill and Miss Turpin had full responsibility for the whole flock during the day. She kept the lambing yards in order and about 70 lambs were born while she was in sole charge.'

Fruit picking and market gardening seem almost effete compared to the cold and isolation of hill farming, but here too land girls were expected to put their backs in, whatever the weather. Three of them in Norfolk scooped the productivity prize for picking out an astounding 9,930 and 9,920 tomato plants in eight hours, while a girl in Lancashire, described by her employer as a 'jewel among land girls', set an impressive record for cutting cress – eighty-six and a half dozen punnets filled in four hours – or 260 an hour.

With fruit picking as with most other open-air jobs the weather made all the difference. A girl working in Essex describes the camaraderie of a day's apple picking 'attired in sou'westers and macs – a day spent wading through the mud that the tractor churns into huge puddles as it carts boxes of wet apples, tying pieces of string round your wrists to stop those icy trickles of rain up your arms, carrying boxes that seem twice as heavy because they are so damp – and an evening drying muddy clothes.'

When the sun shines, on the other hand, 'there are huge jokes about practically nothing at all as we ride up to the orchard behind the tractor, a pleasant break for elevenses, cheerful discussions as picking buckets are filled – a day flies by as we strip the trees. The apples are exquisitely coloured: James Grieve, juicy, easily bruised, with a pale green to deep orange tint; rich red Worcesters; Monarchs, green and delicately tinted with pink; Cox's Orange Pippins, sunrise and sunset coloured and lastly, Bramleys, which rely on taste and not appearance.'

The drying up of imports forced a certain amount of experimentation on conservative British farmers. Early on in the war the Government was keen to extend flax production, which had been imported from Holland and the Baltic. Flax was used in the manufacture of all sorts of things – aeroplane wings, webbing for parachute harness and ropes and thread. Moreover, a by-product of flax was linseed oil, which was a valuable animal feed. A girl working in Huntingdonshire describes with patriotic pride the first flax harvest from land that was sea bottom a hundred years earlier.

For centuries the problem has been to keep drained the ever-flooding land. The continuous sinking of the soil has necessitated the cutting of dykes and the installation of increasingly powerful pumping units. What justifies this prodigious expense, this unending expense? The answer is that the Fens can boast some of the finest soil in England for the growth of wheat, potatoes, sugar-beet, fruit – and now flax.

Last autumn I spent seven happy weeks helping with the flax harvest on the Whittlesey Wash. Among the workers were seven land girls, three permanently employed, the others having joined for the season. We pulled the flax, we stacked it, we carted it . . . Sea bottom a century ago, virgin soil until last year the Whittlesey Wash is an experiment in agriculture. England was at war and its rich potentialities for production could no longer be ignored. Ploughing began in April in soil that defeated everything less formidable than caterpillar tractors. Wide dykes were cut to drain the flooded furrows. The drilling of the flax was completed early in June and the potato land prepared. The scene is peaceful, filled with eternal things that no wars can change. Nevertheless the Fens have gone to war again and once more are playing a vital part in the nation's history.

Land girls were the last group of people to learn the ancient and deeply hierarchical art of threshing, the process by which the dry grains of corn are separated from the straw. Today it no longer exists as a separate procedure – thanks to the advent of the combine harvester. In the time of the Land Army the cut corn was stored in ricks. When it was deemed ready and when there was little other work to do on the farm – usually around November – the farmer would arrange for the threshing machine to call – they were hired from contractors on a daily basis and went from farm to farm. From then until all the corn was threshed and bagged in sacks ready for sale, practically all other farm work ceased and it was all hands on deck. Unlike the efforts of the combine harvester, whose driver works solo, threshing was extremely social, requiring at least five and often up to a dozen workers. Two worked on the thresher itself, one cutting the bonds that bound the sheaves, one feeding the loose corn into the drum. Other workers stood on the rick and pitched sheaves to the cutter, while yet more removed what the machine spewed forth. As with many agricultural procedures, a rigid pecking order was observed. Cutting bonds was the plum job, while the newest recruit invariably got the dirtiest and most uncomfortable chore – clearing out the chaff, the remnants of the corn husks, or the cavings, which were the broken and mangled bits of straw, both of which produced a choking dust which penetrated ears, eyes, mouths, noses, lungs and clothing.

The threshing machine, a direct descendant of the great steam engines of the industrial revolution, possessed more charm than our combine harvester. It was, however, a machine of great power and potential danger and one land girl in Kent lost a leg after it became caught in the drum. Threshing was extremely strenuous work and girls employed as threshers were supposedly entitled to extra rations of cheese, tea and sugar, extra soap, and a shilling a day on top of their pay. Land girls living in hostels were entitled to get the bath first when they were threshing. Dorothea Abbott, a librarian from Stratford-upon-Avon, says the first threshing machine she saw was painted red, 'like a gipsy caravan but was hung about with all sorts of belts and wheels and cogs in the manner of a Heath Robinson drawing'.

New land girls were invariably assigned to the worst job of removing the chaff from underneath the thresher. If allowed to pile up this could clog the machine. Dorothea, sent off with no training to her first farm remembers being torn between feelings of admiration for the machine and those who knew how to operate it and exasperation at her own clumsiness. 'I watched fascinated while the machine shook out the chaff underneath, poured out the grain into sacks one end and produced boltings of straw at the other. Beside me a tall youth was raking short pieces of straw known as cavings into another sheet. I didn't realise how lucky I was, for at many farms one person has to cope with both chaff and cavings. As it was I felt I'd got my work cut out keeping the chaff under control.'

What impressed Dorothea was the rhythm with which the skilled hands worked together.

> I was able to watch the two men on the top of the rick pitching sheaves to the bond cutter on the top of the machine. His job was to cut the string round the sheaves while the man beside him fed the loosened corn into the drum with a pitchfork. If he let too much down at once there would be a groan in the rhythm of the machine.
>
> We were well under way now, with chaff and cavings pouring out. The boltings of straw clicked down steadily to be carried away on pitchforks by two men who were building the strawrick. Every time I came back from the shed there was a positive Everest of chaff waiting to be flattened. It was warm work and chaff spilled down the neck of my shirt every time I flung the bundle over my shoulder. It clung to my hair and I realised now why most of the girls from the hostel had been wearing headscarves turbanwise when they set off for work.

The dust got everywhere, as did the spikes of barley which had a habit of getting stuck in the navel and needed removing with eyebrow tweezers. Many land girls decided that threshing epitomised the gulf between the magic of life on the land as suggested by Land Army recruitment posters and the prosaic reality.

Without protective clothing threshing did nothing for a girl's looks. A glance in the mirror, after an hour or two's threshing shocked one girl: 'Dirt was in the corners of my eyes, up my nostrils and on my lips. There were clean streaks where the sweat had run down my face and I seemed to have lost my pageboy bob. I was a brunette, but thistledown clinging to my hair made me look prematurely grey.'

In time, the huge rise in wheat cultivation and the subsequent need for more threshing led to land girls forming their own gangs. In most cases the driver, responsible for starting up and overseeing the running of the machine, was a man. But there was a small number of girls intrepid enough to take over the running of the threshing machine itself. Vera Petrie who came from Tonbridge in Kent, worked on an all-girl team.

> Our driver was a girl called Olive Bass. She was a little tiny thing. She was responsible for driving the threshing machine right up close to the stacks, getting it started and seeing that it continued to run all right. When she first started she was quite a novelty, but by the time I joined she had been doing it for about a year and the farmers were all used to her. We were quite a sight going along the road. There'd be the tractor in front, then the threshing machine, then our caravan, which was where we had our lunch and sheltered if it was wet, and then the trusser which tied the loose straw into bundles.

Threshing was one of the few jobs in the Land Army where promotion was a possibility. The most competent girl could become the forewoman. This gave her some authority over her workmates and made her responsible for time- and wage-sheets, in return for which she earned more money. In the early days, however, one can appreciate the irritation of farmers on a tight schedule when they found that they had been sent untrained labour. Dorothea Abbott describes one farmer's frustration at discovering that out of four land girls he has been sent not one knows how to thresh.

> I was told to start unricking, another job which wasn't as easy as it looked. Half the time I found myself trying to pull up the

sheaf I was standing on . . . Suddenly the farmer's son was at my side, suggesting we should switch jobs. 'I'll do that and you try passing them on to Josie.' This sounded better, but as I'd never handled a pitchfork before, the sheaves landed at my feet quicker than I could pass them on. I could see Josie was having a struggle to swing them up to the bond cutter on the top of the drum.

I'm pitching my bloody guts out . . . and the farmer keeps giving me black looks because the corn's not coming through fast enough.

Aware of the problems presented by chaff dust Kent War Ag. distributed 'glamour bands' to its threshing gangs. The *Land Girl* eagerly took up the idea and published a pattern. 'To make these "Glamour Bands" you take two strips of material 30 ins long by 8 ins wide. Lay one strip on top of the other, then round off one side so that one edge of these strips is absolutely straight and the other edge is curved towards the end. Next join the strips across the ends and down the curved edge for 6 ins. The effect will then be of a child's bonnet, ending in long side pieces. This is worn with the bonnet part over the head and the loose ends are crossed, tied round the head and knotted in front.'

Girls who worked on threshing machines swopped advice on the best sort of protective clothing. A girl working in Shropshire thought no precaution too great. 'I wear dungarees with the overall coat on top, buttoned round the neck, if the top button is missing a silk handkerchief or scarf tied round the neck, an old beret on my head or scarf and anti gas goggles.'

As the land girls' skills increased, so did the confidence they displayed in taking on the men on their own ground. They began to enter ploughing competitions. A Scottish land girl won two first and four second prizes in two ploughing matches in which she was the only woman competitor. In time many tackled tasks in public that they had never attempted before, like the girl who decided to have a bash at shearing at an agricultural show.

There were crowds round the pen waiting to see me start, so my face was feeling like an overgrown beetroot as I entered and laid down my shears. Three Lincolnshire Long Wool sheep looked as big as horses but I made a grab at one and managed to down it, me falling on top. He gave me a fine smack under the jaw, leaving a lovely green patch and a tidy smell. Some of the crowd laughed – others were sympathetic but I was too busy to notice.

When I had done the first sheep the sweat was rolling down my face but the praise of the crowd gave me more pluck to tackle the next and I was able to get on better when I could keep my mind off the crowd and on my work. I think I have tried nearly every job on a farm – hedging, stacking, thatching, plashing, tractoring and I have never been beaten by one. I do think if you try a job and are interested in your work you will win . . .

And not content with tackling any paid job that they were put to land girls, so fearful of the farmyard at the start, began to acquire a reputation for heroism beyond the call of duty, reacting to emergencies in the same way as would a seasoned farmhand. They were not intimidated either by rogue bulls or fire. A girl in Essex saved her employer's life when he was attacked by a bull. The *Land Girl* reported: 'There was no one else present and she drove the bull off with a pitchfork, shut it in another yard and then helped her employer into the house.'

Not long afterwards they were congratulating Mary Simmons in West Sussex who drove off a bull which had attacked the cowman and got him down. 'She got the bull into his pen and then managed to carry in the cowman who had two ribs broken. He would almost certainly have lost his life but for this volunteer's courage and presence of mind.' L. Thomas from Lancashire was also commended for saving a fellow worker who had been knocked down and seriously injured by the bull to which he was attending. 'Miss Thomas beat the animal off with a hay fork.'

It was always said of old farmhands that they would put their animals before themselves. If this is the case, Joan Collinson proved she had won her spurs the night she woke up and saw a flickering glow coming from the farmyard where she worked near Doncaster. 'I looked out of the window and saw all the buildings where the animals were going up. I stuck my feet in my wellies, banged on the boss's door and rushed out to rescue the animals. It was the calves in particular I was worried about. I didn't stop to think what to do, I just dived in. There were sparks everywhere and the upper floors were falling in . . . When the Fire Chief asked who led the animals out the farmer said, "the little lassie here." '

Betty Gingill

(née *Attwood*). Joined Land Army at 17.
Land Army 1942–5.
Home town: Hayes, Middlesex.
Civilian occupation: student librarian.

I wanted to go into one of the Services but my father, who was a chemist, forbade it. He had fought in the First World War. He said, 'No daughter of mine is going to be an officer's groundsheet.' I told him I didn't know what he meant and he said, 'That's another reason for your not going in.' I sneaked off to London, walked into the Land Army recruitment office in Oxford Street and joined. When I told my parents they thought it was the biggest joke they'd ever heard. I was a dainty little thing. My father gave me a fortnight at the most. Then I heard that there was a shortage of girls in the Timber Corps and was asked if I would mind transferring.

My first billet was a private house in Wroughton, a village just outside Swindon in Wiltshire. It was a far cry from the kind of life I was used to. There was a double bed which I was to share with another girl, with metal strips instead of springs. The bedding consisted of two torn sheets, two two-inch thick flocked mattresses, two threadbare blankets and two thin quilts. It was December and despite putting both greatcoats and the rugs from the floor on the bed we both woke at 4 a.m. frozen to the marrow. We huddled on the edge of the bed waiting for the breakfast call. When it came it was one slice of bread and marge and a cup of very stewed tea. Our landlady's husband went out very early and she warmed up what he had left. We lived there from December to March and in all that time, despite the fact that we were stacking timber all day, we never had one cooked meal. It was always toast or bread and cheese. We were constantly hungry. It was scandalous as the landlady was getting paid. But instead of buying food she would got to the pub every night. Once she and her husband went away and left us to fend for ourselves completely. That was the only time we did get a hot dinner. A neighbour took pity and cooked us a meal. The problem in the Timber Corps was that we didn't have the same county-based welfare network as the land girls did. Our welfare officer was based in Bristol at head office. We complained about our billets, but the wheels turned slowly and it was March before we were moved.

It was in Wroughton that I had my first experience of the colour bar. I knew that whites looked down on blacks in America from *Gone with the Wind*. One day in the street I was stopped by a black US serviceman – there was an American hospital not far from the village. He asked me directions to a place I didn't know. 'I'm sorry,' I told him. 'I can't help you.' He must have thought I meant that I wouldn't help him – because of his colour – because he said, 'I'm awfully sorry I stopped you in the street. Will I have made trouble for you?' The thought that I hurt someone that much still troubles me.

I worked alongside Italian prisoners throughout the war and found them charming. At the first place they knew we were hungry and used to give us bits of dried fruit from the rations. At the next place, which was near Cowey, I worked in the sawmill. Fortunately I never had to push the timber through the saw. I took it away after it had been sawn. We all developed a healthy respect for those saws. One day an Italian who had been working the saw switched the works off, walked over to the office, propped himself up against the wall and asked the staff to call an ambulance. The girls in the office realised there had been an accident but there was no panic. The man was incredibly brave; he just held his hand under his other arm. He had taken a couple of fingers off with the saw.

My last billet was in a wonderful house in Clanville, near

Andover. It was owned by a concert pianist whose husband was overseas. It was a motley household consisting of two elderly women who had been her and her husband's nannies when they were children, two conscientious objectors, three or four other Timber Corps girls and a mystery German, who was not a prisoner and whose family were rumoured to be friends of Montgomery's. We all cooked our own food there. The Italians used to make pasta using dried egg. They taught me and I still make it now. My brother was fourteen years younger than me and I used to have him to stay during his school holidays. These Italians had left young families at home and they used to love to talk to my brother, eventually they got their wives to send them some of their children's school books so that they could see how they were progressing. I wasn't interested in the politics of war – at seventeen it was all way above my head – but I remember that while my brother's reading books used sentences like – 'the cat sat on the mat' the Italian ones had: 'This is the house where Mussolini lives.' 'When we see Mussolini we salute.'

13 : The Timber Corps

'Let it never be forgotten that members of the WLA Timber Corps won the war! We felled the trees and cut pit props so that the miners could cut coal to enable munitions to be made for the Army to fire. If it hadn't been for us – well, it doesn't bear thinking about.'

Win Arnold, an eighteen-year-old wages clerk when she joined the Timber Corps in 1943, may be overstating her case – but not by much. Many people today have probably never heard of the Timber Corps, since they associate the Land Army with sheaves of corn and fluffy lambs. But during the war female foresters, who thought nothing of wielding six-pound axes and driving monster caterpillar tractors, were providing the timber, not just for pit props, but for telegraph poles, road blocks, ships' masts, ladders, railway sleepers, gunmats, mobile tracking to support tanks, newsprint, tent pegs and even crosses for soldiers' graves. After the war a small number of Timber Corps members were regarded as sufficiently experienced to be sent to Germany to try to salvage equipment from abandoned sawmills.

Before the advent of the combine harvester the corn was stored
in ricks until dry and then threshed by an elaborate machine
which separated the grain from the straw. Threshing was a filthy job,
and there was a rigid pecking order in which
men bagged the best tasks.

Clearing the broken bits of straw, or cavings, from the bottom
of the machine was the dustiest and most hated part of the
threshing operation and invariably went to the newly recruited land girl.

Many girls had been terrified of cows before joining up.
Yet scores came to find caring for livestock
the most satisfying aspect of their new lives.

In the days before refrigeration, getting the milk off the farm
and into people's homes was an urgent task. Girls had to learn
to master their mode of transport, whether pony and trap,
lorry or motorbike, with minimal tuition.

At a time when food was scarce the rat was declared to be
a public enemy second only to Hitler. Despite the disgusting nature
of the job, land girls took to rat catching as a patriotic duty.

These land girls look delightful, dungarees rolled up
to make the most of the sun. But hoeing remained a hated,
back-breaking task – as was turnip thinning (below).

Forestry enjoyed a more glamorous image
than farming. But the work required
considerable stamina and expertise.

With imported cane sugar threatened by U-Boat raids in the Atlantic,
the campaign to persuade British farmers to grow sugar beet took off
in earnest. Here land girls from London stack sugar beet
ready for the lorries that will take the crop to the factory in Lincolnshire.

The day's work done, the best moment is when
the boots come off. With rubber a disappearing commodity
after the fall of Malaya, Land Army gumboots
were regularly condemned for their leakiness.

Conditions in
WLA hostels were
frequently basic,
rather in the
spirit of a girls'
boarding school.

At the outbreak of war Britain's forestry industry was only slightly less run-down than farming and was characterised by a similar state of dependency. The majority of timber used for telegraph and pit props was imported. The desperate nature of the situation and the girls' willingness, however, had the same galvanising effect on timber production as it had on farming. Within a year of its inception the Timber Corps was responsible for twenty-six sawmills in the New Forest alone and girls were confidently handling all the tools of the seasoned forester – axes, cross-cut saws, bushmen, chainsaws, spokeshaves for bark stripping, sledgehammers, canthooks, billhooks, wedges and grinding stones.

The conviction that a German invasion was imminent – and the discovery that there would be very few road blocks available to stall the invaders – led in October 1940 to a recruitment campaign within the Land Army for home-grown pole selectors. Volunteers were interviewed by their District Officer and, if found suitable, were sent for four weeks' training to one of England's great forests – the Forest of Dean, the New Forest, the Savernake Forest . . . Often the girls were shown the ropes by veteran pole experts from the GPO. Although pole selecting was not heavy, the work required considerable stamina. There were few cars available and girls, who worked in pairs, were expected to walk everywhere. One girl's District Officer, clearly unaware of the difficulties these girls faced endlessly having to find new billets, quixotically suggested horseback riding as a solution – 'But the thought of asking for lodgings and rations for horses as well as for ourselves was a bit too much.' Countrydwellers in the Forties didn't travel great distances. Buses often operated only once a week on market day and in some isolated parts only on Fair Days, which were once a month. Sometimes girls moved as often as three times a week. This created problems with laundry, boot repairs and keeping up with mail which was often received weeks late.

Orienteering, a skill many women struggle with at the best

of times, was made still more difficult because, in anticipation of the German invasion, all signposts had been taken down and getting lost was a daily hazard. One girl observed ruefully, 'I didn't know the New Forest was so big till we started to walk through it. Twice we got lost and my friends from home sent me a compass.' Journeys were made more arduous by the fact that, because pole markers were itinerant, they had to carry their belongings with them. One pair of girls, thrilled at finally being allowed to start out as fully fledged pole markers, decided travelling light was the best plan and sent most of their belongings home in parcels, keeping only changes of under-clothes and uniform. 'But after three weeks, in which it rained every day, and the difficulty of getting things dried, we had to have some things sent back to us.'

They walked phenomenal distances and became exception-ally fit. One team spent some time in the New Forest, lodging in eight different billets and walking an estimated 600 miles. '. . . We are walking all the time we are working and when you get into, say, 50-acre woods and have to explore from one end to the other, going up and down the lines of trees, one can soon cover a few miles.'

These pole markers were expected to be totally self-regulat-ing and many grew to love the challenge of their free, nomadic existence, relishing, in the heart of these ancient forests, the timeless loveliness of a wild, secret landscape known to few. One girl, who worked in the isolated countryside of north Wales, explains how they worked: 'We had all our instructions by post, just a plan of the wood and the nearest station being given . . . These places might be anywhere up to 12 or 15 miles from the station . . . The houses were miles apart, and Mrs Jones would tell you to try Mrs Hughes just over the mountain. And when you got to Mrs Hughes she did not take hikers . . . We got ourselves an *AA Handbook* which gave us the market days, and if we could we tried to move on those days.' One mammoth journey involved travelling from Bala to Lake Vyrnwy, which as the crow flies is only about 12 miles, but without a car involved a huge detour. 'To do this we took a taxi for 7 miles, went about 50 miles by train, and then had to get down to the lake, which was 3½ miles from our lodgings. There was a gang of Ministry of Supply men working there, so we got a lift to work, but still had about 4 miles each way to walk round the lake to get to the bit we wanted.'

As the war progressed the national need for home-produced timber became too urgent to leave in the hands of a thousand untrained land girls. In March 1942 the first training camp of what would become known as the Timber Corps was set up in Suffolk, under the auspices of the Home Timber Production Department of the Ministry of Supply. A month later the Women's Timber Corps came into being as a special section of the Women's Land Army. Though Lady Denman was also Honorary Director of the Timber Corps the administration, welfare and discipline of members was delegated to the Home Timber Production Department of the Ministry of Supply. The nucleus of the new Corps was formed by the one thousand land girls who were already working in forestry, either for the Department or for the timber trade. Though at this point the girls were asked whether they wanted to stay in forestry or move into farming, the vast majority opted to join the new corps, while some land girls, like Doreen Lingard, left jobs in farming to join the new corps. 'I was on a threshing gang and I couldn't stand the dirt. When the Timber Corps was set up I requested a transfer.'

The uniform of what quickly became known as the Lumber Jills, or teasingly 'pole cats', was similar to that of the Land Army except that the slouch hat was replaced by a green beret (regarded as far smarter) and the badge, instead of a wheatsheaf, featured a fir tree surmounted by a Royal crown. The Timber Corps which combined the appeal of the open-air life with more regular hours than general farming, proved a popular choice. Training centres were set up and before long girls were joining the Timber Corps at the rate of 250 a month. By the end of the first year the strength of the Corps had risen to 3,900 in England and Wales and 1,000 in Scotland. It would probably have risen even higher but in July 1943 further recruitment was stopped, as it was to the Land Army, to force women into other less popular types of war work. From the start the Timber Corps acquired an up-market image which the Land Army would never achieve and which land girls resented. One middle-class girl, volunteering for the Land Army, was told by her recruiting officer, 'You're much too well educated to be a land girl. Why don't you join the Timber Corps instead?' What they see as totally unwarranted snootiness on the part of the sister force rankles with many old land girls to this day. 'They always thought they were the élite,' said one girl. 'I wouldn't like to have done some of the jobs they did – like working in the sawmills. But they weren't expected to master the sheer variety of skills that a land girl in general farming had to take on.'

Training varied according to what the girls would be doing once they started work. The chief task of the Timber Corps girls who worked in Scotland whose vertiginous, pine-clad hills proved a valuable source of much-needed softwood, was felling trees for pit props. Their training, therefore, concentrated on general forestry, though the girls could, if they wanted, learn sawmill work and haulage using tractors and horses. In England and Wales, where the demand was more varied, specialisation began during training. Because of the dense nature of Scottish forests and the consequent scarcity of lodgings most Scottish Timber Corps girls lived in hutted camps in the heart of the woods. Girls working in England, on the other hand, normally lived in private billets. Large country houses were taken over for training where for a month the theory and practice of forestry were taught – felling, cross-cutting, 'snedding' or lopping off the side branches, drawing the trunks out with horses and tractors, working sawmills, loading and stacking pit props. After one week of general instruction girls were allocated to whatever branch of timber production they had chosen.

Attempts were made to look after the welfare of Timber Corps girls, in the same way as the rep looked after the land girl. The central office of the Ministry of Supply in Bristol employed women officers specially trained in dealing with welfare problems, but despite this, many English Timber Corps girls seem to have had a raw deal on lodgings and a shamefully inadequate diet. Betty Gingill, who joined the Timber Corps as a seventeen-year-old and worked in Wiltshire was not served one hot meal from December to March. 'There were three of us. We used to say, "bread and pepper today for dinner." Once one of the girls was so hungry she ate writing paper. The Italian prisoners of war saw how hungry we were and used to give us the few bits of dried fruit that was doled out to them as part of their lunch. We had inadequate bedding at night. The mattress was two inches thick, you could read a newspaper through the blanket. We used to put the bedside rugs over us to try to keep warm.'

Monica Robinson encountered the same gradgrind mentality among her landladies. 'In one billet we returned to bread and dripping for the main meal – having lifted heavy timber all day; at another scrambled egg, made from reconstituted egg powder . . . At night we froze. Two cotton eiderdowns covered the bed: one fat and one thin. We dressed fully to get into bed, carefully placing an overcoat and a threadbare rug from the floor on top of the eiderdowns.'

Strength and suppleness were vital to combat stiffness and aching muscles that wielding unfamiliar heavy tools brought with it and the day at training camps began outside at 6 a.m. with exercises designed to strengthen the muscles used in axe swinging.

The Timber Corps girls were obviously admired by the public. A Scottish newspaper, describing a parade celebrating the first birthday of the Timber Corps, reported:

Crowds of people thronged the streets of Inverness on Saturday afternoon and witnessed a parade of timber girls who are engaged in tree-felling operations in the Highland area . . . Wearing their attractive uniform, consisting of khaki breeches, green pullovers, and jaunty green berets, the girls paraded on Bank Street, where the spectators had an opportunity of admiring the precision with which they carried out drill movements preparatory to marching away. They were led away by the pipers and drummers of the Highland Squadron of the Air Training Corps . . . and the selection of pipe tune 'Highland Laddie' was not inappropriate considering that although not Highland 'laddies' the timber girls are doing men's work.

Timber Corps work offered a considerable variety of tasks. Some girls worked in the forest itself, measuring, felling, snedding and hauling the timber, turning the unwanted branches into huge cheering bonfires. Others worked in the sawmills, a job, like threshing, notorious for its accidents. Vita Sackville-West particularly admired the girls who worked in the mills: 'This is a terrifying task, as anyone who has watched the great toothed circular saws whirring with murderous speed will agree. It is a task which requires extreme care, precision and concentration, for the saw which will travel with prolonged and undeviating ruthlessness up the solid trunk of wood will slice in one second through the soft finger, the pulsating wrist . . . Men have been known to shake their heads and say no, it didn't take their fancy; but the girls of the Timber Corps have done it.'

In fact the only deaths that occurred in the Timber Corps were due more to an act of God than to deadly machinery. In July 1944 two Timber Corps girls in Dumfriesshire were killed when the timber wagon they were travelling in, pulled by a tractor, overturned and crushed them.

A palpable rivalry existed between the Land Army and the Timber Corps, with each accusing the other of lack of expertise. A pole selector wrote waspishly in the *Land Girl*: 'Pole selecting is one of the jobs the Land Army seem to know nothing about, judging from the interest my partner and I have excited on the rare occasions of our meeting them but our bicycles, equipped with paintpot, calipers, bill-hooks, knap-sacks etc. are now well known in many districts where we have at first been regarded as an advance party of invasion.'

Many girls opted to become timber measurers. One Timber Corps girl commented drily: 'We have never managed to rid the Land Army of the conviction that we actually climb trees to find out their height.' An article in *Woman* written by a Timber Corps girl described what was involved in measuring:

> Measuring involves the holding of a long tape along the length of the tree and the encircling of the centre girth with another tape. In muddy weather whichever of us does the girthing is the unluckiest. If you ever try walking round a log which is coated with mud you will know what I mean; but if you go one step further and try to place a tape round its middle, I advise you to wear your oldest clothes. My 'other half' shares my daily life and between us we cope with the office management of the mill and are responsible for the entire measuring of the incoming and outgoing timber. We share a small wooden hut in which we struggle with division, subtraction and addition, brew weak tea and eat queer sandwiches.

Ruth Symonds was an eighteen-year-old secretary with the London department store Derry and Toms when she joined the Timber Corps in January 1943. Within a few months she was making fencing which was used as a mobile 'track' to support the tanks as they rumbled across the soft sand of the Normandy beaches in the D-Day landings. 'I had wanted to join the Land Army the year before, but they said I would probably have to wait till April 1943 to get a post as I was a London girl and had only worked in an office. I was advised to "toughen up" by walking out in all weathers. A friend who also wanted to join suggested we go rowing on the Serpentine – in rain and cold weather – and this we did, to the amusement of the boatmen.' Within a week Ruth was on her way for training in Abbey Woods in Kent.

The hardest part was getting used to the hard army boots – and learning to use the different tools. I didn't do any felling – I found it too heavy. This was done either by the foreman or by English or Canadian troops stationed nearby. Once the timber was down our first job was to cut off all the branches with a billhook. The next step was to burn the branches. After that we had to measure the trunks very accurately, and saw them into correct lengths for pit props and Army telegraph poles. For this we used a cross saw which was operated by two girls. Lastly we removed the bark with a stripper. This was a tool with two wooden handles joined by a curved blade. Wood that was going to be used for fencing we split with a cleaving axe. Someone else used to wire the stakes together. Then they would be rolled up and put on Army tanks ready for use on the beaches.

After the pitprops and telegraph poles were stacked the girls loaded them on to lorries. 'We went with the lorries to the station and loaded the timber on to goods wagons, noting down how much timber we had loaded on to each train.'

However thorough the training, it could never provide all the answers to the problems of felling and removing timber from hostile terrain. Doreen Lingard, a Londoner who sewed brass buttons on Service greatcoats before her call-up at seventeen and a half, says:

We spent a lot of our time felling birch in Lifton, just outside Exeter. You didn't really have to be that strong for felling. It was a knack, like sawing. We had four-and-a-half-pound and six-pound axes. We preferred the six-pound ones. You got on faster with them. The hillside at Lifton was so steep you had to kneel on one knee to get the trees down. And we weren't allowed to leave a stump of more than four inches. There was a railway at the bottom of the hill. Before we started we had to build a wooden support to keep the timber from getting on to the line. As we felled the trees we would roll them down the hill so that they were stacked up against the support. Every Sunday we had a special train. There were about twenty of us. We had to load the whole lot into the goods wagons and take it along the line towards Bridestowe. We were supposed to ride on the wagons, four on each corner, but we used to invade the engine cabin and blow the whistle all the way to Bridestowe. The locals complained about the noise we made but we didn't care. We used to blow it the next week just the same.

Before the Timber Corps started work in a new softwood forest the professionals would come in and select any particularly straight timber for their own priority war needs. Doreen: 'The Post Office would select what they wanted for telegraph posts, the Navy would pick the timber they needed for ships' masts and the US army personnel would pick what they wanted for radio signal masts. They would all be marked up with different coloured crosses. Then we would fell them and draw them out using horses.'

A forest near Clovelly, where they were cutting pit props was a mile and a half from any road and turned out to be an opportunity for fifty-odd Timber Corps girls to build a miniature version of the Burma–Siam railway as featured in *The Bridge on the River Kwai*. Doreen: 'We cut sleepers on the portable saw bench in the forest. Sledgehammers, rails and dogs for fastening the rails on to the sleepers were delivered and we built our own railway. Because the three fields we had to cross were not a level slope and one was marshy we had to build the railway up in some parts with a parapet of pit props. Some of us used to have to stand at the bottom of the first slope, catch the carriages and push them up to the top of the next slope. We even built the bogeys that carried the timber – only the wheels were supplied. We had between four and six bogeys and we used to pile them up quite high with nine-foot timber. Some days there was so much timber the bogeys would be running all day.'

Monica Robinson was selling silk in Debenham and Freebody when she was called up. She spent a year in the great Savernake Forest, near Marlborough in Wiltshire, measuring and felling trees and driving trucks and giant caterpillar tractors among Italian, German and Austrian prisoners of war, Norwegian whalers who had fled their German-occupied homeland and English conscientious objectors.

At the beginning the physical shock was daunting; lifting heavy hardwoods and balancing the long sawn lengths, hoisting them higher and higher, building up tall timber stacks . . . Early each morning two of us, billeted together in Marlborough, cycled out of the town, away up the hill through the morning mists to the sawmill set close to the Grand Avenue, a broad road running through the heart of the forest. Beneath corrugated-iron shelters and scattered over a wide area, large US Army munition dumps were concealed, guarded by soldiers standing like statues against the silvery trunks of the beeches lining the Avenue on every side; perfectly camouflaged in their grey-green uniforms, they delighted in leaping out from behind the trees to startle and challenge us.

The mill was the hub of all activities and from there we rode out on trucks to clear softwoods in outlying areas, at other times remaining in the mill to measure and stack timber. Expertise with axe, cross-cut saw and billhook grew gradually as we felled, trimmed branches and cut measured lengths into pitprops . . . Unwanted brushwood, piled high in the clearing, was set alight crackling and spitting as flames and sparks shot into the air. The pit props had to be stacked in cords, then lifted onto trucks and driven to a nearby station where they were off-loaded into rail wagons to be transported to coal mines around the country . . . We moved on across counties to other forests gaining a variety of skills: measuring standing timber, driving a truck and sitting up aloft on an Allis Chalmers caterpillar tractor winching out huge trunks. Often journeying in open trucks from home to work we grew accustomed to a soaking in winter time with squelching boots and damp clinging overalls seldom fully drying out.

The compensation for all this discomfort and back-breaking effort was discovering the secret heart of the forest, 'observing the birds and animals living among the branches and under-growth, occasionally coming across other forest dwellers: charcoal burners quietly camped beside their kilns, or solitary poachers. We learned the different tree species: hard and softwoods, deciduous and evergreen, foliage patterns: solid oak, beech and chestnut, graceful firs and pines and the slim feathery larch hung with bright crimson flowers in spring . . .'

Timber Corps girls in England usually lived in billets in

nearby towns, cycling to and from their workplace. A few, like Monica Robinson, went completely native, acquiring their own log cabin and living in the forest in splendid isolation.

The cabin was clad externally with softwood offcuts – just like an American cabin in the wild west we thought – and although spartan inside with bare floors and very little furniture, we were proud occupiers . . . In the tiny kitchen cooking over a wood burning stove meant we needed to keep a store of dry chopped wood ready so supper could be started as soon as we returned home from the woods each evening. We sat by the light of a hissing Tilley lamp with our companion – a wild ginger cat who had wandered in from the forest whom we had nicknamed Popeye – plus our only contact with the outside world – a radio empowered by an accumulator. Outside the kitchen door, close to the rainwater butt and chopping block, a large tank held the drinking water supply. Toilet arrangements, always somewhat hazardous when living a life in the open air and in rural accommodation, consisted of a small wooden hut set some yards from the cabin containing a bucket and a makeshift seat. We emptied the bucket every Sunday, carrying it to a distant deep pit. On Saturdays the water tank was replenished. One hot summer's day the high frame of the delivery truck caught on the clothes line stretched between the cabin and toilet – the driver gleefully racing away as we shovelled up the week's mess spilt in and around the fallen hut.

14 : Backs to the Land

The image of the land girl as a sunburnt temptress, ever-eager, despite long hours and a punitive workload, for a tumble in the hay with a farmhand, is a persistent one. The innocent slogan 'Back to the Land' used by the Ministry of Agriculture to tempt girls to enlist, soon became corrupted to a nudging 'backs to the land'. But was this sexy reputation really deserved?

Joan Pountney, who worked as a land girl in Leicestershire, believes it was profoundly unfair. In her opinion the land girl's free and easy reputation, far from making her more sought-after, actually inhibited her social life. 'I lived in a hostel and we used to find it difficult to get the locals to come to our dances. There were plenty of village boys, but the villagers didn't like their sons associating with land girls and there was a lot of resentment from the farmers' wives. They thought you were going to run off with their husbands, though you wouldn't have had some of them as a gift.'

The most blatant prejudice Joan and her friends encountered came from a clergyman. She and five friends from the hostel decided to attend chapel one Sunday morning – the village chapel was right opposite the Land Army hostel. 'We were in uniform and we sat down at the back. Suddenly the minister, who was a real old Bible basher, started thundering about 'heathens living across the road, who hold dances on Friday nights and spend their time fornicating with local boys'. We were incensed. We got up and walked out.'

What was at the root of this prejudice? Was there any justification for it? The urgency and unprecedented freedom of wartime did lead couples who didn't know whether they would meet again to leapfrog conventional courtship rituals. Did the discovery by these young women, so many of whom were city-bred, of the immutable rhythms of nature and the changing seasons, their observation of the unselfconscious sexuality of animals cause them to shed their inhibitions in a way they might not have done in other circumstances? Did land girls behave with less discretion than women in the Armed Services – the WRNS, or the ATS? Did their reputation of availability have something to do with the uniform, which by its very masculinity, drew attention to the curves of the women's bodies? Women in the armed services wore skirts and, with the exception of the WRNS, whose uniform was universally admired, rather unflattering skirts at that. In the Forties it was not thought decent for a woman to wear trousers – even horsewomen usually rode side-saddle – and the outline of a woman's bottom was probably both arousing and rather shocking. One can't help thinking that all the innuendo about land girls' morals contained more than a dash of wishful thinking spiced with a dollop of malice. For, despite their willingness to learn new skills and the unquestioned success of their contribution, land girls encountered a great deal of personal resentment. It came, in part, from the farmers' wives. In the Armed Services men and women mingled unsupervised by their spouses. On the farms land girls worked alongside farmers and their sons and many middle-aged farmers' wives clearly felt threatened by the intrusion of these enthusiastic and, as photographs testify, often exceedingly good-looking young pupils on the threshold of womanhood. Some of the resentment, though, came from the men. In some cases this has to be put down to irrational prejudice – that women had no business doing men's work and could never do it as well. In others, however, it may have had some justification. For in some instances land girls, whose pay was regulated, were paid more than the men they were sent to assist. Joan Chapman who worked as a market gardener in Kent, was sent for by her employer to be told that she would henceforth be paying income tax. 'He told me it didn't apply to the head gardener, who was my direct boss, as he wasn't earning enough. This was a married man with forty years' experience who lived in a tied cottage lit by paraffin lamps. He was always unhelpful. Now I understood why.'

The main reason for treating the land girls' reputation for being free and easy with scepticism is that Britain in the Forties was an extremely formal society, with a degree of consensus about social conventions – among others that sex before marriage was wrong – that is unimaginable today. The land girls may have strode around in unladylike breeches and enjoyed a flirtatious, bantering relationship with the odd farmhand, but the Pill and the Abortion Act were still twenty-five years off and most romantic encounters stopped short at what used to be called heavy petting. As one land girl put it: 'My friends and I used to go out at night in uniform. We reckoned that by the time the lads had undone your belt and pulled your jumper out of your trousers they'd be nackered.'

In wartime Britain it was normal for women without a male escort to be refused service in pubs – many land girls, thirsty after a long cycle ride, found themselves led into secluded back-rooms by disapproving landlords. Women unfortunate enough to bear children out of wedlock would expect to be ostracised by the community if they kept the child, while growing up with the stigma of illegitimacy was deemed an appalling fate to inflict on a child. Most people did not even use Christian names until well acquainted, still less have full-blown love affairs with casual partners. The other factor we have to consider is that, however come-hither they may look to us in their breeches and dungarees, these girls in their late teens and early twenties were less well informed on sexual matters than the average eleven-year-old today. Far from being, as painted by some farmers' wives, shameless seduc-tresses who presented a moral danger to others, they seem rather to have been at risk from predatory men through their naïvety. Joan Chapman shared a flat with Vita Sackville-West's land girl at Sissinghurst Castle in Kent. When I asked her if she had been aware that Vita was a lesbian she hooted with laughter. 'I didn't even know what a lesbian was.'

The consensus that sexual licence was a bad thing meant that those whose job was to look after the land girls took their task extremely seriously. At one stage headquarters became so concerned at reports of soldiers pestering land girls that letters went out to Regional Officers suggesting they give talks on sex to girls living in hostels in their areas. The advice limited itself to the imperative of not mixing one's drinks and saying 'No'.

One Land Army official remembers a County Organiser inspecting a large house with a view to turning it into a hostel for land girls. 'She peered into the distance and asked the Ministry of Works man who was accompanying her, "What are those huts in the far distance?" "Polish troops," replied the man. "Poles," she exclaimed, "And all that bracken . . . oh no!" '

Nothing was too much trouble for these zealous moral guardians in their desire to see virtue protected. A district rep, hearing that the elderly mother of a bachelor farmer had died, leaving the land girl without a chaperone, paid him a visit, aiming to raise the delicate matter of the proprieties. In the end the farmer pre-empted her by informing her drily: 'We sleep under the same roof but not under the same ceiling.'

On occasion, however, the women who ran the hostels turned out to be as unworldly as many of their charges and proved singularly ill-equipped to deal with the boisterous sexual teasing of servicemen.

A flustered approach was made to the County Secretary of North Riding by the warden of a hostel near Doncaster. Dorothy Brant, who was in charge of the northern division of the Land Army, says: 'She was elderly, had evidently led a rather sheltered life and ran her hostel along strict YWCA lines. She was all of a twitter over her girls and some story of French letters. She had got up one morning, found all the shrubs round the hostel bedecked with condoms and was in a great panic about her girls. The County Secretary called on her and noticed scores of huts in the middle distance. "What's that?" she inquired. "A camp," replied the warden innocently. It turned out that they had 4,000 men based less than a mile away, who took delight in alarming her and teasing the girls by offering them this unusual tribute.'

Often the girls' naïvety placed them in greater danger than their reputed sophistication might have. Joan Chapman found herself billeted on what turned out to be the local prostitute in the Kent village of Biddenden. 'I didn't realise at first, though there did seem a succession of male visitors at night. One day my landlady was away hop-picking with her parents when a soldier knocked on the door. He was not going to be discouraged and kept his foot in the door. I was absolutely terrified and complained to Vita Sackville-West, who was my rep. She found me other digs. I discovered afterwards that once a month my landlady dressed from head to toe in black with a black ribbon in her hair. That was her signal to customers that she was unavailable.'

Inevitably there were a small number of girls who did become pregnant, though whether there were more mishaps in the Land Army than in the women's Armed Services is doubtful. The popular perception – many former land girls will affirm this – is that usually an American was to blame. Girls living near service bases were more likely to get into trouble than girls living in farm billets. Dorothy Brant remembers the

Americans, as she put it 'causing trouble in the south'. Most of the time the hostel wardens acted like dragons to protect their flock. One warden who ran a hostel near an American airbase in Lincoln received a request for the girls to visit their base. 'I declined, suggesting instead that they come to the hostel. They arrived in a truck loaded with drink. I said they could come in but that the drink was staying in the truck.'

Joan Pountney remembers 'one or two' girls getting pregnant while she lived in a hostel near Melton Mowbray, where there were a number of service bases, including bases for American and Belgian servicemen. A land girl in Kent gave birth to twins, according to Joan Chapman. 'The opinion at the time was that they were an American's leavings. The thing about the Americans was that they had money and they used to get girls who weren't used to drinking, drunk. As far as this girl was concerned the popular opinion was that she had been silly – but she didn't deserve twins!'

The policy of the Land Army towards pregnancy was pragmatic rather than censorious, an attitude dictated by the manpower shortage. Pregnant girls were sent to special hostels to have the baby, granted temporary leave and then expected to resume their service after giving the baby up for adoption. Joan Pountney remembers one girl being allowed to stay on working in the hostel she lived in until her baby was born. Penelope Greenwood visited a couple of girls who had got pregnant with her mother, Judith Burrell, Lady Denman's daughter. 'Their main concern always seemed to be: "don't tell Mum." And I don't think we did.'

The scandal that awaited a girl who had a baby out of wedlock sometimes led girls to take desperate measures. Dorothy Brant received a call from the County Secretary in Lincoln informing her that a girl in a private billet had become pregnant. 'She had managed to conceal it under her roomy greatcoat and had had the child. Her landlady had become suspicious and had called in the District Nurse. The nurse examined her and she confessed she had taken the baby out and drowned it in the water butt.' In fact, although the girl was discharged from the WLA she met with surprising clemency at the hands of the law. 'The law took a pretty lenient view of infanticide. This was because at that time women were regarded as being mentally unstable for up to two years after giving birth.'

Joan Collinson

Joined Land Army at 20.
Land Army 1942–9.
Home town: Gateshead, Tyneside.
Civilian occupation: Restaurant cashier.

There were thirty of us land girls in the Craiglea Hostel, Darlinton, Co. Durham, plus a warden, cook and assistant. There were rules to abide by – infringement of which brought punishment – discipline was strict. Curfew was 10 p.m. except Wednesdays and Saturdays when we had a pass till 11 p.m., lights out half an hour after curfew when the warden made her rounds making sure everyone was in. We were knocked up at 5.45 a.m. and had to wash, dress, strip beds, folding sheets and the two blankets just so at the foot of the thin straw mattress – the wooden camp-beds weren't very comfortable. Then we'd tidy the room, have breakfast, collect sandwiches and be on our way to work by 7 a.m. Hostel food was adequate but menus never varied. Lumpy porridge with salt, a tiny piece of bacon, half a slice of fried bread, one slice of bread and margarine comprised breakfast. The daily offering of one cheese and one beetroot sandwich had to sustain us all day till the evening meal at 6.30 p.m. Girls working within a 3-mile radius walked or cycled to work, beyond that limit girls went by public transport. After deduction of board and lodging we had the princely sum of nine shillings (approximately £10 at today's rates) in our pockets. We signed for it every Friday in the office. We worked a minimum fifty-hour week, some of us much longer, especially at haymaking and harvest times. We worked seven days a week. Our only break was a weekend every third week from Saturday 12 noon to Monday 7.30 a.m. Our evenings were free unless on punishment duties.

I was assigned with another girl to a farm 6 miles from the hostel, a journey we did by bus. We couldn't be off together – one of us was always on duty with the stockman and when he was off we were both on duty with the farmer. On my duty Sundays I walked the 6 miles to work as there was no bus and I couldn't ride a bike. This meant a very early start as we had to be at the farm no later than 7 a.m.

Back from our labours we had to be washed and changed out of work clothes into dress uniform with beds made by the dinner bell at 6.30 p.m. Not easy with just two bathrooms, and eleven washbasins for thirty girls all with the same deadline to meet. On the bell we filed into the dining-room and stood behind our chairs till grace was said. There were cloths on the tables, which sat eight. One girl from each table waited on the others. The warden and the cook served out the food – meat stew, potatoes and cabbage. Suet pudding was the usual afters – gravy and custard were only distinguishable by colour for both were either lumpy or watery. We took turns at waitressing and there was a roster for dining-room duty – six girls who were responsible for clearing away, washing up the dishes, cleaning the dining-room and pantry floors and resetting the tables for breakfast the next day. Chores completed the warden would inspect our efforts before locking the dining-room. Friends – including boys – were allowed into the lounge, but all visitors had to be off the premises by 9.30 p.m. At that time a plate of bread and dripping and a huge jug of cocoa was taken into the lounge. If you were there you got it, if not you didn't. The tray and contents were removed ten minutes later. We knew what to expect for the evening meal on Saturday – 'cheese dreams' – the leftover cheese sandwiches fried in dripping. With bare wood floors, sparse furnishings, a lockable wooden box under the bed for our private belongings and the obligatory black-out curtains, living conditions were spartan and everywhere icy cold in the winter months. The only comfort was a tiny coal fire in the lounge lit each evening from October to April.

15 : Cool Under Enemy Fire

In many parts of the country agricultural life continued its timeless progress as if Hitler and the Luftwaffe had never existed. But the realities of war were never far away in the south of England. The evacuation of the British Expeditionary Force from Dunkirk in June 1940 brought the phoney war to an abrupt end, while first the German invasion of the Channel Islands and then the installatioan of the heavy cross-Channel gun emplacements at Cap Gris Nez in August 1940 made land girls working in Kent only too conscious of how narrow a stretch of water separated them from the would-be invaders. They watched the first engagements of the Battle of Britain as planes and parachutes dropped all round them. From then to the terrifying doodlebug campaign of 1944 counties in the firing line between London and France were ceaselessly pounded and strafed by bombs, shells, fighter planes and deadly chunks of flying shrapnel from our own anti-aircraft guns. A directive from the Ministry of Agriculture describing the German offensive of the high summer of 1940 reported that 'the principal waves of German bombers crossed the

English coast between Dover and Dungeness, and at least two hundred German planes flew across Kent in a single afternoon'.

While the struggle was at its height five hundred land girls working in east Kent were cut off for two days from all communications with Land Army HQ. Inez Jenkins described their phlegmatic reaction when contact was once again restored, with amused admiration: 'When news came through again, the first message to reach us at Headquarters, if somewhat terse, was reassuring. It came from the tractor girls in the Dover area and was to the effect that they could not go on forever stopping work to take shelter. With the engines running, it just wasn't possible to tell when a battle was overhead, so surely to goodness HQ could do something about tin hats. HQ did – and quick.'

With all this action in the air, fears of invasion ran high. One girl remembers all the land girls in her area being summoned to an urgent meeting in the local drill hall to be taught how to fire a rifle, in reality an extraordinary breach of regulations since civilians were not allowed to carry arms. 'We lay on our tummies and did rifle practice and were shown how to fix a bayonet and use it, practising on a hanging stuffed sack.'

The *Kent Land Army News Sheet* urged its members to prepare for the worst. Farmers, farmhands and land girls were ordered to 'go on producing every ounce of food possible . . . some of our Kentish people have worked unperturbed in their fields with shells screaming over their heads. So can we all and we must. Tractors and other motor vehicles must be put out of action. They are in real danger of being captured by the enemy. Rail and road transport may be dislocated, milk, perishable fruit and vegetables should be sold or given away to those nearby when necessary; nothing should be wasted. Keep your stock and yourself off the roads. For every member of the Land Army, there is a simple path to follow – stick to your job and carry on.'

And carry on they did, watching dog fights between Spitfires and Messerschmitts, dodging shells, in constant danger from machine-gunning from German pilots or from exploding stricken planes and occasionally diving for cover in ditches or among the stooks of corn.

Barbara Morris joined the Land Army in March 1940 and worked as a tractor driver on a farm near Dover which, because of the extent of shelling there, became known as Hellfire Corner. For continuing to work in the fields while air battles were going on almost daily she was awarded the county badge for courage. There was, she says matter-of-factly, just too much work to keep stopping to take shelter.

> It was harvest time and I remember hearing a terrific screaming sound as a plane seemed to be coming down on top of me. I just ran and ran to the edge of the wood nearby but the plane fell some distance away. If we were not sure how things were going to develop, we dived into the shocks of corn; otherwise we would look up and say 'it's all right. It's one of ours', or 'they're going over' and we would carry on. With the noise the tractor made it was not always easy to tell if a fight was going on. We did not pay much attention when planes fell some way off, we were too busy. . . . At the height of the battle we saw many planes shot down. One of our pilots baled out when his plane was shot up. As his parachute descended, he was attacked by a German pilot. He landed badly wounded. His plane fell on the roof of a barn on a nearby farm. On one occasion we watched a flight of Hurricanes passing overhead when one of them suddenly peeled off. As it landed the pilot was flung out. We supposed that he had collapsed from wounds. An American bomber came down in some woods near us. We heard the engine cut out and saw the clouds of smoke; nobody could do anything. All the crew were killed.

The tin hats, designed to protect the wearer from flying shrapnel from the AA guns, were not favoured by the girls. Barbara Morris: 'They were too cumbersome and heavy to work in. I remember when I first heard an explosion from a German cross-Channel gun. It made a tremendous crack. Later we found a piece of its casing in one of the fields. It weighed four pounds! After that we took our tin hats with us wherever we were working.'

Other land girls found it more logical to wear their tin hats in a less conventional way. Joan Faulkner was machine-gunned twice by German planes as she worked. 'We had our tin hats with us but decided it would be better to wear them on our bottoms. As we were so often bending down we thought that was the place most likely to be hit.'

There was a temptation, with so much enemy action, to grow blasé about the danger. Joan Faulkner: 'One day we chased what we thought was a German airman baling out, only to find, as we got nearer, that it was a cylindrically shaped land-mine on the end of the parachute. My God did we leg it fast in the opposite direction. We never chased a parachute again.'

A mixture of patriotism and admiration for the fighter pilots, whose bravery they witnessed on an almost daily basis, led a group of land girls working on the south coast to propose the setting up of a Spitfire Fund. The idea, which was born in September 1940 was the brainchild of Miss E. Cross of West Sussex. 'Do you think the Land Army could buy a fighter aeroplane?' she asked in the *Land Girl*. 'Now that so many of us are in jobs, I think we could raise the money or very nearly, and it would be exciting to think that one of the many fighters that roar over our heads while we are at work, might be our very own. After all, it's not much good for us to get corns on our hands and aching backs growing food if a lot of Nazis turn up to eat it!!'

The Spitfire Fund was a huge success. Land girls up and down the country gave money, put on plays, held dances and sales of work and on 8 August 1941 the first cheque for £1000 was handed to the Minister of Aircraft Production by two land girls. Less than a year later the final amount – an impressive £35,691, was presented to Squadron Leader Barrie Heath by land girls selected for their bravery in the face of challenges such as rescuing drowning airmen, entering burning sites, checking angry bulls and staying cool under enemy fire. The money bought the first Typhoon fighter aircraft. With 'Land Girl' boldly painted on its fuselage it first saw active service in January 1943. To the delight of its patronesses it played an active role in the battle against the Luftwaffe, taking part in convoy protection sweeps over occupied territory, attacking enemy shipping and acting as a bomber escort.

People caught up in the sort of enemy action that was played out remorselessly for four years over the south coast showed remarkable compassion for each other, but land girls were aware that for some farmers the animals were the prime concern. One girl working on a dairy farm near Rye remembers her farmer's reaction as a German plane heading for home decided to have one last go at the enemy. 'I was bringing cows from one of the lower pastures below Rye cliffs when an aircraft flew low overhead. I looked up and was astonished to see German markings on it and the outline of a face looking down at me. I was horrified when the sound of machine-gun fire rooted me to the spot. Then I heard my boss's voice shouting. "Get the cows to lie down." I think he would gladly have traded the life of one land girl for one of his shorthorns.'

Land girls in Kent often found themselves working a double day, out in the fields in daytime and on fire-watching duty at night. In the very dry year of 1940 forest fires were a major hazard. It only took one incendiary bomb and a whole new plantation would be set ablaze. One girl who worked in the Home Timber Production Department found putting out the fires rather exciting. 'Often we were out at night, once being called out to a fire miles away, and as quickly as we got one fire under control, the Germans dropped incendiaries in other places. At one fire I remember the ground being so hot with burning embers that we were taking a boot off and holding it up in the air to cool a bit and standing like a stork on one leg.'

The gritty behaviour of land girls who refused to acknowledge danger attracted approving comment from surprising sources. On 3 December 1940 the *Farmers Weekly* commented:

'In Kent over 200 have worked on steadily in constant danger. Six of them have been doing tractor ploughing in a particularly dangerous coastal barrage area. It is not "done" to shelter until the battle is overhead – otherwise one would be forever sheltering. The tractors were so noisy that the drivers could not tell when the battle was overhead. So frequently they found themselves working with shrapnel falling all round them and even on their tractors. Not one of these girls asked for a transfer. Instead they applied for steel helmets – and got them!'

Lady Denman had been pressing for some form of recognition of the bravery of land girls who carried on working undaunted by enemy action. The doughtiness of Kent farmers and their land girls in the face of repeated air attacks and shelling by the Germans in the early part of 1942 backed up by her campaigning finally did the trick and a small number received bravery medals from the King. One farmer, his wife and their seventeen-year-old land girl, Grace Harrison, who drove a tractor, were awarded the prestigious George Medal and British Empire Medals respectively. The three of them, together with one elderly shepherd, had carried on farming 120 acres through the Battle of Britain after all the other farmhands had left. The only casualties, despite the fact that a bomb had fallen in the midst of the cows, were a couple of sheep. The farm and the trio's sang-froid were praised in *The Times* on 23 May 1942:

The farm is at the nearest point to the Continent and is scarred with filled-in shell holes. The farm buildings are probably the most vulnerable in the country, yet work was carried on throughout the Battle of Britain and ever since. During intense air raids the German pilots machine-gunned the farm and work on the land had to be stopped, but in spite of all the difficulties and dangers there was no change in the routine of milking and attending to the stock. When cutting corn Mr Mitchell and Miss Harrison often had to take cover under the tractor or binder when German pilots were machine-gunning. On one occasion, when Mr Mitchell was driving the tractor, a balloon

175

nearby was shot down in flames. The burning fabric fell across the tractor but was quickly extinguished by Mr Mitchell, who then carried on with his work. Mr and Mrs Mitchell, with the help of Miss Harrison, remained at the farm and not only saved their own crops, but also those of other farms which had been evacuated.

Interviewed by the newspapers, the young Miss Harrison's phlegmatic comment was 'But the war is only a side show after all. The real show is the farm.'

As well as the national awards for bravery, Kent's War Agricultural Committee was so impressed with the courage shown by land girls in their county that in July 1941 they decided to award some of them with their own 'fortitude' badges.

By the last year of the war everyone accepted that land girls working in Kent had more than answered the call of duty. On 18 October 1944 the King and Queen made a visit to Dover and Folkestone and twenty land girls who had worked in the shelling area were presented to them. The following month all 4,000 land girls working in Kent were sent a message by the Queen congratulating them on their bravery in continuing their work under enemy fire. The message, addressed to 'Members of the Land Army Working in the County of Kent', and sent out by Lady Denman from Balcombe Place read: 'I am commanded by the Queen to express to you Her Majesty's admiration for the magnificent way in which so many of you played your part under direct fire from the enemy. The Queen wishes me to say that you have rendered an incalculable service to our country throughout the most testing times and that, as patron of the Women's Land Army Her Majesty is more than proud of you.'

It wasn't only Kent land girls who knew there was a war on. The total evacuation of 35 square miles in south Devon in the autumn of 1943 as British and US troops launched a full-scale live ammunition dress rehearsal for the D-Day landings brought the reality of war to the south-west. As popular family beaches like Slapton Sands were transformed into theatres of war (this area was selected because geographically it so resembles Normandy) 3,000 people were evacuated and 200 farms requisitioned, turning some of the richest acres of farming land in the country into desert. But while the animals were all moved to safe areas, the grain, which had not long been harvested, would be needed for bread the following year. Johnnie Luxton, by now a proficient thatcher, was one of three land girls bussed in daily to these extraordinary ghostly acres to thatch corn stacks against the winter rains. She remembers still the unnatural silence that pervaded those fields as the Allies gathered for the final assault.

> We were picked up every morning by lorry from our hostel in Totnes and driven out into the country. We were dropped at a particular gate and directed to the ricks. Other land girls had harvested the corn and built the ricks. It was self-sown corn, which had grown from the grain that dropped from the drying stooks at the previous harvest. It was poor quality but because it was wartime it was needed. There we found the ladders and the reeds and everything we needed. It was double summer time then and so it was still light at eleven o'clock at night. We never saw anybody, except, occasionally, if we were high up on the rick, an American jeep going past, usually with coloured servicemen in it. It was so quiet it was eerie. There were no animals, no farmers, no sound. I don't even remember birds singing. As we walked to the gate at dusk the only thing you'd hear were the crickets.

No sooner had the troops left for the D-Day offensive of 6 June 1944 than the first doodlebugs appeared with their sinister whine which cut out just before they dropped. The first fell on Kent and London on 13 June. State-of-the-art weapon though they were, these flying bombs frequently failed to reach their destination. Of the 8,000 doodles intended for London, in an intensive bombardment which lasted eighty days, five-eighths fell on Kent and Sussex. Kent took 2,400, Sussex slightly fewer. The volume of doodlebugs which rained down in a triangle between Dover and Romney Marsh with London as its apex led to Kent becoming known as 'Bomb alley'. Land girls displayed the same stoicism in the face of this new danger as most showed towards the work they did. Brenda Lister was in bed in her cottage billet with two other land girls when an exploding VI demolished the back of it. Miraculously they were all unhurt and managed to pick their way out through glass and rubble. Another girl who was fruit picking near Rainham in Kent, says with quiet understatement that it was 'quite frightening' to be at the top of a tree on a ladder swaying in the breeze when the doodlebugs were coming over. 'One morning while we were cycling to work one cut out overhead. We leapt off our bikes and into the ditch expecting the explosion. Instead we heard a very strange sound nearer at hand. It turned out to be the cable of a barrage balloon, cut by the VI flying bomb and falling close behind us.'

Vita Sackville-West, writing in November 1944, was lost in genuine admiration for the land girls' behaviour.

> The workers in the fields were more exposed than anyone else to a danger which arrived at such speed and from which there was no available shelter except perhaps a ditch which might be several acres away. But, so far as I can make out, not many land girls bothered to run for the ditches. They just stood and watched, and then got on with their job. One of them is reported as having burst into tears as a doodle escaped the fighters and travelled on towards London. . . . A special word should, I think, be given to those girls who were working along the Kentish coast. They had not only the bombs to face, but also the really appalling noise of the Ack-ack barrage to endure. There was no sleep for them, during all those weeks, unless it was the sleep of utter exhaustion. We had the barrage inland for about a fortnight and learnt how sleepless nights could tell on one's resistance, but then the guns were removed to the coast and remained there till the nuisance ceased. There was no respite for those girls, and they deserve all honour for carrying on as they did, when they must at times have felt absolutely dead to the world.

Casualties, mercifully, were extremely few. A land girl in Kent lost her leg when she inadvertently stepped back into the drum of the threshing machine while watching an aerial dog fight. Another girl who was standing outside her caravan watching a chase got shot in the arm by the bullets intended for the doodle. She was so badly injured that it was thought she might have to lose her arm. Vita Sackville-West went to see the girl's companions after the accident. 'They seemed a bit shaken by this incident, but when I asked them what they were going to do, they replied: "Oh, just carry on." And they did.'

Land girls were particularly selfless where animals were involved. After a raid on Canterbury ten out of eleven land girls from a house which had been bombed reported for work next morning at the usual time. The eleventh apologised for being late due to having to be dug out of the debris. During another night raid on Canterbury another girl bicycled through the burning town to the farm where she worked because she was worried about the cows. She then returned at milking time. She too was awarded the County Badge for Courage. Mystified at the Press interest, she told journalists, 'It was my job to look after the cows. As for going back to milk them, the milk was wanted and the cows needed milking, and that was all there was to it.'

As the tide of the war started to turn, land girls sensed that perhaps the long years of marking time defending the home-land were coming to an end. Several girls saw mysterious convoys of lorries and tanks rumbling through Kent villages in the summer of 1944. Margaret Garland remembers the scene: '. . . a very large convoy going through the village, so long it took two and a half hours to pass. Two days later it returned with white crosses painted on the vehicles. One of the men said, "we shall hear something soon." We had battle training grounds near us and had seen many tanks and troops. A day or so later, we were working in the field, when about 8 a.m. a woman ran out of a nearby house shouting "it has started". Our feeling was: "at last we could fight back." '

Mary Twyman, a land girl in Kent during the heavy bombardments of 1944–5, worked on a dairy farm and had a milk round. 'In spite of air raids and shelling milk had to be delivered daily; so on a bad day when the siren sounded the "All Clear" we seized a hand crate and hurried round to the houses within walking distance.'

On occasions, however, even the most sophisticated military operations had to yield to the unpredictable ways of country life. 'By the late spring of 1944 troop convoys were constantly on the move in and around the town. I was delivering to houses on the main London road one morning when, after leaving milk at a house surrounded by trees I heard the rumble of heavy vehicles, followed by the screech of brakes and the blowing of horns. Hurrying up the long drive I found my horse had pulled the cart across the main Dover to Canterbury road to graze on the grass verge the other side, bringing to a halt a long line of army lorries. My appearance caused hoots of laughter, wolf whistles and good-natured, if somewhat uncomplimentary, advice.' The troops in question were Canadians, recently arrived and stationed in nearby barracks. But any resentment Mary Twyman may have felt at the lack of sympathy her wayward horse elicited notwithstanding, she soon had cause to bless the Canadians. The following September they stormed the German cross-Channel guns at Cap Gris Nez. 'How grateful we were to them for bringing to an end the four years of enemy shelling which caused so many civilian casualties and destroyed so much of our town.'

From 1941 when they first arrived from the Mediterranean, the ranks of farm workers were swelled by thousands of prisoners of war. By July 1943 more than 37,000 prisoners – mainly Italian – were working on the land. The following year an acute labour shortage on the farms caused the Ministry of Agriculture to request an additional 37,000. Many of this second and last wave were German and Austrian. Many farmers when offered the choice, still opted for male workers

The great thing about being in the Land Army was that,
unlike the women's services, who insisted on skirts and
stockings, you could get a tan.

Land girls relax in the sun during a rally near Canterbury.

In a society starved of young able-bodied men, land girls
were frequently condemned as predatory and sexually available.
In this photograph, featuring men from the Pioneer Corps
taking a break from a land reclamation project,
it is not easy to decide who is stalking whom.

In isolated country areas the opportunity for
boy to meet girl was often limited to the local pub,
where a girl needed a male escort to provide respectability.
Land girls were often refused service in the bar
by censorious publicans.

Service dances were popular with land girls, especially those organised by the Americans. These offered more drink, better music, and, if their critics are to be believed, more sex.

Land girls march through Maidstone in December 1943, the year the Land Army reached its peak strength.

Land girls frequently left the force to get married, though some
only took the day off, returning to the farm as usual
the following day. This bride is treated to an unconventional
guard of honour formed of pitchforks and hayrakes.

The Government's crassly unfair decision to exclude the Land Army from the generous post-war gratuity scheme offered to most other workers led to the resignation of Lady Denman and lit a new flame of militancy in the ranks of the Land Army.

(*Above:*) Realising that Servicemen based abroad could not be brought home overnight, the Government belatedly launched a Land Army recruiting campaign in 1946. Yet it had already announced that land girls would not receive post-war gratuity payments. The irony of this was not lost on the veteran socialist cartoonist Vicky.

(*Left:*) Lady Denman campaigned tirelessly to improve conditions for the Land Army, who were excluded from perks enjoyed by the women's services. One of her triumphs was to secure one week's holiday with pay, not just for land girls, but for all agricultural workers.

The Queen Mother, seen here inspecting a parade of land girls
with Lady Denman, was a dedicated and active patron of the Land Army.

Some land girls were more equal than others. Jean Barker, now Lady Trumpington,
was the only land girl on Lloyd George's estate. Neither dung-spattered nor unduly
taxed, she packed apples and enjoyed lunch every day with the great man.

One of the Land Army's last tasks was, in the spring of 1950, to declare war
on the colorado beetle. Here land girls pour pesticides on the foliage of
the new potato crop.

Women's Land Army girls march to Buckingham Palace for the Queen's inspection
and the winding-up parade. The Land Army was disbanded on 30 November 1950.

over land girls. As it turned out, however, the Italians soon acquired an almost universal reputation for laziness, and as far as land girls were concerned, lechery. Moreover there were constant complaints, both from land girls and politicians that, due to an excessively zealous interpretation of the Geneva Convention, prisoners of war received kid-glove treatment compared to native workers.

'The Italians were disgusting,' says Doreen Lingard who had joined the Timber Corps at seventeen and was sent to clear woods near Salisbury. 'And bone idle. They'd spend all day cutting up one log. We were supposed to be picked up by their lorry every morning to go to the forest where we were working. When we climbed in, their hands would be everywhere and whoever was supposed to be in charge of them did nothing. When we got to the forest you didn't dare go to the lavatory . . . they'd be lying in wait to grab you. We were only kids. It really wasn't fair. It got so bad we refused to go in the lorry with them. We said we'd rather walk to work.'

The Italian prisoners seem to have enjoyed remarkably relaxed supervision, since others tell the same story. Cynthia Brown remembers being followed around on her farm by Italian prisoners.

> They would keep on 'you marry me and come back to Italy'. When I replied 'what would your wife say?' the answer was always the same. 'I have no wife.'
>
> It became so difficult, one day I shut myself in a cellar where I thought peeling onions was preferable to being chased by Italians. I was going to the cowshed looking a fright after a recent extraction of a tooth, when out of the bushes rushed one of them who threw his arms round me and kissed me. There were cheers and clapping from the others who tried to follow suit. I cannot help thinking that today I might have got off rather worse. I stamped my foot and cried, 'no good. Go away.' But they went on shouting 'Good. Good. You are beautiful.'

Occasionally prisoners could be violent. One land girl hoeing in a field in Kent narrowly avoided being killed by an

Italian prisoner who had gone berserk. The prisoner turned on the soldier in charge of the gang, who were hedging, and decapitated him with his hedge hook, seized his rifle and ran across the field to the girl. He fired at her but missed and then fled towards some woods. He remained in the woods for several days, with the army camped round it. He was eventually discovered by a farmer in the bedroom of a nearby farm and shot dead.

The poor old Land Army came bottom of the pile whenever it came to perks. But surely the most insulting example of official insensitivity is to be found in the way that enemy prisoners were accorded more humane treatment than our own volunteers. Prisoners enjoyed far better working conditions than land girls, they worked a shorter day, were better fed, were provided with more luxurious transport and benefited from ludicrous protection from inclement weather. Whereas land girls usually had to cycle to work from their hostel, often quite a distance, and worked an 8 a.m.-till-5 p.m. day, Italian POWs came to work by lorry, or even in some instances by coach, at 9 a.m. and were collected again at 4 p.m. The reason is that the prisoners were the responsibility of the Government and the Government was zealous in its observation of the Geneva Convention with respect to the humane treatment of prisoners of war.

The unfairness of the situation was bitterly resented by land girls. In the end the discrimination was so obvious and so widespread that it became the subject of a Parliamentary debate. In a report in the *Daily Sketch* of 15 February 1945, under the headline 'Italians Better Off Than Land Girls', Mr Henderson Stewart, Liberal MP for Fyfe East, claimed land girls were less adequately clothed and less respectfully treated than prisoners. 'I've seen girls standing up to their knees in mud in cold misty weather wearing leather boots needing repair . . . alongside Italian prisoners who wore good rubber boots and battledress. The prisoners were treated by the farmers with respect, whereas the girls were treated with ill respect.' It was one more example of the official indifference with which the land girls had to cope.

16 : Some More Equal than Others

It is tempting to believe that class barriers came down during the Second World War, with gentry and factory workers, secretaries and housemaids forgetting their differences as they stood shoulder to shoulder against the common foe. But in reality the England of the Forties remained a rigidly class-bound society. Class distinction dictated the pecking order of country life even more than it did in cities, with the landed gentry rarely mixing with tenant farmers and farmers not expecting to socialise with their farm workers. Even within the apparently egalitarian ranks of the land girls some were decidedly more equal than others.

The administration of the WLA, as we have seen, was carried out by women from the landed gentry and professional families who acquired their jobs via the social network. Often these women had little empathy with the young girls in their charge, having never mixed with them. On the other hand we have already observed that the majority of the girls who did the manual work came predominantly from artisan families. Their behaviour could, on occasion, be both startling and gauche.

One countrywoman who was a child during the war remembers the shock generated one hot summer's day in Devon by lorry loads of land girls going past wearing only pink bras above the waist. Another woman who entertained hungry land girls to tea remembers how overawed and shy they could be when in the presence of those they regarded as their betters. 'They would stand round the walls stolidly devouring their cakes and sandwiches as if stuck there with glue. Afterwards there would be a horseshoe of crumbs round the edge of the room.'

Some members of the upper classes, far from applauding the girls for their hard work and patriotism, made it clear that war or no war land girls were social inferiors. Two pole selectors were treated to an appalling display of English snobbery when wet, tired and hungry after a day spent tramping Somerset in search of straight timber, they finally arrived at a hotel. 'We were asked if we wanted dinner. As our funds were so low we dared not have any, but asked for bread and cheese and tea. The girl there said would we have it in the bar or dining-room as we were wet. Miss Tuffield said the bar, but I said the dining-room, so the dining-room it was. There I realised my mistake as the other guests were all in evening dress, and let us know how disgusting it was to let the Land Army in their hotel. Two left their dinner and went out. We could have eaten it, we were so hungry.'

Volunteers who came from well-to-do backgrounds tended to be made a special fuss of in the newspapers, as if their gesture was somehow more patriotic than that of the mere factory girl. A newspaper photograph of a dark-haired land girl handling day-old chicks was captioned gushingly: 'Many society girls are playing their part in this war and among them is Miss Joan Street, who has joined Britain's biggest battalion of the Women's Land Army, namely Hampshire. Miss Street is the daughter of Lady Tottenham, wife of Vice-Admiral Sir Francis Loftus Tottenham.' If a girl from an educated background did become a land girl she could expect to be treated differently from her more humble colleagues, at least when it came to social matters. Doris Taverner, from Birchington, in East Kent, who was a lady's maid in a large private house in Broadstairs before joining up, was shown how to milk cows at a training centre the other side of the county in Bethersden. Among their number was the daughter of the Mayor of a local town. 'We all lodged in the house but Una, the Mayor's daughter, who didn't know one end of a cow from the other, was treated quite differently from us. When we came in at night we'd go into the kitchen for a quick coffee and then be expected to go up to our rooms. Una would be invited into the drawing room to have coffee with the lady of the house and any officers they might be entertaining. We weren't expected to mix with the officers. They used to leave their tunics hanging outside the drawing-room. Once as a prank one girl cut the pips off their tunics. Una was teased too. One night we filled her pillowcase with flour.'

And if the class system saw to it that an educated land girl received more respect from her hosts, so the more social clout an employer of land girls could deploy, the better equipped his girls would be. Land girls who worked for some of the great titled landowners even had access to better uniform. Jean Procter, attending a rally in Chester, was dazzled by the appearance of the land girls who worked for Lord Derby. 'We had scraped the muck off our breeches as best we could. They were patched and faded . . . When Lord Derby's girls joined the parade they were all in brand-new uniform with armbands that looked as if they'd just come out of the box.'

Often even if they were educated land girls were treated little better than servants, on their farms. But there were exceptions. The small number of land girls who came from established families tended to be regarded as the social equals – if not superiors – of their hosts. Hilary Deedes (née Branfoot) who married Bill, now Lord, Deedes in 1942, was the daughter of a prominent shipbuilder on the Tyne. A country girl by birth – they lived in Northumberland – she joined the Land Army because she loved animals and had always wanted to be a farmer, though her sex and class forbade it. Even before joining up she preferred to wear breeches, though she was supposed to change when she came in from riding. When war looked likely, much against her father's wishes, she bought five Jersey cows whose milk she sent daily to the local regiments and messes. She lent one of her five horses to the blacksmith and turned her own hunter into a plough horse, working land which hadn't been ploughed since the time of the first Land Army in 1917. She worked as a land girl for two farmers in her native Northumberland. 'For me it was a dream come true. It was what I wanted to do. In normal circumstances I wouldn't have been allowed to work. We were gentry and there was no question of girls like me getting jobs. At home the groom had already joined the Services, the gardener was about to be called up . . . Father said "just join the Land Army . . ." '

Lady Deedes's background meant that, while she was prepared to work as hard as anyone else, there was no question of her being paid. 'I remember my pay was supposed to be fourteen shillings a week. But the farmers I worked for were very hard up. They couldn't have afforded to pay me. I got on very well with the wife at the second farm I went to. She was a well-educated woman who had been to agricultural college. From time to time Father would send over a case of champagne or a couple of bottles of Port and Flo and I would stop work in the middle of the morning and have a glass of champagne.'

One of the advantages of being a patrician land girl was that you were spared the malicious teasing so many others had to put up with. Lady Deedes says that if the local men disapproved of her they didn't show it. 'My family was well known. People just saluted when they saw you.' Lady Deedes believes she won the farmhands over not through her competence – but because of her language. 'The men had had it impressed upon them that they were never to swear in front of the land girls. One day one of the cows was being difficult and they overheard me shouting "come on you bloody old sod" at her. They were rather impressed.'

If Hilary Deedes won her spurs despite her privileged upbringing, Jean Barker, another well-connected land girl, abandoned the life after just a year, out of a mixture of boredom and loneliness. Now Baroness Trumpington, the seventeen-year-old Miss Barker had been allocated as a land girl to Lloyd George who owned a large fruit farm. This was at the suggestion of her grandmother who had been a close friend of Lloyd George and his first wife, Dame Margaret. 'The idea was that I should go to Churt, in Surrey, to harvest Lloyd George's delicious raspberries and pick and pack his Coxes. Of course I was treated very well and I really don't remember any aching muscles. I stayed in the house (Miss Stephenson, destined to become the second Mrs Lloyd George, was discreetly accommodated in her own bungalow) and used to be invited to lunch with Lloyd George who was an absolute darling.'

As one of the Land Army's Regional Officers, Dorothy Brant spent a lot of time visiting the houses of the county women who had taken on local administrative posts. She found observing how they coped with life in reduced circumstances in the enormous houses fascinating. Many rose to the challenge magnificently and actually enjoyed the experience of playing house for the first time.

The Bingley household was a perfect example of how the aristocracy responded to the wartime spirit. Lady Bingley was the Chairman of West Riding county committee. She had been a Halifax before her marriage – her brother had been Foreign Secretary under Neville Chamberlain. She lived at Bramham Park near Wetherby. It was a beautiful house with beautiful gardens. If I couldn't find an hotel to stay in, when I was travelling on behalf of the Land Army, I had an open invitation to stay with Lady Bingley, provided I didn't mind having my dirty sheets from the last time. They would be folded up after I left and stored in the linen cupboard, marked with a label with

'Miss Brant' written on it. Lady Bingley always got up at 6 a.m. to do her share of the housework and spent the rest of the day involved in various war work charities and committees. But it was at mealtimes you really noticed what changes these people were having to adjust to. We would start off in the hall, which had a blazing log fire. Then, when dinner was ready, we would walk through the vast house, past the vast kitchen, all shrouded in linen sheets, to the butler's sitting-room. This had become the family dining-room, while the butler's pantry had become their kitchen. After dinner Lord Bingley washed up while I dried. Their butler had joined the local police, but if the Bingleys were giving a dinner party he would come back and be the butler again for the evening.

Some society women actually found satisfaction in being forced to play a part in the running of their households – and some were appalled at the conditions their own servants had been expected to work in.

Miss Brant remembers conversations about the change in social conditions with Lady Beryl Groves who lived in the splendid Revesby Abbey in central Lincolnshire and who was a member of her county committee. 'The house had been taken over by the Army but Lady Beryl continued to live in a few rooms with a maid. She told me, "I was brought up never to do anything and I do so enjoy being able to lay the table now." She told me how once, as a child, she had gone to put a log on the fire. Her mother rebuked her, observing "Ladies do not do that. You ring for the footman." When I think what some of those sort of people had to adjust to, when they were not young, I am full of admiration.'

Not everyone rose to the challenge, however, and some gentry families – and many farmers' wives too – looked on land girls as heaven-sent replacements for the servants they had lost. It was the job of officers and reps to admonish unscrupulous employers who were abusing the system, removing their land girls if the abuse continued.

One particularly brazen example of abuse took place under Dorothy Brant's nose. 'I had been staying with a woman whose husband had been MP for Louth. She was very large, red-faced and ungainly, but she had an exquisite small house, filled with the most delightful things. I was treated like Royalty. The maid woke me, opening the curtains, bringing me breakfast in bed and a *fresh hot water bottle*. Imagine my embarrassment when, as I was ready to leave, my car, which had been washed, was brought round by the land girl.'

It was stated expressly in the *Land Girl Manual* that WLA members were only to be employed in food production – 'They are . . . never used on nurseries growing flowers or in parks or private gardens, except where the latter have been turned over to food production.'

A commercial horticulturalist was found to be bucking the system when land girls in Cornwall began to complain of an itchy eczema-like rash on their hands. A decision had been taken at the beginning of the war to allow the well-established export of spring flowers from the Scilly Isles and the West Country to the United States to continue. The itchy fingers complained of by land girls in the area were eventually diagnosed as a disease promoted by handling daffodil bulbs. The employer was deprived of his land girls.

If a land girl found she was being asked to carry out duties that contributed more to the comfort of her employer than the war effort she was entitled to complain to her local WLA rep. But in some cases this proved difficult. Joan Chapman spent her three and a half years in the Land Army working as a gardener for a retired general and his wife in a lovely old house in West Kent. She was collected from the station by an enormous Bentley driven by a disdainful chauffeur, who tipped his cap, asked 'Are you for General Drummond?' and dumped her outside an end-of-terrace house. This turned out to be her digs. Her efforts contributed nothing to the war effort, but she felt complaining to her local rep, who happened to be Vita Sackville-West, would have been tricky, as it was Vita herself who had allocated her to her neighbours, with whom she was extremely friendly. 'I felt really bad about the fact that I wasn't helping the war effort. The Drummonds never sold anything. I spent my time pruning roses, growing arum lilies, training peach trees and picking raspberries for private dinner parties. I wish I had known how many others were, through no fault of their own, in the same position, as it worried me dreadfully at the time. Vita was friendly with the Drummonds. They had lost all but a boy and their old head gardener to the Services so it seemed to her the natural thing to allocate me to them.'

As the only land girl on the estate Joan's physical sense of isolation was heightened by the constraints of class. 'I had had quite a responsible job in London before joining the Land Army. So I wasn't from the labouring class. But I wasn't county either so I wasn't received by the Drummonds. I was neither fish nor fowl – but effectively I was a servant.'

Vita was not only one of the West Kent reps but also the official biographer of the WLA. But despite the patriotic and socially egalitarian ideals of the Land Army embodied by Lady Denman herself, those who knew Vita say that she never really grasped how people outside her class lived and was extremely reluctant to drop her own standard of living to accommodate the war effort.

One aspect of the war effort Vita couldn't – or wouldn't – understand was that you got money to buy feed for your animals in direct proportion to the amount of produce you sold. Vita had three cows at Sissinghurst – the lovely Tudor home she bought and restored with the money she made with her successful novels – with a land girl to look after them. 'The trouble was she hardly sent any of the milk away. She kept it for her own use – and she made butter. Vita was a great butter eater. She would tell her land girl, "I have a keen butter eater coming to stay today, so be sure that I have plenty of lovely creamy milk." Peggy could not stand the prospect of her cows not getting proper food, so she used to get up early and go and pinch cattle cake from the neighbouring farm.'

Barbara Pawlowski

(née *Wright*). Joined Land Army at 16.
Land Army 1943–6 – dairy and general farming.
Home town: Chester.
Civilian occupation: Zoo keeper.

I was so keen to join the Land Army I lied about my age and forged my dad's signature to get in. You had to be seventeen and I was only sixteen. He opened my call-up letter and he was disgusted that I'd lied. 'If you go you needn't come back,' was his response. I left for my first farm the next morning. He had a point, being angry. Forging his signature was a crime really, but my mother had died when I was eight and I was quite headstrong. All through the war I met people who had enlisted when they were under age. I'm sure thousands did it. You wanted to do your bit for King and country so you just filled in the form and went.

I'd left school at fourteen – my dad was an electrical contractor whose business had been badly hit by the slump in house building in the pre-war years. I started out as a trainee hairdresser and beauty therapist, but a bout of bronchitis followed by jaundice caused the doctor to prescribe an outdoor life. I went as a farmhand to friends who were farmers. They had daughters who worked on the farm so there was no division of labour. I learned to hand-milk, which stood me in good stead later and helped prepare the mounds of vegetables for lunch every day. After that I went as a junior keeper to Chester Zoo. I started off with the birds and foxes and then graduated to the lions and bears.

The thing I remember about my first billet, after I joined the

Land Army, was hunger. My landlady was a childless widow with a very small appetite. She hadn't a clue how to feed someone who was doing manual labour. When I arrived – in an MG sports car driven by a friend who had a garage in Chester – she was wearing a black silk dress with a white collar. She used to change every afternoon. Women did in those days – even my mother – after they had done the chores. She dismissed my friend without even offering him a cup of tea and then served me tea and two wafer-thin sandwiches containing three strawberries in jam. The house was quite civilised. It had a bathroom and a garage, where I was expected to take off my wellies. She told me I would be sleeping in her dead husband's bed. Breakfast the next morning was a piece of toast. She pointed me in the direction of the farm, which was about a mile and a half away, and left me to it.

When I arrived I was met by the bailiff – the actual owner was a wealthy man who owned cotton mills. His job was to tell you what to do each day. He'd ask you to do something, watch to see you did it properly and then leave you to it. There were four other land girls on the farm so we were no longer a rarity. My job was to milk the cows. They had machines at the farm, but cows that had just calved were hand-milked and cows that had been machine-milked would need 'stripping off'. We used to start bringing them in at 3.45 a.m., which meant getting up at 3.30 a.m.

I used to walk to the farm from my billet until my County Organiser got me a bike. It was an American bike and I assumed the brakes were on the handlebars. It wasn't till I found myself going down a steep hill that I realised they weren't. I landed up in a ditch at which point I discovered American bikes had their brakes on the pedals. I stayed at my first billet until my landlady told me I would be sharing a bed as she was taking in another land girl. I told her I wouldn't put up with that. After that I moved up to the farm and lived in a caravan with another land girl. That was much more fun. We ate well. When we were harvesting we got extra rations – cheese, marge, meat . . .

My first farm was really nice but I decided I wanted a change and went to my County Organiser. She thought I was mad but I wouldn't listen. The next farm was much smaller and belonged to the Master of the local hunt. I was billeted on the bailiff who was about forty-five and lived with his mother in a cottage. It was a miserable place with neither conversation nor laughter. You just got up, worked and went to bed. There was hot water in the cottage. I got hot water for sterilising the milking equipment, but I was expected to wash in cold – and my time was rationed. 'Be quick about it,' she'd shout through the door. I wasn't allowed out except to go to church on Sunday. I wasn't supposed to read either, though I used to read by torchlight under the blankets. The mother was a funny-looking woman with one tooth that stuck out in front like a pickle stabber. I doubt if either of them could read or write. 'Books drive you mad. I knew someone who read books and she's insane,' she'd say. The country people didn't like us townies. To them we were intruders. My landlady showed her feelings for me one Christmas Eve. I had been invited to a party by a friend I had met at church. My landlady told me I would have to be in by 10 or I would be locked out. At 9.30 I told my hostess I would have to go or else I should be locked out. They were all appalled and persuaded me to stay on. Eventually they all decided to escort me home, thinking that if they were all there, she'd relent. As we came to the cottage I found the door was locked. I knocked and a head appeared at the bedroom window. The landlady told everyone else to go home as it was nothing to do with them. 'Don't worry,' they assured me, 'she's bound to let you in once we've gone.' As soon as they'd gone she announced, 'you can sleep where you like but you're not coming in at this time of night.' So I went into the shippon, got a couple of bales of straw and snuggled up to my favourite cow, an old Jersey called Celandine.

17 : Party Time

Land girls had the reputation of being very sociable. Country people, weaned on the puritan philosophy of early to bed early to rise, insinuated that the high spirits of the interlopers went beyond the bounds of decency. They marvelled at – and disapproved of – the way girls who had spent all day in the fields had the energy to go drinking, dancing and flirting at night. But these were girls in the prime of life, teenagers, many of them, and most had come from towns and cities where there were plenty of things to do in the evening. However isolated they were, they were determined to have a social life.

Not all land girls, however, spent their free time jitterbugging the night away with predatory GIs. Many remember being so tired after their day's work that most evenings were spent lying on their beds, reading, writing letters and mending endless pairs of holed socks. There was something quite boarding-schoolish about the hostels, with girls entertaining themselves listening to music, holding sing-songs and making things for each other.

In the characteristically arch language of the *Land Army*

Manual, Shewell Cooper had urged land girls to find things to do to entertain themselves. 'There is no reason why little parties should not be arranged for a few girls in any town or village. Sometimes the girls themselves arrange these and perhaps pay a visit to the local cinema together or meet for a game of cards or a good gossip round the fire. The Land Army volunteer must be prepared to help with her own welfare and she can do much to make her own life happy if she tries to make others happy too.'

Their motives may have been less pious than Cooper was hoping. None the less the ingenuity land girls put into creating a social life for themselves – often in the depths of the country where there never had been much to do – is impressive. The long days devoted to what were often numbingly repetitive tasks, weeding and singling limitless fields of beet, fetching the cows home for milking twice a day, carting and spreading muck, must have made some form of escape absolutely vital. Besides they were all at the age where boy will do anything to meet girl. The ends they went to to create an atmosphere of cheer in the midst of wartime austerity, and the pleasure they took in what to us appear unsophisticated treats, are touching. What would today's clubbing teenagers make of the two girls at a hostel in Warwickshire who cycled six miles on a dark windy night after a day's threshing just to get a sprig of mistletoe to decorate their Christmas party?

Clothing rationing created impressive displays of resourcefulness when civvies were the order of the day. One girl, short of a dress to wear to a dance, remade a mauve taffeta eiderdown and wore that. With curly hair scraped up at the sides Betty Grable-style (*the* fashionable hair-style to wear) most girls washed their hair on the morning before a dance, hiding their pipecleaner or metal 'Dinkie' curlers under 'turbans' made of First Aid bandages. What to wear on one's legs when silk stockings had all but disappeared was a problem. Some girls swore by rubbed-on coffee or gravy browning. Marjorie Cullen found the answer in builder's sand.

'In the hostel we were in, the bath was against the wall so there was only room for four of us to sit on it at one time. When we were going out we would all sit with our legs in the bath and apply the wet sand like a paste. When it dried we brushed it off into the bath and it left a brown stain which looked like a tan. Then we would stand up while a friend applied the "seam". For this we used either an eyebrow pencil or a child's crayon. We often got the giggles doing this as it was so silly. Then the "seam" would go crooked.'

As an eighteen-year-old in a hostel near Wainfleet in Lincolnshire Peg Francis remembers the girls swapping records on the wind-up HMV gramophone.

We used to dance and sing to Vera Lynn, Glenn Miller and Bing Crosby. We had some lovely sing-songs. Amy, who was a cockney, would weep over 'Home Sweet Home'. Jean had her own gramophone and sets of Ivor Novello's shows. She used to sing 'A Woman's Heart' in her odd quavery voice. None of the girls liked classical except me. Once I forced them to listen to Gigli from *La Bohème* on our one radio. A friend and I got round Matron one night and persuaded her to let us stay up to listen to Donald Peers on the Light Programme for twenty minutes. We had to be sure to put the lights out and check once more that the windows and doors were locked.

One of the bonuses of hostel life was the way girls from different backgrounds exchanged skills. 'Doris had worked in a laundry,' recalls Peg Francis. 'She ironed our shirts beautifully. I could mend so I kept the ladders in people's silk stockings from running too far. Edie was good at setting hair; some girls knitted, some crocheted . . . One thing that was off rations were flour bags which were made of fine linen and cost 6d each at Boston market. We used to put transfers on them, embroider them and then give them to girls as wedding presents.'

For many, a night out meant nothing more exciting than a trip to the local. Miles away from towns and cities, and usually with only a bicycle for transport, dressing up was a clean pair of dungarees, while the entertainment was a game of darts. At half a pint for sevenpence, cider was the cheapest drink and a favourite with land girls – often with catastrophic results for their bicycles, since punctures were a besetting hazard cycling in black-out darkness. Marjorie Cullen remembers cycling back with some friends singing lustily after a night on cider, only to discover in the morning that she and her friends were to be fined ten shillings each for cycling without lights. 'I don't know who reported us, but a ten-shilling fine off pay of £2 a week was not funny.'

Dances were the event everyone looked forward to. They were held in village halls, market halls, corn exchanges, hostel dining-rooms, forces canteens. By today's standard they were wholesome and innocent affairs. Smooching was frowned on, and the evenings invariably kicked off with a Paul Jones to make sure there were no wallflowers, before graduating to a vigorous Hokey Cokey.

The energy the girls found to whoop it up after a hard day on the land impressed many members of the older generation. A woman arriving to take over a hostel in Cheshire, expecting to find a troop of weary girls, discovered a hectic twenty-first birthday party in full swing.

It was some party. Twenty girls . . . ten friends, sixteen employers with their wives and families and twenty-four Artillerymen from a nearby camp joined in games, dancing and a feast to celebrate both the twenty-first birthday of Joan Arden and the New Year. . . . One of the dormitories had been cleared to make an extra reception room . . . The whole house was decorated with festoons, lanterns and gaily coloured streamers, while as for the dining-room – well, one of the guests summed it up neatly: 'Coo,' I heard him say, 'if little Ol' 'itler could see this he'd die of rage' . . . I no longer regard members of the Women's Land Army as poor, tired mites. A more cheerful, hard-working, hard-playing lot I've never met . . . they are tough! They can take it.

People today go to parties mainly for the sex interest.

During the hungry war years, however, the boy-meets-girl imperative seems to have been closely rivalled by the desire for a slap-up meal. Dances provided a welcome excuse for a spread, with favourite dishes being the ones that today would be served at a children's party. Dorothea Abbott, whose hostel held a Christmas party one year, says the two most memorable aspects of the evening were seeing each other out of uniform – and the food. 'We derived a huge kick from dressing up for it . . . Most of us lived in slacks in the evening, and as a visit to the Sergeants Mess or a dance at The Hut involved a long cycle ride on a cold evening we tended to wear our walking-out uniform of greatcoat, green jersey and best gabardine breeches. Consequently we had never seen each other dressed up . . .'

The food, looted from parental larders and from queuing at successive cake shops in nearby Stratford-upon-Avon, was the highlight. 'I hadn't seen so many colourful jellies and blanc-manges since a friend's twenty-first party soon after the outbreak of war. Our families were not well supplied with friends and relatives in the food trade and what we had was strictly on the ration. It was obvious from looking at the loaded table that some of the girls must have friends in the right quarters.'

Hostels with sociable wardens held regular dances for their girls particularly if there were servicemen stationed nearby to act as partners, but rules were strict. Wardens, often elderly and unmarried, had a nose for illicit alcohol and unseemly hanky panky and their charges delighted in outwitting them. Joan Faulkner celebrated her twenty-first birthday at a hostel in West Kent. 'We had the Air Force from Malling, the Army from Hunton and some sailors from Chatham. The rule of the hostel was no alcohol on the premises, so we pulled up crates of beer through the bedroom windows, while our warden kept watch at the front door.'

The dances often ended as early as 10 p.m. and Matron was apt to patrol the premises sniffing out sin. One serviceman who was going out with a land girl based at a hostel in the Midlands delivered her back on his motor bike in time for the ten-o'clock curfew. 'Matron was waiting outside the door. "Time to go in now," she said. You couldn't even kiss your girl good-night. When they had dances at the hostel there'd usually be an interval of fifteen to twenty minutes. Matron would be watching those girls like a hawk.' Some were prepared to turn a blind eye – for a consideration. Peg Francis had an Irish matron who was fond of flowers. 'When we wanted a late pass we'd have a whip round and buy her a huge bunch. We'd knock on her door – "Oh my, my! Thank you," she'd say. "How late will you be out?" '

The dances where servicemen were hosts tended to be more popular. The food was more copious, there was alcohol and often a band instead of the gramophone which was all most Land Army hostels ran to. What's more the men usually sent a lorry to fetch the girls, which spared them cycling there and back. The Americans were particularly popular – a fact which caused the occasional outburst of violent resentment among British servicemen. The Americans had more money, wore elegant gabardine uniforms which were far smoother to the touch than the scratchy serge of British uniforms, and were enthusiastic exponents of the new rumbustious style of dancing which caused the girls' skirts to fly up, revealing tantalising glimpses of stocking tops.

Joan Pountney was in a hostel near Melton Mowbray in Leicestershire with the 82nd US Airborne Division camped nearby.

> We used to go to dances at the Corn Exchange in Melton on Wednesday nights. There'd be servicemen of all nationalities there – English, American, Polish, Czech . . . The Americans had all the latest records. I'd seen jiving before, but not the way they did it. I was dancing with one chap and all of a sudden he swept me off my feet and swung me between his legs. Some chaps would pick you up and throw you over their shoulder. It was great. We always had to leave at 11 as we had to be in the

hostel by 11.30. Our driver would always end up threatening to leave us behind if we didn't come at once.

Many of these Americans were black and land girls were forbidden to associate with them. 'A deputation from the War Ag. came to the hostel and warned us that we would be in trouble if we fraternised with the black servicemen,' says Mrs Pountney. Some of the girls found this ruling offensive and defied the authorities by becoming friendly with some of the black soldiers. But mixing with black Americans was seen by some British as a double betrayal. Joan was with a group of land girls in a pub in the village when a huge fight broke out.

The pub was packed with soldiers, British and American. I was sitting with some land girls at one table. A group of black servicemen were at another over the other side of the pub. One of the black chaps had been very kind to a friend of mine, giving her lifts and so forth. The Americans started to sing – 'Bless 'em all' – and my friend said, 'I'm going to buy him a pint to say thank you.' She got half-way over with the pint when a British paratroop sergeant walked over to her and knocked the glass out of her hand, saying the Americans singing a British song was an insult. That was it. They smashed the place to pieces. The landlord rushed over and told us to leave through his quarters. 'If you get caught up in this I'll be in trouble with your people,' he said. There were a good many local men walking round with black eyes the next day.

The thing about service dances was that anything was possible. Nothing was allowed to stand in their way. Marjorie Cullen remembers waking up in despair to find a deep fall of snow had cut their hostel off on the day they were due to be holding a dance for the Sergeants Mess stationed eleven miles away. 'We thought it would be called off but no way! The Captain at their camp sent the snow plough out – to clear eleven miles of snow!'

Class barriers, as we have seen, did not disappear during the war. Officers, NCOs and other ranks each had their own dances and people did not expect to mingle socially with their superiors. One of the smartest events in the country social calendar was the Young Farmers Ball, famous for its professional band and lavish buffet. One girl recalls the excitement this event caused in her hostel: 'Most of the girls were hoping that some farmer's son would invite them – what a forlorn hope. Daddy would not like his son to socialise with a land girl.' In the end, however, the wife of the farmer for whom this girl worked got permission for her to attend – even though it went on till 1 a.m. Seeing how the other half lived – in the middle of a war – was a revelation. 'The girls were as thrilled as I was. It was a long-dress affair but no one could rise to that. There were offers of earrings, bracelets and even a pair of silk stockings. My mother sent my best dress and underwear . . . What a night it was. The band was superb and I hardly sat down. The buffet was everything we had heard. There were home-cooked hams, chickens, beef, trifle with thick cream, home-made meat pies and cakes of every description It was hard to remember it was wartime. . . .'

18 : A Love Affair with the Land

People who work on the land would not do anything else. This is as true today as it was fifty years ago. There is an elusive satisfaction that comes from working with nature – watching the sleek brown furrow of autumn mist with the green of the first seedlings to erupt triumphantly into the dense gold thicket of late summer; bedding grateful animals down snugly on cold nights, observing the perennial marvel of instinct-directed birth – which outweighs long hours, discomfort and the low pay that is still, so unfairly, the farm worker's lot. Land girls – often to their astonishment, since the first few months of dealing with irritable employers, primitive billets and sore bodies did not augur well – succumbed in droves to the sensuous charm of the land, to its smells, its sounds, its look, its feel. Fewer girls left the Land Army than abandoned far better paid jobs in munitions factories and five thousand of them stayed on after the Land Army was disbanded in 1950. They expressed their feelings through their work and with their spirits, bombarding the *Land Girl*'s office at Balcombe Place with drawings, articles and a torrent of poetry – so much

203

that the best was distilled and published as a book – with which none of the Women's Auxiliary Services could possibly compete.

For many, their years in the Land Army represented a cherished initiation into a world of hitherto unimagined grace. One girl, on the verge of leaving the Land Army, wrote in 1950, 'In the WLA I have found so much to interest me and cause me joy it is difficult to pick out one particular pleasure. My earliest recollection is of those September mornings in 1939 when I was sent alone into an orchard to gather windfalls just as it was getting light. The day was newly born, the grass spangled with dew and the plaintive song of a robin gave me exquisite joy. Through the years of dairy work and market gardening I found pleasure in many things – the sound of milk in the pails, the symmetrical planting of a cabbage field, the flight of birds, the smell of apples waiting to be picked.'

Many girls found an exhilarating sense of poetry, not just in nature, but in the effect of their own labour. A girl who had escaped from Norway to join the Land Army describes the excitement of being allowed to go out ploughing on her own for the first time: 'When I saw those furrows stretching behind me, like the wake of a ship only brown instead of white, and knew I had done it all myself, I thought I should fall off the saddle with the thrill.'

Life on the land could be hard and monotonous, but a girl working in Kent maintained that for her the beauty of the landscape and the grace of the animals more than compensated for the discomfort.

I straightened my aching back and gazed with considerable lack of enthusiasm at the field of sugar-beet which seemed, in the haze of rain, to have assumed gigantic proportions. What a prospect! A whole morning of trimming sugar-beet ahead of me and already, at half past seven, my feet felt cold and damp, rain was dripping dismally down my neck, and the beet, slimy with mud, slipped from my icy fingers. A warm bed was my idea of heaven at that moment, but I seemed to recall dimly that there had been times when I was glad to be up before the rest of the world, mornings when the cool air had the exhilarating tang of wine, and the lambs on their stiff woolly legs leapt under the cherry trees. Dark winter mornings, with the stamping of hooves and the jingle of harness from the stable as I clattered by over the iron-hard ground, hurricane lamp in one hand and pail in the other. Summer mornings and long hot days in the cornfields with shared jugs of tea ... the smell of a sweating horse, the incredible softness of a horse's nose. The big yellow harvest moon and the frosty silver moon of a few months later. The magic of a white winter morning and moonshine, with the footprints of Thumper the rabbit making a delicate pattern on the smooth snow.

I straightened my back once more – strange it did not ache so much now. It had stopped raining, and in the soft autumn sunlight the beet field seemed quite small and friendly. Soon it would be lunchtime. I sighed with satisfaction. 'Thank heavens I joined the Land Army!'

City girls found it hard to adjust to work which often taxed their bodies to extremes. But in time they derived satisfaction from the way those bodies hardened and grew strong as they adapted to the demands of hard physical work. This feeling is eloquently described by a girl working in Surrey:

One's first impressions are of wrestling hopelessly with inanimate objects far more vengeful than any live enemies; of winds cutting ruthlessly through clothes, bullying straw and hay into wild involuntary dances about the yard; of cold hands curled up inside damp woollen gloves, wet breeches clinging to the knees, and icy iron handles of an unbelievably heavy dung barrow. There are nightmare thoughts every evening of the next morning; six o'clock in a strange cold dairy or a long cowshed full of shifting unknown cows; thoughts of taut great udders full of unwilling milk; of legs ready to strike wickedly and of the grotesquely triumphant sound of a kicked bucket clanging on a concrete floor. The miserable feeling of being dung-spattered and tired, of dragging the shovel to the wall and propping it up, of it falling to the ground and of having to prop it up again before plodding the long mile home. But gradually the broom begins to lose weight and become an active and indispensable ally and there is ease and a vigorous pleasure in handling the fork, shovel and hay knife, while even a bitter wind or driving rain makes one realise with a sense of exhilaration the heat and strength in one's body. Sometimes there is moonlight at six o'clock; the church windows glitter as one speeds past and the time by the church clock can be seen as well as heard. There are black starless mornings; one's boots ringing up the village street; faint lights from a few small thin curtained windows, occasionally the muffled birr of an inmate's alarm clock and a 'good morning' from someone else who passes by on a dimly lighted bicycle at the same hour . . .

Certain jobs on the farm appealed more than others. Haymaking and harvest recur as happy memories – a time when land girls were warm and bronzed, and the countryside was at its shimmering, sensuous best. This girl made use of the long hours driving the mower at haymaking time to test her growing botanical knowledge.

On a hot sunny day in June there are certainly worse places to be than seated on the back of a mowing machine. One soon grows oblivious to the drone of the tractor, the purr of the knives and the clickety clack of the connecting rod and although an eye must be kept on the machine and the knives must be raised and lowered at just the right moment at every corner there is plenty of time to look around, . . . We started early while the lavender scarves of mist still hung in the valleys promising heat later in the day. The first few turns on the outside of the field took us along the rose-scattered hedgerow and the air was heavy with the perfume of honeysuckle and the pungent meadowsweet. As the ripe grass fell before the knives little puffs of pollen hung for a while in the still air as though imitating the light fluffy clouds that drifted in the eggshell blue sky. I began to amuse myself by seeing how many varieties of grass and wild flowers I could recognise; there was ryegrass of course and cocksfoot, dogstail, catstail and sweet vernal, which gives the new-mown hayfield its unique fragrance. There was purple and white clover, a sprinkling of buttercups and here and there a patch of golden Meadow Vetchling or a handful of big white daisies . . . During the afternoon the sun blazed down with furious intensity. Tea was . . . eaten as we sprawled in the shade of a convenient oak . . . later in the evening the clouds began to disperse showing the sickly white face of a ghost of a moon ... Now I began to calculate how many more turns would be necessary to eradicate the remaining island; but appearances, as ever, were deceptive and it was some time before the last swath was laid low. Then leaving the field to its four, six and eight-legged inhabitants who were no doubt mourning their lost abode we made our way homewards under a sky that was a flaming sea of crimson, scarlet and gold.

An extraordinary number of land girls chose to express their feelings in poetry, proof if ever proof were needed, that to them these seasonal tasks represented far more than a job of work. Harvest proved the most fecund source of inspiration as in 'Early Harvest' by an anonymous land girl.

The corn is carted.
The full wains swayed and down the rutted road
There came at evening the last heavy load.
The wagoner, light-hearted,
Called it a day.
The corn was carted.

The corn is carted.
A sickle moon upon the stubble gleamed,
Up to the flying clouds a searchlight streamed.
A wailing siren started
For not too soon
The corn was carted.

The corn is carted
The bombers came, tired workers at the farm
Not for the first time heard the shrill alarm,
Now, not a man downhearted
Saw creeping flame.
The corn was carted.

The corn is carted
We said goodbye when it was springing green,
But death has ploughed a furrow in between
Us, since the day we parted,
And where you lie
The corn is carted.

The corn is carted.
The feeble seed which broke the heavy clod

At length was ripened by the hand of God.
Young, strong, and eager-hearted,
For England's need.
The corn was carted.

Sometimes, as in the delightful 'Harvest Home' by Enid Barraud, working in Cambridgeshire, the fecundity of the land becomes an image for young love.

You are my harvest home, the last rich sheaf
My tired arms shall gather to my heart.
Long are the days from snowy winter seed time
When we ploughed, harrowed and drilled the dormant grain.
Long are the days through biting winds of March,
And April's laughing showers and May's sweet green,
And June's long hours – the blazing days of summer
With the heat shimmering from the sun-parched land
And the silver hay piled high in scented loads,
Oh long the days of dull July, the sullen
Of weary August and her dragging toil,
Till with a mighty shout came gay September
And the sheaves ranged in their four-square shocks,
And the carts creaking and the horses straining
And our hearts spurring our arms to beat the sun.

The fields are quiet now, the corn is carted:
The harvest moon dreams on the empty land.
And I am free to cry 'Te Deum!' with my hand in yours
My tired arms may gather to my heart
This last rich sheaf. You are my harvest home.

Many of the most appealing poems take as their inspiration the simple beauty of the countryside, savoured all the more because to these girls, with their urban roots, it was fresh. 'Undowered', by Audrey Hancock who worked in Warwickshire, is a simple, elegant expression of what many land girls felt.

Mine is the moonlight-silvered winding river,
Mine are the trees that grow, the birds that sing,
Mine are the happy woods, the friendly wildflowers

For, having nothing, I have everything.

Mine is the splendid sun, my bridge the rainbow,
Mine are the shining darts the rainclouds fling,
Mine are the winding lanes, the curving hillsides –
For, having nothing, I have everything.

The boist'rous wind is my familiar playmate,
The beauty of the dawns and sunsets bring,
The chattering streams are mine, and I am happy –
For, having nothing, I have everything.

Sometimes, as in the poem 'October 1940', the eternal nature of the seasons' cycle serves to emphasise the uncertainty of man's future.

Today I gather from the orchard grass
Apples and shrapnel – windfalls shaken down
When angry gusts tempestuously pass.

Tonight above the dark surrounding town,
Shellbursts and stars will decorate the sky
With dangerous beauty, devastation's crown.
A lunatic balloon, adrift on high,
Trailing its shadow by a silver thong,
Above the sailing leaves goes sailing by.

Sirens and robins share their autumn song,
As War and Peace alternately take wing,
Chanting antiphonally all day long.

And I, impartially harkening,
Nevertheless continue, hour by hour
Confident planting for a doubtful spring

The cabbages that others may devour,
The tulips I may never see in flower.

Land girls' poetry did not always deal in weighty philosophical concepts. 'The Gardeners', written by an anonymous Gloucestershire land girl, gives a light-hearted insight into what it felt like to be abruptly transformed into a surrogate male.

Johnny Brown was wont to grow

Stocks and asters in a row.
Marrows of enormous size
Hollyhocks that won a prize,
Peas and beans both large and stout
And endless things for bedding out.

Johnny Brown has gone to sea
And left his hallowed ground to me,
So, clad in manly boots and breeks,
I toil amid the beans and leeks,
Casting flowers from their bed
And putting onions in instead.

One day when Hitler is no more,
Johnny Brown will come ashore,
Seize again his spade and hoe
And stocks will flourish in a row.
And – if I'm not too worn and plain
I'll be a woman once again.

The beguiling, androgynous nature of the Land Army's contribution to the war effort occasionally inspired poetry in members of the public. The following verses, in which the poet contrasts the lily-handed Beatrice of his civilian life with the unladylike farmhand she has turned into, are a witty, yet touching tribute.

I praised her in a graceful rhyme
I made her many a stanza'd vow
I sang her lovely hand:
And now
Ah woman, changeful – swift
As Time
She milks a cow.
Those lily fingers, calming
Care
'As gentle as the voice of Peace'
(I think I wrote) I daren't release
For if I do she'll muss my hair
With tractor grease.
I'd kiss her footprints in the sod
I promised her with ardour
Pure,

Even for that she has a cure.
For, seeing where her feet have trod
I'm not so sure.
How shall I hymn my lady
Fair?
How can my tuneful
Numbers pour
'Mid mulch, manure, machines that roar?
I cannot tell, but this I swear
I love her more.

Dorothy Chalker

(née *Cross*). Joined Land Army at 24.
Land Army 1942–4.
Home town: Street, Somerset.
Civilian occupation: Office worker, Clarks shoe factory.

As I could take a bicycle apart when I joined the Land Army they thought I could be a tractor driver. I was sent to a hostel where there were fourteen girls. We went out daily either by van or cycle to farms within a 12-mile radius. I've heard about twenty-eight days' training but as far as I'm concerned you learned on the job. We would arrive at the farms by 8 a.m., but it depended on the work – and the weather – whether you were back for tea at 6.30 p.m. Usually it was much later. Harvest time 1942 was particularly wet and we didn't finish harvesting till 11 November. The first time I drove a tractor was about one week after joining the WLA on the road at the top of the Cheddar Gorge, 'supervised' by another girl with two weeks' service and who had never driven on the road before. We were hauling tanks of water for a school camp set up for children who came to help with farm work during their holidays. We gained experience with tractors by hauling trailers, which we helped load, to the rick.

After about two months my friend Daisy and I were transferred to another farm – 800 acres of mostly arable land and 3 miles from any shop, pub or village. The other hands consisted of three conscientious objectors, we two land girls, a mechanic, and Old Harry who was a dab hand at repairing dry-stone walls, should someone's tractor give them a gentle shove.

On this farm we did everything. We lime-washed the cowsheds when it was wet, we caught sheep for maggoting and dipping and learned the ins and outs of ploughing, cultivating and sowing by drilling seeds.

After about a year I left the farm to marry and as I'd had a good grounding in tractor work was transferred to a War Agricultural department near home. This meant being sent out to farms within a radius of 10 miles to plough, reap, cultivate, roll or anything else on your own. Up on the farm there was always someone else to help.

My equipment consisted of a Fordson tractor with lug, or spike wheels. This was for going through mud. If you had to drive along a road you had to bolt on four road bands to make the wheels smooth. I also had a trailer – not much more than a floor between two wheels, a 40-gallon drum of paraffin, a 2-gallon bucket and a funnel for filling the tractor, an assortment of tools – wrench, hammer, spanners, the implement for the particular job, i.e. plough, my bicycle and food for the day. The depot foreman would give me the address and nature of the work and off I went.

Sometimes the field to be worked was some distance from the farm. When you got there the road bands had to come off before you could unload and get started on the job. Unbolting obstinate road bands in icy weather was a task I dreaded. Sometimes fields were across railway lines and you had to manage the gates yourself. A rough idea of the local railway timetable was a distinct asset. As I was now down on Somerset wet lands the nature of the soil was very different from the limestone of Mendip where I was before. The natural field barriers were often rhines, or ditches – not stone walls. If you got too near the edge you had to know a trick or two to get yourself out. The foreman would usually turn up once a day and the farmer was interested to see the work in progress, but generally you were alone.

19 : The Fight for Fairness

As early as 1942 an official from the Ministry of Agriculture had announced that there was no support from the authorities for the inclusion of ex-land girls in any scheme for post-war education and training. This was a straw in the wind, a foretaste of the far more disgraceful discrimination that was yet to be announced and which would split the Land Army down the middle. True to form Lady Denman vigorously contested the fairness of the decision. 'I find it strange that any committee could think it reasonable that a civilian nurse should be eligible for training as a veterinary surgeon but that a member of the Land Army should be debarred from this advantage.' By the beginning of 1944, however, it became clear that the Ministry of Agriculture had failed to persuade the War Cabinet that the Land Army should be included in the Reinstatement in Civil Employment Act. Sketching a scenario where a land girl's job in civvy street had been taken by a girl who subsequently joined some other women's Service Lady Denman once again took up the cause. 'It would seem most unfair that the second girl should be held to have a prior claim for reinstatement.' She campaigned with equal energy for a fair deal for land girls over clothing coupons and grants, but without success. By the autumn of 1944 it was clear that Mr Hudson, the Minister of Agriculture, had lost the fight; land girls were to be excluded from all post-war benefits.

Yet despite this it was the Government's intention to maintain the Land Army at full strength. In what seems an act of pure malice the Government proceeded to rub salt in the wound by announcing, through the medium of Ernest Bevin, Minister of Labour, that resettlement grants of up to £150 were to be extended to Civil Defence and other Auxiliary workers but not to the Land Army. This was to be dealt with by the Ministry of Agriculture. On Friday, 16 February 1945, realising that her position was untenable and bitterly disappointed for the land girls whom she – and indeed the rest of the country – believed were being treated so shabbily, Lady Denman sent a letter of resignation to Mr Hudson. Before delivering it she told Pressmen that she had accepted, albeit reluctantly, that post-war benefits were being given only to men and women in the Forces but the announcement that the benefits were to be extended to Civil Defence workers while being denied to the Land Army was 'the last straw'. Lady Denman wrote:

> The LA is a uniformed service recruited on a national basis by a Government Department and the work which its members have undertaken, . . . is in my view as arduous and exacting as any branch of women's war work and of as great importance to the country. Yet they have been refused post-war benefits and privileges accorded to such other uniformed and nationally organised services as the WRNS, the ATS, the WAAF, the Civil Nursing Reserve, the Police Auxiliaries and the Civil Defence Services . . The position is a serious one for Land Army members who will have as great need as those in other services of Government assistance in the problems of resettlement . . . I have protested against the omission of the LA from various Government schemes and also against the decision . . . that capital grants to assist in re-starting business enterprises will be available after the war to men and women who have served the whole time in the Forces, the Merchant Navy or the Civil Defence Services but not to members of the WLA . . . I have reached the decision to resign

only because I have held the view that one of my chief functions has been to get a square deal for members of the LA and I have felt personal responsibility for policy affecting their welfare.

Lady Denman's feelings at the Government's rebuff, according to her granddaughter, Penelope Greenwood, were 'anguish and anger'. 'She felt totally let down, devastated that all the hard work and discomfort land girls had put up with for so many years had not been recognised.'

The following month Lady Denman wrote a moving farewell in the *Land Girl*, expressing her sadness, but also her hope that girls returning to the city would do their best to fight for improvements in the standard of living of countrydwellers. 'To those of you who go back to the towns I ask you not to forget the country. Remember it not only as an incident in your own life . . . but give the countryside your practical interest. You know the value of agriculture to the nation, you know the avoidable disadvantages under which country people live. Make townsfolk realise some of this (especially Parliamentary candidates when they ask you to vote for them) and the countryside may not be as neglected in the future as it has been in the past.'

It was not only those directly affected who were incensed at the injustice of the Government's attitude to post-war gratuities. The public reaction, too, was one of dismay, for the Land Army was by now popular with the general public. A leader in *The Times* declared: 'no fine distinctions must be allowed to debar the members of the WLA from their due reward on demobilisation.' The Queen herself was appalled. She sent a telephone message through her Lady-in-Waiting saying, 'The Queen will do anything she can to help.'

Balcombe was inundated with messages of support from individual farmers, from National Farmers Union branches and from land girls and their parents. A letter from one land girl, widely printed by a sympathetic Press, summed up the injustice. 'I joined in June 1939. I have lost my pre-war office job (they sacked me when I volunteered) and as far as the Government is concerned my future would be completely blank – my sole souvenir of five and a half years' loyal service a rather battered scarlet armlet – not even a discharge badge.' Almost all the newspapers supported the land girls' case. The *Daily Sketch* carried an emotional plea for fair treatment by an anonymous ex-land girl. Under the headline 'Heartbreak Army' she wrote:

Some 60,000 to 70,000 girls have been waiting and watching during the past few days. They are the girls of the Women's Land Army, and they've been waiting for and watching the announcements about Service grants and gratuities, just to see if, by some incredible miracle, their existence has at last been noticed by the Powers That Be. The answer still seems to be 'Include me out'. Is it good enough? These girls have had the roughest deal of any from the word 'Go'. They have fallen between two stools at every turn. Because they have always been employed by the individual farmer, not by the Government, the Government seems to have repudiated all responsibility for them except to say they may not leave their jobs, or even change them, without official sanction.

They are, in fact, like other civilian war workers, civil defence personnel etc. Not even that. They were not included in any scheme for providing comforts. No gloves or scarves or other knitted comforts were ever issued to them, and yet their relatives could not get coupon-free wool to knit things for them. They have no works canteens with off-the-ration meals. And now apparently there are to be grants or gratuities to war workers shifted about – but not to the Land Army. When a land girl is forced to resign on medical grounds she forfeits every stitch of her uniform, even the little metal badge. True, she gets a few coupons in return – but the more reckless she has been in demanding replacements the more coupons she will get. If she has been careful, wearing her things till they are patched and mended and patched and patched – well it's just too bad, but you can't expect full coupon value for very badly second-hand things can you? She gets no sort of discharge badge to bear witness to honourable service, no matter if she has served from the first day of the war and won every possible diamond for good service and the Proficiency Badge as well. I'm not claiming that the land girl has done more than her duty but I am saying that this duty, well and truly done, should receive similar recognition to that accorded to people in any other form of war service.

Everyone believed the Government would be forced to back down but Churchill insisted in a statement on war gratuities that benefits could not be extended to the Land Army without opening the door to unending claims from other classes of industry who received industrial or professional rates of pay. Although she had now resigned, leaving the administration of the Land Army to Mrs Jenkins, this was too much for Lady Denman. She dealt with this piece of sophistry in a circular. Her case was that Churchill's argument was absurd. Land girls, she pointed out, had consistently been paid far less than women industrial workers and land girls' pay was 8 shillings and 6 pence a week less than that of women Civil Defence workers who were eligible for the benefits. In any case, she argued, the land girls differed completely from industrial workers in three ways. They were members of an officially designated 'Army', they wore a state-supplied uniform and they had accepted a pledge of mobile service.

A month later the question was raised once more in the Commons. Nearly two hundred MPs signed their names in support of three motions put down by MPs in protest at the Government's decision to exclude the Women's Land Army from all post-war benefits granted to other war services. The Prime Minister was asked to receive a deputation from all three parties and the issue was debated in Parliament. Churchill, however, stubbornly insisted that the Land Army must be treated in the same way as munitions and other industrial workers. What caused the Government to take up this highly unpopular position, dismissed by many MPs as 'mean and niggardly' and 'most disappointing and totally inadequate', we shall never know. Could it have been personal dislike of Lady Denman? No one is more zealous in his beliefs than the convert and Churchill had started his political career as a Liberal Minister in Lloyd George's Cabinet. Could Lady Denman's faithfulness to the Liberal cause and keen social conscience have constituted a thorn of reproach in Churchill's ultra-Tory side? Penelope Greenwood believes that personalities did come into it and that Ernest Bevin, Minister of Labour in the coalition Government, played his part in putting the knife in. 'The Land

Army was the victim of male chauvinism. It lacked friends in high places. Bevin was particularly chauvinistic. He refused to recognise anything my grandmother did. She was always cursing him.'

The Government's obduracy is particularly hard to understand as the recruitment ban which had been put on in August 1943 to channel more female labour into the less popular munitions factories, had been lifted. Realising belatedly that the men would not be returning immediately from the forces, and that the army of prisoners of war on whom many farmers had heavily depended would be soon repatriated, the Government had urged the Land Army to advertise jobs on the land. In January 1945 an announcement in one county newsletter stressed that new recruits were urgently needed – 'so please tell your friends and if they wish to enrol they should apply to their Ministry of Labour Employment Exchange for permission to be considered for employment . . . and so help the war to an early victory.' In the end, aware of its predicament, the Government was forced to make some concessions. On 16 May 1945 Mr Hudson announced that land girls would receive state help in training for agriculture or other work, comparable to that afforded to Civil Defence and Auxiliary War Workers. The Government undertook to pay £150,000 to the Land Army Benevolent Fund and on demobilisation it was decided that land girls were to be allowed to keep their greatcoats – provided they dyed them blue – and their shoes.

In the dawning era of post-war militancy, however, this was not considered good enough. Militant land girls, many of whom had joined the Agricultural Workers' Union, set up a fighting fund of £1000 and formed a committee demanding a three-point charter. They demonstrated with placards in the streets of London, lobbied the Minister of Agriculture and Churchill himself and – in some hostels – took the unheard-of step of going on strike. One newspaper carried a report of 200 land girls meeting at Caxton Hall in Westminster to support the charter – 'Fewer restrictions, twice as many coupons on demob, 2s a week gratuity and an additional grant to their benevolent Fund are the demands made by the charter signed by 1000. The girls carried posters showing that ATS girls get 160 coupons against the Land Army's 20–35 and the ATS get six weeks' paid leave but the land girl only one.'

The demands of the charter, as drawn up by the chairman of the Charter Committee, twenty-three-year-old Miss Joyce Sancho, were (1) war service gratuity, (2) pensions for sickness and injury and (3) guarantee of jobs or training for new jobs on leaving the Land Army. When the new Minister of Agriculture, Tom Williams, refused to meet a deputation of their members they added a further demand to their list – equal pay with male agricultural workers.

Once again the Press was sympathetic. A reporter on the *News Chronicle* relayed the unfairness of the land girls' situation compared with girls leaving the Army.

> The leaders told me they were paying their own expenses and would forfeit two days' pay. They have been trying to pay the expenses of the charter – an organisation formed to represent the interests of land girls – by holding dances and whist drives. Complaints centred on no gratuity. 'The ATS get 8/6d per month of service. We are allowed 20 to 35 coupons when we leave but no clothing allowance; the ATS get 160 coupons and a clothing allowance of £12.10s. If we give a week's notice to leave we get no unemployment benefit, but the ATS get a paid demobilisation leave.
>
> 'When we leave we do not qualify for unemployment benefit and one of the things that the Charter stands for is a post-war settlement scheme such as is enjoyed by the ATS. We are allowed ten extra clothing coupons a year and have to use all those, and whereas the ATS are allowed to keep their uniform we have to give practically all ours up.
>
> 'Our wages are 48s a week and we pay 20s to 25s for board and out of what is left we have to buy cigarettes and snacks, pay for laundry, underwear, odd fares, entertainment, cosmetics and boot repairs. Some of the girls have had six years' experience and can be counted as skilled workers. They do tractoring, milking, hoeing, threshing, fruit spraying and all sorts of jobs.'

The land girls' cause was also taken up by women's magazines, some of whom were worried, however, by the growing mood of militancy. An article in *Woman* in 1946 claimed the land girls' rights were being discussed by the whole country.

If anyone doubted the worthwhileness of the work done by our land girls, the controversy about the Service gratuities settled it once and for all. For weeks now the 70,000 girls have been front page news, and everybody has joined in the fight – if you wanted an argument on a bus, train or in your own home you just mentioned their names and got down to hard facts.

People took their part on the score of the really tough jobs the girls do; we remembered that it isn't fun to get up at five o'clock or anything but back-breaking to pick potatoes, or cheap to live far away from home with only two free railway vouchers, or exciting to work throughout the year with only one week's holiday – taken in winter.

But in spite of all these arguments Mr Churchill personally announced to the House of Commons that the WLA is to be counted as an auxiliary arm of industry, and so not eligible for the Service gratuities.

It is disappointing but perhaps the final chapter has not been written. Many MPs feel that the girls of the Land Army fall half-way between the girls in industry and those in the services and their excellent work should be recognised by post war benefits. . . . It isn't so long ago is it that it seemed equally hopeless to expect equal compensation for women injured in air raids. In the meantime there is work to be done by the land girls and it would be a pity if these hardworking land amazons slacked off, or worse still, if there were any unofficial strikes. These methods would defeat their own case. The land girls know they must work just as hard this year and they want new volunteers to help them. There are many vacancies and I hope that those girls who had decided to work on the land when they were old enough won't be discouraged by this gratuity controversy.

The high command of the Land Army – Mrs Jenkins had taken over as Honorary Director after Lady Denman's resignation – deplored the trend to militancy and continued to plead the power of persuasion. 'We cannot forbid these parades but the organisation cannot associate itself with them,' she wrote. 'We have been doing our best to get better conditions and we do not think that a useful purpose will be served by these parades.' The National Union of Agricultural Workers offered its backing to the land girls, while making clear it too deplored direct action. An article in the *Landworker* in April 1945 explained the union's position.

> In protest at the decision of the Government excluding WLA from war gratuities a number of hostels in various parts of the country resorted to strike action. Most of the girls were members of the Union. They were induced by our organisers and by officers of the War Ag Exce Cttees to return to work pending the parliamentary debate on war gratuities. A large number of letters from WLA members were also received at the head office. A special meeting of the Executive committee was held in London on March 19 when the following resolution was passed.
>
> 'While the Executive Committee of the National Union of Agricultural Workers cannot support the action of members of the WLA in going on strike and deplores the fact that this has happened in certain districts they consider that, in view of the fact that the Government has extended to certain auxiliary services the principle of gratuities and the WLA was recruited on the basis of an auxiliary service in agriculture, the Government should have regard to their action in respect of other auxiliary services. The Union represents a large number of members in the WLA and feels justified in this expression of opinion on the action of the Govt.'
>
> The resolution was sent to Mr Churchill and to Mr Hudson on March 28th.

As a result of this protest by the NUAW an all-party meeting at the House of Commons unanimously called on Churchill to receive a deputation from the WLA before the debate in the House. Marion Nicholson was one of three ex-land girls who made up that deputation, receiving leave of absence from her job at Pearl Insurance. 'We were shown into a committee room where we were invited to sit down. There were MPs – all men – on both sides of us. Churchill and Anthony Eden sat at the top. Churchill looked just the way he did in his photographs, but didn't say much. His mind was already made up. The others fired questions at us, asking us why we thought we should get a gratuity. Some were clearly on our side, but clearly not enough as we didn't persuade them.'

Ashamed of its Government's ill grace, the public did its best to show its gratitude to the land girls. Those who took part in the Victory Parade of 8 June 1946 found the response of the crowd as their contingent marched past deeply moving.

The July 1946 issue of the *Land Girl*, was almost entirely devoted to victory. Margaret Pyke, the editor, wrote:

> The reception the Land Army got in the Victory Parade was almost overwhelming to the volunteers who took part in it. 'It wasn't even like a dream, it was like floating', writes H. Taylor (East Suffolk), 'the roaring came and went and for about half a mile I floated and my arms and legs went by themselves.' P. Smith (Surrey) found herself 'hoping the reception we received was really ours and I believe it was. At one rather quiet spot a woman's voice said: "These are the girls we should cheer" and we were given a rousing one. I nearly burst with pride many times.' W. Goolden (Hampshire) says the noise was so terrific that it was difficult to hear the band playing just behind. All these impressions were borne out by those standing in the watching crowds. At all points the green jerseys of the Land Army were the signal for a special outburst of applause. J. Brown (Hertfordshire) sums it up – 'we who thought we were a Forgotten Army realised the people of Britain had appreciated our effort.' In fact, this was the first chance the nation has had to show what it thinks of the WLA and it expressed its opinion in no uncertain voice (even a police horse neighed in salute). It was a tribute to all members of the Land Army and also to all agricultural workers. The men and women whose steady purpose and skilled work keep us fed are rarely acclaimed, but on June 8th the nation took its chance.

Zoe Hill took part in the Victory parade in London.

> From Kensington we went to Hyde Park in buses. There we saw all the various Allied Armies marching to their positions. It was interesting to see all the smart and colourful uniforms so closely. It was then I began to feel excited and to realise I was one of them marching in the Victory Parade. The march had begun and we could hear faintly cheering crowds and the distant strains of band

music. Then came our turn to follow on. As we went through Marble Arch, the crowd seemed to burst upon us suddenly, cheering and shouting themselves hoarse. It was then a peculiar emotional feeling came over me. Afterwards I found we all experienced the same feeling, men as well. I went cold all over, my face felt stiff, I wanted to cry, my knees went weak, and for the first five minutes I didn't see a thing distinctly. There seemed a blaze of colour everywhere, and an almost deafening amount of cheering. I was walking in an absolute dream. I thought it couldn't be me walking in one of the greatest parades in history, with the biggest crowd ever looking on . . . I marched on – on down Oxford Street, Charing Cross Road, Northumberland Avenue, Bridge Street, Whitehall, past the Cenotaph . . . up the Mall to the Saluting Base, a really beautiful sight. The Queen dressed in a soft shade of mauve and Queen Mary in powder blue, as were the Princesses . . . The Queen was just looking interested until the WLA drew level, then she gave us a lovely smile. . . .

Four other girls and myself went for a walk, as if we hadn't done enough walking! Making our way through Hyde Park and St James's Park we arrived outside Buckingham Palace, just in time to see the King and Queen and the two Princesses come out onto the balcony. Then we walked down Whitehall, nearly getting our feet trodden on by a police horse; who should we see go by but Mr Churchill and Mr Eden in a car.

We ended up on the Lambeth side of Vauxhall Bridge to see the fireworks. It was a grand sight. Searchlights changing from red to white, blue to green; the finest show of fireworks imaginable; various buildings floodlit and the whole reflected in the river. At 11 o'clock we made our way back to the hotel. My legs and feet were twice their normal size and my heels were sore. Weary and thoroughly worn out . . . The end of a perfect day and one I shall never, never forget.

Even after Lady Denman's resignation the Queen continued to take her duties as patron of the Land Army as seriously as ever. By 1945, despite the need for labour on the land, numbers had dropped to 54,000. On 7 December the Queen was a guest at a Christmas party held at Mansion House by the Lord Mayor of London to mark six years of the Land Army. After presenting golden armlets to 235 of the earliest recruits the Queen made a stirring speech.

You came in those distant days six years ago, with your great gifts of youth and strength and with high purpose, to serve your country in her hour of need, and never have British women and girls shown more capacity or more pluck. On the farms and in the fields, forests and gardens, you took your place in the Battle for Freedom, and through your endurance and your toil you supplied the needs of this Island and sustained the life of the nation.

I realise how hard your work has often been, how lonely sometimes, far from home and family, in strange and unfamiliar surroundings and conditions, but your courage, your resourcefulness and your almost unfailing cheerfulness carried you through every difficulty.

You have gained a great reputation by your skill and your selfless service and as your Patron I am indeed proud and I rejoice with you and with your devoted officers that the Land Army should have won for itself so fair a name and should so truly deserve it . . .

Sadly neither public affection nor Royal patronage were sufficient to allay the impression that where the Land Army was concerned officialdom felt no need to roll out the red carpet. In August 1946 a march through the streets of the City of London by 750 land girls with six years' continuous service went practically unnoticed by passers-by. The girls were receiving armlets from the Queen at Mansion House. The journalist who wrote it up for the *Manchester Guardian* of 24 August evidently felt the pathos of the situation:

> The citizens' goodwill towards the girls on lonely farms is real and deep. But there was little to demonstrate it earlier today when 750 of the six-year-service girls marched through the City. Few realised the march was taking place and the veterans of the farm and forest in greatcoats and breeches had small crowds to cheer them. The biggest was at St Paul's. Some elderly men of the City raised their hats as the women passed with only one band to play them on their way . . . But a rare occasion should have been more generally honoured. One passer-by obviously thought so. He called for three cheers for the girls from the other sightseers after they had been played into Guildhall to the tune of 'A Farmer's Boy' and 'John Brown's Body'.

20 : The Land Army Stands Down

Fun though they were, the raft of rallies, celebrations and
victory parades that saw out the summer and autumn of 1945
could not blot out the issue many land girls had to face; what
to do now that the war was over. For those engaged to
homecoming servicemen the choice was easy. The future for
them spelt marriage and babies. For girls who had never
worked before joining the Land Army, or who felt, as many
did, that they had outgrown their old lives, the prospect of
returning to the parental nest provoked mixed feelings. For
these were no longer the puny, gauche, homesick teenagers
whose presumption in believing they could do a man's job had
provoked so much scorn in farming circles. They had grown
into strong, independent and capable women who knew their
worth. They had worked hard, they had coped in primitive
conditions, run their own budgets, won the respect of their
employers, had love affairs . . . Far from apologising for not
being as good as a man, many had joined a trade union and
supported the demand of equal pay for equal work. They had
hugely enjoyed the female companionship they found in the

226

hostels, the hectic social life that goes with the uncertainty of war, the satisfaction that comes from a task well done and the freedom of life in the clean open air . . .

At the end of April 1944 the headquarters of the Land Army had moved back to London. It was from Nos 4 and 6 Chesham Street, London, SW1 after VJ-Day that land girls received a letter informing them that they were free to seek release from the Land Army if they wished. Some, though by no means all of those who chose to leave received a letter from the Queen. As time went by efforts were made to make the message more personal.

A Sussex land girl who left the Land Army in November 1944 received a brief, impersonal message: 'The Queen wishes me to say that you have rendered an incalculable service to our country throughout the most testing time and that, as patron of the Women's Land Army, Her Majesty is more than proud of you.'

Three years later a girl resigning from the Land Army in September 1947 received a rather more thoughtful message in which her name and dates of service had been inserted. 'By this personal message I wish to express to you . . . [member's name typed] my appreciation of your loyal and devoted service as a member of the Women's Land Army from [date joined] to [month and date left] . . . Your unsparing efforts at a time when the victory of our cause depended on the utmost use of the resources of our land have earned for you the country's gratitude.'

The clear-sighted organisational skills of Lady Denman on the one hand and the vigour and commitment of Robert Hudson, the Minister of Agriculture with whom she worked throughout her Land Army years, had played a major role in getting British agriculture to meet its ambitious annual production targets. A measure of their success was that by the start of 1943 food imports had dropped to half a million tons, the lowest since the start of the war. The Land Army was still a hugely popular choice with young girls and, but for the recruitment ban in August 1943, by the spring and summer of 1944 numbers would have exceeded 100,000. Without Lady Denman and Robert Hudson, however, the muddle that had characterised Government farming policy before the war returned. No sooner had letters gone out offering serving land girls their release than the Government realised that without the army of prisoners of war who had played a vital role on farms throughout 1944, and with many servicemen still occupied overseas, they needed a further 30,000 land girls.

The winter of 1947 was bitterly cold and snowy. One land girl now married to a farmer who had farmed an adjoining farm to the one she had worked on in Oxfordshire, was cut off by snow for more than a week. She and her husband had the heartbreaking task of pouring the milk away, or feeding it to the pigs as the roads were impassable. 'One day I walked to Banbury through the snow. I walked over hedges, across fields and snow-covered roads, which you couldn't follow, to get food as our village shop had run out of necessities and there were no freezers then. I carried back flour, meat and bread. The snow was so bad at one stage that the stable roof collapsed with the weight of it on to our horses. I managed to pull aside the wooden beams to go in and lead the terrified animals out and calm them down.'

As the war neared its end Inez Jenkins and Margaret Pyke continued to encourage land girls to think about peacetime careers and qualifications. In her farewell in the *Land Girl* Lady Denman had expressed hopes of a peacetime future in which women would occupy responsible jobs on the land. '. . . many of you will want to stay on the land,' she had written, 'and for you the Ministry of Agriculture is planning courses to give you the opportunity of adding to your knowledge and to help you fill responsible jobs. I hope that I shall live long enough to see many ex-members of the Land Army in charge of herds, managing farms and gardens, holding posts in Farm Institutes and training centres and working in research.'

The pages of the *Land Girl* at this time teemed with articles on socially useful jobs like teaching, nursing, laboratory work, the police and even veterinary medicine which it was hoped that a new era of equality and emancipation would open up to women . . . But they were at pains to stress that competition with men in the workplace should not be the cornerstone of a woman's life. In an editorial in the *Land Girl* of August 1945 Margaret Pyke expressed the belief that raising happy and loved children is the most worthwhile career of all. Feminists will doubtless dismiss Mrs Pyke's philosophy as lacking in radicalism and conniving at men's domination, but those who feel that the equality campaign has not provided the solution to the dilemma of work versus family may feel she was ahead of her time.

Young women who grew up in wartime may feel themselves the equal partners in work and in struggle with their men comrades and be justly proud of their achievement. Equality of work and pay is, in fact, one of those things women are at present struggling for and they have achieved it in some branches of industry, after proving that they could, in fact, do their work as efficiently as the men. But is there not another side to equality and is it quite certain that every woman's highest aim lies in measuring up to masculine standards of work? . . .

Western man and Western woman have more or less relegated the struggle of the sexes to the privacy of the home . . . Officially the husband and father is still the head of the family but in many cases this is only a position of honour and the real leader may be the mother. Understanding her husband and her family, giving them her sympathy . . . she becomes the indispensable centre, the haven and refuge for the male and female members of the family alike. This aspect of the woman's domestic life is very often not sufficiently recognised and valued. Her drudgery . . . is made the excuse for regarding her contribution to the family as inferior . . . The truth is, however, that enduring this drudgery by means of her powers of love she is showing herself not merely the equal of man but capable of the most important achievement on which the continuance of civilisation rests . . . The young woman of today is determined not to allow herself to become the drudge she thinks her mother was. Smaller families have made it possible for the woman to follow a career if she so wishes. Yet the conflict between a home and a career, children and ambition, is raging in many a young mind . . . There is no doubt at all that many young women who have been allowed to work in congenial jobs will want to continue in them. . . .

. . . the most vital task of woman can be found [in] her contribution to peace. While the nation's elected leaders are planning ways and means of patching up the world after a devastating war, the future of this generation and the next depends on the lives they are leading now in their homes. The woman who is building a home now, who is deciding to bring up children, is the guardian of the peace of the world as much as any man in uniform. She can bring up her children to be happy and free and to know real love so that they may later love in turn and keep the peace.

There is no career which can compare with this one and the woman whose talents are all centred round the home is able to do work of vital importance . . .

In the immediate aftermath of the war there was little change in farming methods. Except in certain parts of the south mechanisation was still a futuristic dream. Horse- and man- or woman-power was still the order of the day. Peg Francis, a Grimsby girl whose besetting fear was that the war would end before she was old enough to join the Land Army, joined in 1946 when numbers were down to around 54,000. She was sent to work on the endless potato fields of Lincoln – but won a respite because of the snow that winter.

We had to dig ourselves out of the hostel and help clear the roads outside too. The River Steeping froze solid and we skated by Tilley lantern. Then all the water pipes froze solid, so we shovelled – clean top snow for cooking, middle-grey snow for washing etc. – the rest for 'hygiene'. Imagine! two buckets of water from melted snow standing on our coke stoves.

At work we cleared roads, made sacking wind-break sheets ready for taatie riddling time! My friend Joan and I painted implements, putting identity marks on hoes, spades, petrol tins. Suddenly the snow disappeared and it was taatie setting time and work began in earnest.

The Women's Land Army had been a response by a beleaguered nation to an emergency. The last issue of the *Land Girl* appeared in April 1947 and was replaced by a free *Land Army News* until November 1950. In 1948 the county committees which had underpinned the day-to-day life of the land girl, matching girl to farmer, finding billets, issuing kit . . . were dissolved. The announcement at the end of October 1949 by Mr Tom Williams, the post-war Minister of Agriculture, that the Land Army was to be disbanded should have come as no surprise. Even so the news was received with a howl of protest by the very people who had initially so scorned it. The National Farmers Union was particularly outraged, claiming that the decision had been taken without consulting them. An article in the *Manchester Guardian* of 23 October 1950 reported that 'all through and since the war the majority of farmers employing WLA volunteers have had nothing but praise for them'.

An important market gardening company in Surrey, Messrs F. A. and A. W. Seckrett, who had been among the largest employers of land girls in the south of England, was quoted as saying they thought it was a great mistake to disband the army, particularly in view of the new demand on labour which would be made by the rearmament programme. 'Many of the women will continue in private employment on the land, and they are undoubtedly the pick of the original Land Army. There will be very few whose employers will willingly dispense with them on the excuse that the uniformed army has ceased to exist. There is, however, a persistent feeling that something will be lost by the removal of the corporate spirit of the WLA as an organised entity.'

There was considerable sympathy for those land girls who were keen to stay on the land but who were unsure how they would find work and make ends meet – henceforth they would have to buy their own work clothes – without the umbrella support of the county office.

An article in the Farmer and Stock Breeder of August 1950

quoted an agriculturalist who had helped train the first batches of land girls in 1939 as 'very sorry to see them disbanded,' adding:

'This view is echoed by farmers all over the country as well as by Agricultural Committees, research stations and other organisations well served by the WLA.' The writer ended by urging country people to do their best to look after those land girls who did not wish to return to their former lives.

'. . . There are still thousands of land girls looking for some out-of-door work. It is to be hoped that none of those wanting to stay on the land will be prevented through lack of knowledge of where to apply for posts, or inability to find lodgings which are not too expensive. These girls have done well by the industry, and it is up to country folk to see that they are given a chance to apply for any suitable posts which may be available in the next few weeks.'

In fact, despite the goodwill of farming organisations, the last months of the Land Army's existence seem to have left many girls with time on their hands. Girls living in hostels remember days when they didn't go out at all, but did hostel cleaning duties instead. Some of the jobs they were deployed on bore little relation to farming. One group was sent out to pick pebbles off a golf course, while another was supplied with picks, mattocks and shovels and sent to break up the concrete foundation slabs of a demolished Army camp.

The last battle to be fought by the Land Army in the year it ceased to exist was the Colorado Beetle Campaign. The black and yellow striped insect was a fast breeding pest which threatened to destroy the national potato crop at a time when carbohydrates were still in desperately short supply. To combat the invader 18,000 acres in Kent and Sussex were sprayed as a precautionary measure. In 1950 twenty-three outbreaks were recorded over the whole country of which eleven were dealt with by the Land Army. Teams of girls were sent out into the countryside armed with giant syringes filled with DDT and carbon disulphide to inject into holes in the ground along parallel lines marked out with string. Vera Smith and Pat Matynia had been in a Land Army hostel near Dorking in Surrey for four years when they learned that the hostel was to close in June 1950. 'We wanted to stay on the land,' Vera recalls, 'so we elected to transfer to Kent and join the Colorado Beetle campaign. We were sent to Malling House Hostel in West Malling, near Maidstone. There we met the third member of our team, June Golding, who was also to be our car driver. There were several teams like us, deployed across the country in potato-growing areas. We visited scores of farms inspecting potato fields for the tell-tale signs of the dreaded beetle. It was during a routine inspection of a field that I noticed the tiny bright pink beetle larvae on a single potato plant. From that point it was all systems go. Our boss, Sholto Rolfe, chief entomologist at Wye College laboratory, was immediately informed. A large area of potato plants was dug up and destroyed. The bare ground was marked out and injected with insecticide.'

By the time the stand-down parade of the Women's Land Army took place on Saturday, 21 October 1950 the force in which over eleven years nearly a quarter of a million women had served numbered just 8,000. Five hundred of them marched past Buckingham Palace that day. The land girls who had been selected to take part in the farewell parade were put up in what was known as the Deep Shelter, an air raid shelter, specially equipped with huge double-bunked dormitories and basic washing facilities deep beneath the rumbling trains of Clapham Common Underground station in South London. From there they were taken by coach to Wellington Barracks in Knightsbridge to rehearse for the march past of the next day.

A Dorset land girl thought the newsreel men would have got a better story if they had taken their cameras into the Deep Shelter, where an atmosphere of schoolgirl excitement prevailed.

The flitting of scantily attired figures (if stalwart land girls can be said to flit) up and down those huge underground dormitories . . . the massage of tender knees not yet recovered from the unequal struggle, with nearly 200 spiral steps to fresh air and daylight and back again; the wash place with its splashings, splutterings and frequent gasping groans as the cold water assailed one's anatomy . . . what memories we shall all treasure.

And so to bed – reached by a series of gymnastics which would have been the envy of any thoroughbred monkey. While many a dull thump reverberated as some unfortunate cranium made contact with the shelter roof. At length land girls stopped giggling over the multitudinous witticisms which accompany such an occasion and the last lemonade bottle had fizzed. The bunk springs ceased creaking and silence settled slowly over all – to be broken only by the interminable rumbling of the Underground railway overhead.

A girl who had come up to represent West Sussex felt that the parade brought back to the memory of Londoners 'the forgotten army of green berets, green jerseys and farm breeches' which was once such a familiar sight. In her opinion there was only one cause for regret – 'that all the girls we represented could not be with us to share the thrill of the band playing "God Save the King" while we stood in the courtyard of his home, the excitement of touching his State coach, the aches and the pains of our square bashing that nearly broke our hearts and almost reduced the sergeant to tears but which gave us confidence and bearing . . .'

The abiding memories of the momentous day for a girl from Dorset were the drilling – and the blue eyes of the Queen.

The rehearsal on Wellington Barracks square began with a little levity but the sergeants of the Coldstream Guards quietly and politely impressed us with the dignity of our surroundings and of the task in hand – learning to march and form an open square. Marching behind the band of the Irish Guards from Wellington Barracks to Buckingham Palace was a wonderful moment, hardly to be believed and at the same time most proud. We stood at ease in an open square round the quadrangle of the palace. The Queen came, with her Minister of Agriculture . . . and spoke to several girls, one of whom was standing in front of me so that I could see the Queen's lovely blue eyes and hear her quiet, pleasant voice . . . Her Majesty then spoke to us all from the dais and received gifts of produce from the counties . . . Next we went by coaches to Ludgate Hill and marched through the Great West Door of St Paul's for the National Harvest Thanksgiving.

The speech the Queen made contained genuine warmth which must have gone some way to making the land girls feel that, in spite of everything their efforts had not been unappreciated.

. . . The story of the Land Army has been one of a great response by women of our country to the call of duty in the nation's hour of danger and need. They could not have done more for their country than they did. By their efforts they helped to ensure that our country contributed its utmost towards its food supplies and for this the nation owes them an everlasting debt.

The Women's Land Army has always been recruited from volunteers, and I like to think that its greatest strength lay in the free spirit which has always inspired the people of these islands to their greatest achievements.

The Land Army attracted girls from every kind of different occupation and I have always admired their courage in responding so readily to a call which they knew must bring them not only hardship and sometimes loneliness, but often danger. By their hard work and patient endurance they earned a noble share in the immense effort which carried our country to victory. Yet their task did not end when the war was over, for they stayed at their posts through the difficult years that followed. Five thousand of those who served in the Land Army have decided to remain on the land. There can be no greater tribute than this to the happiness with which their work rewarded them. Now the time has come to say goodbye, because the job has been done, but the sadness which many feel at the parting should be outweighed by pride in the achievement. Moreover, the Land Army will not, in any case, be only an affectionate memory, since it will live still in the shape of the thousands of members who have settled down in the countryside as the wives of farmers and farm workers, or who are themselves continuing to work in agriculture when the Organisation itself comes to an end.

I thank you for all the splendid service you have given your country. In field and forest, garden and orchard and dairy, the work of the Women's Land Army has always been worthy of the ageless traditions of those who have toiled for the land they loved . . .

It was an eloquent tribute. The degree of genuine involvement felt by the Queen in the Land Army cause can be gauged by an almost unprecedented revelation of Royal feelings the following year. Presenting Lady Denman with the Grand Cross of the British Empire, King George VI told her: 'We always thought that the land girls were not well treated.'

What began as an experiment, dictated by a nation in peril, accompanied by scepticism on the one hand and youthful patriotic naïvety, on the other, had ended as a triumphant example of co-operation – between town and country, men and women. All had been enriched by it. Women had acquired skills they had never been dreamed capable of and in so doing had achieved both self-fulfilment and the respect of their employers. They had worked uncomplainingly at tasks their bodies were not designed for, often in atrocious weather, occasionally under enemy fire. They had run farms single-handedly when their employers were incapacitated; many had shown heroism beyond the call of duty – rescuing terrified livestock from blazing barns and fellow workers from dangerous bulls. Never again would these men dismiss women as helpless creatures. They resolved the sex war in a way we who came after them can only admire – and possibly envy – through partnership.

Postscript

On 19 August 1995 for the first time in forty-five years eighty land girls marched through the streets of London. They formed part of the procession celebrating the fiftieth anniversary of VJ-Day. They were not, of course, in uniform. That had had to be surrendered when they left the force. But it was not only the distinctive green and red armband, kept safe all these years, or the black banner displaying the Land Army badge, that caused them to stand out from the rest of the marchers. Though most of them were over seventy and the weather that day was so scorchingly hot that several other marchers passed out, the land girls were distinguished by a palpable quality of vigour and good humour. Margaret Drage (née Barnett), who had gone as a seventeen-year-old typist to help run the secretarial side of the WLA headquarters at Balcombe Place in 1939, took her thirty-eight-year-old daughter Elizabeth Prior to see the procession. 'They all had a similar expression on their faces, a very determined look, as if they wouldn't take no for an answer. They looked as if, even now, they were ready for anything . . .'

It is a quality one notices at land girl reunions which still take place regularly up and down the country. All the participants are grey-haired, many are grandmothers, but that has not made them frail or retiring. Old land girls have a certain spring in their step, a look of purpose in their eye. You are in no doubt that these are capable women.

It is tempting to look at those who so doggedly showed that when required they could do a man's job, and see them as heralds of the equal-opportunity-based feminism which is an integral part of the thinking of today's young women. It has become a cliché to describe the immediate post-war era as one in which women who had tasted independence and self-fulfilment were forced back once more into the thankless enslavement of *Kirche, Kinder und Küche,* while the newly demobbed men 'stole' their jobs. This is not how they saw it at the time. Women who were young in the Forties do not think the way their daughters think. They did not question the *status quo* to any great extent. They were reverential – towards their social superiors, towards the Royal family – in a way we of a more cynical age find hard to comprehend. 'We knew our place,' as one land girl put it. They did not quarrel with the received wisdom that men were the breadwinners and women the raisers of children. That a mother might pay someone to look after her children while she did a job of work was barely thinkable. Those who welcomed back sweethearts they feared they might not see again found deep fulfilment in the prospect of marriage and babies.

The countryside, however, can be as seductive as any lover. Without the war hardly any of these girls would have discovered the satisfaction of working on the land. Those who fell under its spell during the war suffered real pangs trying to readjust to their former, monotonous urban lives. Marion Nicholson, back at her old office job at the headquarters of the Pearl Assurance in London's High Holborn, felt so cooped up she rushed out to Lincoln's Inn Fields at every opportunity 'just to get some air'. Her dream of running a smallholding, a venture which would have delighted Lady Denman, sadly, never came true. Phyllis Nichols, back at her job making playing cards in a printing works, found the once familiar smell of ink made her nauseous: 'I kept going to the door to take deep breaths of fresh air.' Five thousand couldn't bear to go back to town life and just stayed on. Some, tough and fit through a lifetime in the open air, are still at it. Barbara Morris, who fearlessly drove her paraffin-fuelled Fordson tractor through four years of shelling in the Dover area, winning a medal for her courage, never returned to her 'monotonous' pre-war life as a shop assistant. Instead she stayed on at the same farm, ploughing, harrowing, muck carting, harvesting . . . graduating to a self-starting tractor when diesel power came in. 'I wasn't thought of as an oddity, not around this area. Everyone knew me. They used to set their clocks by me cycling to and from the farm each day. I loved the work. I couldn't imagine doing anything else . . . There weren't many jobs I couldn't do on the farm. I could carry a two-hundredweight sack of corn . . .'

In Bilsington, on the edge of Romney Marsh in Kent, Hilary Deedes, who has just turned eighty, still keeps over twenty sheep, a mixture of Jacobs and rare breeds, whose wool she spins on her collection of spinning wheels. She also keeps about thirty Bantam hens, tending to them all in the much patched fawn drill milking coat she got from the Land Army at the outbreak of war. When visiting the agricultural shows at which she shows her sheep Lady Deedes sleeps in a tent. Her husband, a former Cabinet Minister and editor of the *Daily Telegraph*, who sees himself as possessing the advantage of 'enjoying the show without lifting a hand', says he is quite used to their coming home from a party at 1 a.m. and seeing his wife 'vanishing in evening dress to put the hens' light out'. Though she no longer shears the sheep herself, Lady Deedes thinks nothing of trudging across frozen fields with hay on icy mornings when the east wind whips across the marshes from the Continent, or of getting up in the night to help with a difficult birth. 'She's always very calm,' observes Lord Deedes, 'even if there's a terrrible tragedy and a lamb is born still. I think it's a hallmark of the old Land Army to take nature's setbacks in your stride.'

Dinah Pengilly defied a farmer father to join the Land Army. With no marriage plans after the war she declined to submit once more to the paternal yoke. Instead she 'ran away' to try farming in post-war Europe. After eight years in Denmark, Holland and Germany she was about to try Finland when she was temporarily grounded. Her uncle's bull attacked her on a visit home, breaking seven of her ribs. She wrote about the dawning brave new world of intensive farming still unknown in Britain for one of the last issues of *Land Army News*. 'This is a very old farm but during the past year it has been rebuilt on modern lines. The stable is lovely; I have never seen a better one. The cow house has windows on both sides and is very light and airy, water and electricity installed. We have pig houses to hold more than a hundred pigs – they also have electric light and water. The loft above the pigs' house has a concrete floor so that if there was a fire in the loft the floor could not burn and the pigs would be quite dry underneath if it rained before the loft was rebuilt. Herr Hansen has a Fergusson tractor. He also has his own threshing machine and mill, both worked by an electric motor. All our water is also pumped up from a well by electricity.'

Now seventy-four, Dinah still works on a farm in Totnes eight miles from the one she worked on as a land girl. 'It's about a ten-minute ride on my bike. I don't milk cows or do lambing now, but I still climb ladders picking apples and plums; twice a day I walk right round the farm making sure the cattle and calves are all right and I look after the vegetables in the greenhouse.'

If anyone has proved themselves these women have. But are they really accepted by the men they work with – or does a new generation of farmers need to be convinced all over again? Kathleen Hickmott drove a tractor during the war. At seventy-four she still mows the orchards at the fruit farm in East Sussex where her husband is manager. Kathleen believes the old prejudice still survives. 'It's all right for me. My husband is the manager and he knows what I can do. But the chauvinism we put up with in the war years is still there. The other day I came in on the tractor and got off to open the shed and put it away. By the time I came back a young boy had hopped on and was driving it, giving me a look that said "I'll do this. You're only a woman." '

Not that this competitiveness interferes with Kathleen's pleasure in her work. 'I left school at fourteen and for six years I worked in the Co-op laundry in Birmingham. I was twenty when I joined the Land Army. After the war they offered me my old job, but I could never have gone back to all that heat and steam. I can't think of anything that could bring me more satisfaction than working on the land. I used to love mowing when we drove the old-fashioned machines with the long blade jutting out at the side, seeing the grass fall over in that wonderful rhythm. Ploughing was my favourite. To turn round and see a good straight furrow behind you was a real pleasure.'

Dinah Pengilly, Kathleen Hickmott, Hilary Deedes and all the others who threw off the shackles imposed by their sex and embarked on a lifelong love affair with the land owed their introduction to it to the Land Army. It seems appropriate, therefore, to end with a poem written by Hebe Jerrold, a fellow land girl:

> War, which has brought to others fear,
> Pain, sorrow, slavery and death,
> To me has brought what I held dear,
> And longed for but could not possess.
> Has given me wide stretch of sky,
> The sailing clouds, the wind's sharp breath,
> A roof of leaves, the wild flower's eye,
> Bird song, all woodland loveliness,
> Health, vigour, deep content, and faith

That at its source our stream runs clear.
What have I done? I never meant
To be a wartime profiteer.

Select Bibliography

Dorothea Abbot, *Librarian in the Land*
Adrian Bell, *Corduroy*
————, *Silver Ley*
————, *The Cherry Tree*
Anne Hall, *Land Girl*
Gervas Huxley, *Lady Denman*
Knighton Joyce, *Land Army Days*
Joan Mant, *All Muck, No Medals*
Vita Sackville-West, *The Women's Land Army*
Arthur Street, *Farmer's Glory*
Sadie Ward, *War in the Countryside*